The Origins and Development of Food Policies in Europe

Edited by
John Burnett and Derek J. Oddy

Leicester University Press

London and New York

Distributed in the United States and Canada by
St. Martin's Press

Leicester University Press
(Pinter Publishers Ltd.)
25 Floral Street, London WC2E 9DS, United Kingdom

First published in 1994

Distributed exclusively in the USA and Canada by St. Martin's Press, Inc., Room
400, 175 Fifth Avenue, New York, NY10010, USA

British Library Cataloguing in Publication Data

A CIP catalogue record for this book is available from the British Library

ISBN 0 7185 1474 2 (hb)
ISBN 0 7185 1694 X (pb)

Library of Congress Cataloging-in-Publication Data

The Origins and development of food policies in Europe/ edited by John Burnett
and Derek J. Oddy.
    p.   cm.
    Includes bibliographical references and index.
    ISBN 0–7185–1474–2 (hb), 0–7185–1694–X (pb)
    1. Nutrition policy – Europe – History – 19th century – Congresses.
    2. Nutrition policy – Europe – History – 20th century – Congresses.
    3. Diet – Europe – History – 19th century – Congresses.   4. Diet – Europe –
    History – 20th century – Congresses.   5. Food supply – Government policy –
    Europe – History – 19th century – Congresses.   6. Food supply –
    Government policy – Europe – History – 20th century – Congresses.
    I. Burnett, John, 1925–   .   II. Oddy, Derek J., 1931–   .
    TX360.E8075   1994
    363.8'56'094–dc20
                                                                93–5647
                                                                CIP

Typeset by Mayhew Typesetting, Rhayader, Powys
Printed and bound in Great Britain by Biddles Ltd., Guildford and King's Lynn

Contents

List of contributors

Professor John Burnett, Professor of Social History, Department of Government, Brunel University

Dr E. Margaret Crawford, Department of Economic and Social History, The Queen's University, Belfast

Dr Maria Concetta Dentoni, Faculty of Law, University of Cagliari, Sardinia, Italy

Professor Mats Essemyr, Gotland College of Higher Education, Visby, Sweden

Dr Adel P. den Hartog, Department of Human Nutrition, Wageningen Agricultural University, The Netherlands

Dr Marjatta Hietala, Renvall Institute of Historical Research, University of Helsinki, Finland

Dr Sally M. Horrocks, Centre for the History of Science, Technology and Medicine, University of Manchester

Professor Thor Øivind Jensen, Centre for Social Research, Department of Administration and Organization Theory, University of Bergen, Norway

Dr Eszter Kisbán, Department of Ethnology, Magyar Tudomanyos Akademia, Budapest, Hungary

Dr Hanna Krajewska, Archives of the Nineteenth Century, Warsaw, Poland

Dr Christoph Maria Merki, Institute for History, University of Berne, Berne, Switzerland

Professor Mats L.W. Morell, Department of Economic History, Uppsala, Sweden

Professor Derek J. Oddy, Professor of Modern Economic History, University of Westminster

Dr Lydia Petránová, Institute for Ethnology, Czechoslovak Academy of Science, Prague, Czech Republic

Dr Peter Scholliers, Belgian National Foundation of Scientific Research, and Free University of Brussels, Brussels, Belgium

Professor Alan Swinbank, Department of Agricultural Economics and Management, University of Reading

Professor Hans J. Teuteberg, Historisches Seminar, Westfalische Wilhelms-Universitat, Münster, Germany

1 Introduction[1]

John Burnett and Derek J. Oddy

The inaugural meeting of the International Commission for Research into European Food History was held in Münster, Germany, in 1989 when participants from 14 countries reviewed the current state of food history research: the papers were published as *European Food History: A Research Review*, edited by Professor Hans J. Teuteberg (Leicester University Press, 1992). At Münster it was agreed that future conferences, to be held biennially, would address substantive issues in food history, and that the 1991 meeting would be devoted to the development of European food policies, principally in the nineteenth and twentieth centuries. This was regarded both as an important subject in its own right, but additionally it was hoped that it might provide a relevant historical background to the emerging harmonization of European Community policies. The conference, held at Brunel University, West London, in September 1991, brought together contributors from 15 countries, whose edited papers are contained in this volume.

As the most basic of human needs, food has been an object of public control since the earliest civilizations, the regulation of price and quality being traceable to ancient Egypt and the city-states of Greece and Rome. Such controls were essentially a product of urbanization and the growth of consuming populations which were unable to supply their own food requirements. The commercialization of food production and retailing, and the increasing number of stages between growers and consumers, gave opportunities for rigging the market in various ways, for charging exorbitant prices, giving short weight and reducing quality by adulteration, especially in periodic times of scarcity. In most Western European countries throughout the medieval and early modern period, states attempted to control such abuses with varying degrees of success, principally through local urban administrations: in England, for instance, the Assize of Bread and Ale dating from 1285 vested in magistrates the power to regulate the price and quality of these commercially produced basic necessities. Such controls were motivated, at least in part, by a widely-accepted belief in a 'just price' to the consumer and a fair profit to the producer, that there existed a 'moral economy' which underlay commercial transactions and should, where necessary for the public good, supersede market forces. In the process of advancing industrialization in the eighteenth century such views came under increasing attack: in France the Physiocrats urged the case for *laissez-faire* policies and in Britain the Classical Economists from Adam Smith onwards argued that public interests were best served by unfettered competition and the freedom of each individual to make the best bargains for himself. In this spirit the medieval Assize of Bread was swept away between 1815 and 1836 in the belief that free competition between bakers would alone ensure bread of the best quality at the lowest price. Throughout many of the more industrialized European states this became the received wisdom for much of the nineteenth century: earlier food controls were removed, allowed to lapse, or were found to be beyond the administrative ability of local authorities to enforce in the face of rapidly-expanding urban populations.

Against that background, the conference was largely concerned with the emergence of new food policies better adapted to the demographic and economic changes of modern times. But if history is about change, it is also about continuity. The most enduring source of social policy in Europe has been charity, the obligation to help others less fortunate than oneself, which was enjoined by Christianity since its foundation and has continued to inspire many voluntary services until the present. Several of the conference papers illustrate the significance of philanthropy in the initiation of food polices, most typically perhaps Krajewska's paper on the charity institutions of the Protestant Augsburgian Community in Warsaw, which provided hospitals and homes for poor children and women. The detailed dietaries which have survived show the gradual improvement in standards as nutritional knowledge developed in the late nineteenth century and fruit, fresh vegetables and milk were added to the menus. The feeding of poor children, both by voluntary charities and by publicly-funded poor law institutions, was a longstanding provision in almost all European countries, but escalated in the nineteenth century as child populations increased and the development of schooling systems brought the problems of poverty to public attention.

The papers by den Hartog and Burnett illustrate the voluntary initiatives for the feeding of poor schoolchildren in The Netherlands and England, showing how these formed the basis for later public provision. Although humanitarian concerns here were first driven largely by religious motives, political influences became important in increasingly democratic and secular societies, where pressure grew from liberal and left-wing parties to make school feeding a state obligation as part of the educational system. The contrast between the two countries is interesting: while in both the initial involvement of the state was only tentative, in Britain it blossomed into statutory provision between 1944 and 1980, yet in The Netherlands, argument over the division of responsibility between state and family has persisted throughout the twentieth century. In these cases the determination of need was a political judgement – neither Britain nor The Netherlands invoked science in the way that Norway did. Jensen's paper, by contrast, shows how such links between science and state policy were more successful when they accorded with economic interests than when they diverged from them.

The growth of scientific knowledge and the increasing ability to analyse and quantify the constituents of foods was therefore an important influence on the development of food policies. As Teuteberg states, advances in chemistry were critical in the detection of adulteration in which Friedrich Accum was a key figure in both Germany and England. From 1820 onwards the exposure and publication of food frauds by him and later chemists and doctors was the essential prelude to the enforcement of effective legislation against adulteration in the 1870s. The paper by Horrocks demonstrates the ways in which scientists began to be incorporated into some sectors of the British food industry between 1870 and 1940, especially into some of the newer consumer industries such as chocolate where quality control was particularly important. Considerations of public health have often been at the forefront of food policies, and have not uncommonly conflicted with commercial interests. Hietala presents a case study from Helsinki at the turn of the century where food issues were principally concerned with the improvement of hygiene.

Several papers are concerned with the introduction of new foods, illustrating how, in general, food habits are remarkably conservative and resistant to change. In her study of innovation, Kisbán shows how a new food, the potato, took up to 90 years to achieve acceptance in Sweden, Poland and parts of Austria and Hungary. Even when there was strong official encouragement for its use, as in Transylvania, its adoption required 70 years. But consumers' resistance to new foods was not always based on mere prejudice. Crawford argues that when during the Irish famine of 1845/6 Indian meal was imported as a substitute for potatoes, it was not only disliked but resulted in outbreaks of scurvy and eye diseases since it lacked the vitamins provided by the former diet. New food products may also encounter strong opposition from the vested interests of existing producers, as the example of saccharin by Merki illustrates. Laws were initially passed against it in order to protect beet-sugar manufacturers in Germany, which drove it into a black market organized from Switzerland. Saccharin only came into acceptance during sugar shortages in World War I, though even then it had to face competing interests for its constituent, toluene, which was also required for explosives.

The restriction of food supplies and the resultant rationing systems in wartime have had obvious effects on food policies. Governments have had to allocate scarce resources to both military forces and civilian populations in order to sustain both fighting strength and morale on the home front. Several papers illustrate the administrative difficulties of establishing rationing systems in the First World War, when there was often reluctance by the authorities to impose compulsion and a lack of efficient machinery to enforce it. In Bohemia, as described by Petránová, the rationing system became increasingly inadequate as the War continued, so that by 1918 there was a widespread black market and evident signs of malnutrition in the civilian population: food shortages became a main element in the rise of Czech nationalism and demands for separation from the Austro-Hungarian Empire. Dentoni shows how in Italy food shortages produced an ideological conflict between liberals unwilling to interfere with a free market and interventionist politicians who by 1917 succeeded in introducing strict rationing: in this case, it was the lifting of food controls in the summer of 1919 which caused food shortages and serious rioting. In an occupied country, Belgium, Scholliers shows that in the absence of a benign government, food control fell to the work of a voluntary agency, the Comité National: here, food intakes were at an extremely low level, resulting in malnutrition and rising death rates during the last two years of occupation. Nevertheless, the food policies developed in Belgium became an important precedent for wider social policies after the War. In many European countries both the First and Second World Wars stimulated greater intervention by the state, illustrating the thesis of Richard Titmuss that total wars require the support and sacrifice of the whole population which can only be assured by the promise of a better world to come.

The papers given at the conference have been grouped in this volume in an order which tries to establish points of comparison wherever possible: life in wartime, the needs of groups at risk, the search after quality control, and institutional diets are all cases in which food policy emerged as a response to heightened social and political awareness or when the framers of policy, and those who carried it out, turned for guidance to the scientists. In any study not planned purely on comparative lines, there are bound to be limitations in the extent to which papers match, so it may help readers if we try to formulate a general European model of the development of food policies from the late nineteenth century onwards provided that it is recognized that there have been considerable variations in its timing in the different countries and regions of Europe.

With the rise in population in the eighteenth century and the beginnings of industrial development and urbanization, the growth of food policies was of major importance to sustain such economic and social change. In this introductory phase, which can be seen in a number of countries as early as the middle of the nineteenth century, food policies were frequently philanthropic in origin and therefore highly selective in their impact. In this respect, since philanthropy was widely associated with religious practices, there was no clear divide between the form taken by food policies in pre-industrial society and the newly-developing urban-industrial society of the later nineteenth century. The philanthropic approach came under scrutiny by the end of the nineteenth century as poverty persisted – and, it seemed, became more visible – despite the growth of wealth generated by industrialization. As public disquiet developed about the extent of poverty, the issue became politicized and food policies, while seldom formulated by governments, became the means of trying to raise the food intake of the poorer members of the population above the level of the restricted diets which were widespread in pre-industrial Europe, and which inhibited growth and made nutritional deficiency diseases likely to occur during any period of privation.

It is difficult to separate some aspects of this form of government intervention from the second phase of food policies in which governments became concerned with both industrial and military manpower and used concepts of national efficiency to justify their intervention. War, or impending war, as in the first quarter of the twentieth century, gave some sense of urgency to this kind of intervention though, since the science of nutrition was still developing, the efficacy of food policies was, perhaps, unclear and government enthusiasm seemed to ebb and flow to the extent that a sense of national emergency was present. Given an economic climate which saw no major role for government intervention, food policies could be resented as intruding in the labour market and distorting the wage-bargaining process. In interwar Britain, for example, the Trades Union Congress was a major source of resistance to supplementary income allowances to meet the needs of women and children, fearing their introduction would lead to an erosion of the working-man's wage.

Both these early phases in the development of food policies were related to the selective identification of 'groups at risk' and meeting their needs, rather than the provision of across-the-board solutions to general questions, such as the effects of poverty on human health and growth. However, public health measures designed to limit food adulteration and improve standards of hygiene did have general effects on the whole population. In the third phase, generated by social reconstruction plans of the Second World War, food policies became associated with Welfare State programmes. Like other aspects of such plans, they acquired the principle of universality as governments accepted the responsibility of meeting various health targets, notably following the first definition of health by the World Health Organization in 1948. This phase assumed universal provision by governments of welfare foods or dietary supplements, statutory fortification of some foods thought important in the diet of poorer sectors of the population, and state provision of subsidized meals as in school-feeding programmes. It was also concomitant with the post-war growth in food technology over which governments felt it necessary to exercise some supervisory role. The phase was an undoubted success, as nutritional deficiency diseases disappeared and a secular trend in growth developed in post-war Europe, although in many cases the key lay as much in full employment and economic prosperity as in state provision. In addition, success was qualified by the appearance of the diseases of affluence which began to be seen in Europe from the late 1950s and 1960s onwards.

By the 1970s, when the post-war boom was over and governments were troubled by rapid wage-price inflation, the fourth phase in the development of food policies in Europe began. The 1970s ushered in a period of disillusionment with Keynesian-inspired policies as social welfare provisions absorbed an ever-increasing share of gross national product. Despite the emphasis on planning in the 1960s, the changes in the 1970s, by and large, resulted not from evaluation of the success of social provisions but rather from concern at their cost. In this fourth phase, the citing of choice became a new rationale which enabled governments to limit high-cost universal services to selectively targeted groups, to introduce optional provisions and to begin considering ways of dismantling their welfare states.

Notes

1. The editors, in their role as the conference organizers, wish to express their thanks to the sponsors listed below, whose financial support made the meeting possible and met the travelling expenses of the East European participants. These were The British Academy, The Nuffield Foundation, Glaxo plc, Nestlé Ltd, Northern Foods Ltd, Tate and Lyle Ltd.

   The conference administration was undertaken by the Centre for Access and Continuing Education, the University of Westminster.

   The editors are grateful for permission to reproduce the paper by Professor Alan Swinbank. This article was first published in *Food Policy*, vol. 17, no. 1, February 1992, pp. 53–64 and is reproduced here with the permission of Butterworth-Heinemann, Oxford, UK.

PART 1: DIETARY POLICY IN WARTIME

2 Black bread and social peace: Italy's dietary politics during the First World War

Maria Concetta Dentoni

In recent Italian historiography dealing with the First World War, one of the most neglected topics is an account of the organizations working in the field of 'Approvvigionamenti e Consumi'[1] (Supplies and Consumption), a complicated name for a quite simple problem – how to feed the military and civilian populations in order to continue the war and possibly, at the same time, avoid revolutionary uprisings.

Of fundamental importance in understanding the political and social dynamics of the war years, the wartime management of food supplies was not without consequences during the early post-war years as well: the hypothesis on which my research is based is that the events connected with victualling in the years between 1915 and 1918 saw the beginnings of a longer-term process culminating in the rioting of July 1919.

Known as the 'moti per il caroviveri' (revolt against high food prices), these episodes have never earned a place of their own in contemporary historiography. The pre-eminence assigned to the term 'political' in the narrow sense of 'organized'[2] – borrowed from an implicit working-class model, although not always consciously – has led to their being classified as marginal, as hunger protests of pre-industrial memory.

How can we avoid comparison with the schizoid character[3] of the eighteenth century bread riots on which Thompson exercised his irony? In fact, how are we to reconcile the myth of the working class in 1919 and 1920 as representing organization and self-government with its contemporary, but apparently changeless, *alter ego* represented by the bully who 'pounds his stomach convulsively and responds only to the most elementary economic stimuli'?[4]

Beyond the brilliant sketches of social history of which Thompson was a master, it is still on the basis of his 'moral economy' that the revolt against high food prices of 1919 might qualify for the title of political protest. And it is in a return to an analysis of the war years that we can find the justification for this statement.

During the war, more than military discipline, it was the creation of a widespread propaganda machine, preying on the hopes of the masses for possible future economic and social improvements during the post-war years, that guaranteed the maintenance of that minimum of consensus necessary to bring the conflict to an end. Together with the slogan 'land to the farmers', the efforts of the Propaganda Office at the front and the promises of compensation made to the soldiers and their families, it was the direct intervention in the management and distribution of prime necessities that fostered the myth of a future state guaranteeing social justice, a solution to the basic problems of life – above all food supplies – the fair sharing among all citizens of available wealth and hardships and the certainty of punishment for those who refused to abide by the rules. This included, especially, merchants – the 'starvers of the people', as they were so often described in the war years.

At the source of these widespread hopes was the creation of a series of food distribution organizations which, as in the societies under the *ancien régime*,[5] had the primary duty of defending consumers from the perils and speculations of the marketplace. Giving the lie to the fundamental rules of modern economic doctrine by their very existence, these wartime food control bodies detached moral validity from the laws of the free market, proposing in their place the obligation of solidarity between the ruling class and the poverty-stricken masses.

As a consequence, a whole series of measures, which over the centuries had always been welcomed by the working classes and consumers in general and, above all, had been regularly adopted, with greater or lesser reluctance by the governing classes, regained respectability. The first of these, the symbol of a specific political, rather than economic, idea, was price controls – that is, the establishment of price ceilings by the authorities.

It goes without saying that price controls alone were not enough to deal with the food crisis the country was going through. On the contrary, as liberal theoreticians maintained, it was quite often the very fixing of price ceilings that led to the disappearance of goods and an increase in black market activities or, still worse, to a sharp decrease in production.[6]

The advocates of state intervention replied to the arguments and protests of economic liberalists by extolling the deterrent value that the very idea of price controls would have on hoarders, and continued to point out the obvious unfairness of certain prices that only the imposition of state price controls could eliminate. Finally, although admitting that the mechanisms triggered by state control were less efficient than those of the free market, necessities of a higher order, of public peace and quiet, would in any case commend their adoption.[7]

However, once the existence of a 'fair price', to which shopkeepers were obliged to keep, had been established, the price control mechanism brought with it a series of controls, impositions and prohibitions which, being functional to that mechanism, necessarily led to the adoption of rationing. In fact, since the fundamental law of the free market, the law of supply and demand – which grants the possessors of larger amounts of money the right to purchase larger amounts of goods – was no longer operative, it had to be the function of the State, on appointing itself both supplier and distributor (the hated 'shopkeeper State' of the liberalists), to determine by law the rules by which the little available was to be distributed to all.

In its declared universality, the rationing system softened the blow of the reduction in goods available and also guaranteed that they would be distributed. This was a factor in helping to eliminate food queues, breeding places of discontent where crowds could gather and pose a serious threat to the maintenance of law and order. Rationing was also supposed to work as a corrective measure against inequality, and present the government as a higher authority participating in the problems of the many and involved in trying to ensure that the hardships imposed by the war would be borne equally by all.

In a short time, those who had been chosen to direct the various bodies which succeeded one another in the job of superintending Supplies and Consumption, began to voice the need for democracy in the distribution system. They became the theoreticians of new formulations such as the 'associated economy' or 'State Socialism'.[8] Despite the differences in name, these systems implied the age-old paternalism of pre-industrial societies and aimed at the same result: that is, to guarantee harmony between the lower social classes and the dominant groups.

With the end of the war, and with the threat to law and order removed, or at least reduced, the means that had been necessary to maintain it were reviewed and eliminated – first among these being State 'interferences' in the free exchange of goods. In the period of transition, those who wished to leave unchanged the wartime aspects of state co-ordination and rationalization, in a scenario that '. . . elsewhere had actually served', as Mori commented,[9] 'to mark the beginnings of a possible attempt at organized capitalism', were defeated. The masses detected in this a reneging on the promises made to them during the war years and, as a consequence, they expressed their discontent.

Thus, just as the English coal-miners had done in the eighteenth century, the Italian masses in the early post-war period took to the streets, convinced that they were 'defending traditional rights and customs' shared by the majority and sanctioned by previous measures decided by the authorities;[10] the crowds in 1919 appeared to be protesting against the 'offence' to the principles of the moral economy which, at the war's end, were to be abandoned. To prove the existence of this parallelism blunting the distinction between industrial and pre-industrial attitudes,[11] a great deal of evidence is offered by the records kept by the different bodies – police, undersecretariats, ministries – which dealt with Supplies and Consumption in increasingly complex ways as the war proceeded. Together with the re-establishment of the material living conditions of the lower classes, these records bear witness to the birth of the idea of 'future well-being', the negation of which was to bring about the explosion – at first undifferentiated, then more and more conscious and organized – of dissent and outrage among the lower classes.

The problem of food supplies, most of all cereals, had been badly neglected during the period of Italy's neutrality. When this problem was then tackled without an overall policy for dealing with it, the solution already appeared to be almost beyond reach as early as 1915.[12]

Production had fallen owing to a lack of human and animal power, fertilizers and machinery; imports were hindered by poor transportation facilities and discouraged by the Allies' insistence ('advice').[13] Consequently, the Italian government had had to adopt not exactly the system of food rationing cards proposed by the British, [14] but at least the use of milling techniques that helped to reduce the amount of wheat that had to be imported. Thus, in March of 1916, the extraction rate of flour, which had already been set at 80 per cent instead of the usual 70 per cent, was raised to 85 per cent; fine and coarse bran was added to the flour. Later still, experiments were carried out using substitutes, or surrogates, such as the flour of rice, corn, chestnut and lupin, with the idea of making this foodstuff, which was by then bread in name only,[15] less appetizing.

Baked in large loaves, and made even less appealing by its soggy and all but uncooked dough, wartime bread was the first example of the war against waste, declared by the Italian government for the duration. Other examples of this austerity policy which, in theory, was to involve all social classes indiscriminately were the decrees against luxury items, with the imposition of two consecutive meatless days, limitations on the production and consumption of sweets and the reduction of working hours for shops.[16]

It goes without saying that restrictions of this kind had from time immemorial been in force for a great many Italian people, especially those living in the rural areas.[17] Thus, the effect of these decrees by the authorities was more formal than substantial. The purpose of this legislation – in a logic reminiscent of the *ancien régime*, with price controls imposed but not respected, prohibitions, fines and, later on, rationing – was more to demonstrate that the authorities were working to ensure that the hardships deriving from the war were being shared to the same extent by all, depending of course on individual possibilities and needs, than actually to cut back on consumption. The rich, who were used to buying luxury articles, meat and going to the theatre, were to cut down on these activities to which they were accustomed, just as the poor, as was only fair, were to give up what *they* were accustomed to. That this meant partaking of bread containing practically no wheat flour, and eating less of it to boot, even when it represented the only food available,[18] and giving up the little meat they had from time to time been able to eat, which was to be reserved for the delight of the persons of higher social class . . . well, this was the sacrifice that the Nation asked of its less fortunate citizens.

To explain these 'obvious' concepts, to teach the mothers of working-class and peasant families who 'generally know nothing about the cooking of food' and have 'no idea, for instance, of the high nutritional value of broad beans and other bean varieties, peas, chestnuts . . .' and who, consequently, did not know that 'in the kitchen, foods costing little can go a long way',[19] a whole army of 'Ladies', the Dames of the Service Committees, the charity organizations and the various patriotic associations, all charged with sacred zeal, not to mention the blessings and financial contributions of different organizations, including the State, was ready to do combat.

Encouragement and grants, although already established under the Salandra government, acquired special importance when, in January 1917, the organization promoting the limiting of food consumption became a government Commission, the chair of which was assigned to the Republican Comandini, formerly the head of Civil Assistance.

The timing of the inauguration of this new body, although on the one hand it reflected the progressive deterioration of the country's food situation, on the other hand was a token of the different attitude with which the new government of 'national unity' led by Boselli attempted to appear before the masses. This image replaced the logic of 'silence and obedience' of the Salandra government[20] with the use of propaganda and the search for social consent.

Fundamental to this change in policy was the end of the masses' silent neutrality and the revival of socialist peace propaganda.[21] What was at stake, besides the usual problems connected with maintaining order, was the very continuation of the war. What would happen if the threat of a peasants' strike, or more precisely a peasant women's strike (one of the principal targets of renewed socialist agitation, especially on the part of the revolutionary faction and the young members of the party), became reality? This would bring about a consequent, further reduction in available foodstuffs and, above all, a defeatist contagion spreading from the families to the soldiers at the front, who were mostly of peasant origin. With the buckling of the home front, and with hunger and revolution feared by many, especially Nitti,[22] the breakdown of the morale of the armed forces and a subsequent humiliating withdrawal from the conflict would follow.

It was in the light of these dramatic forecasts that in November 1916 – not by chance at the height of the women's protests and while the socialists were propagandizing the peace motion they intended to present in Parliament – the Boselli government created the first body specifically charged with responsibility for propaganda in Italy. A second creation was a committee for the limiting of food consumption which began its work in January 1917 in the sector in which the anti-war germs were festering most dramatically, that is, the food crisis. Its message was addressed to those who were called upon, exclusively and dutifully, to deal with the problem of food – the women. This meant all women of course, rich and poor, urban and rural, but with special emphasis on the peasant women in their triple role as managers, producers and, at the same time, vehicles of consent – or dissent, as was feared – among the soldiers.

Replying to Comandini's invitation, many mayors, prefects, school board directors as well as unsung champions of the theory of thrift at all costs, literally inundated the country with leaflets, recipes and theories, all aimed at demonstrating the possibility, not to say the heroism, of 'living well while eating less'.[23]

The National Women's League for the Limitation of Consumption, chaired by Countess Spalletti Rasponi, even came up with a list of new Commandments: 'don't eat bread unless baked the day before'; and 'never serve, even on feast days or when you have guests, more than two courses for lunch or three for dinner' – precepts that the women belonging to the League pledged to abide by and enforce on their honour, in the name of 'love of Country and our Soldiers'.[24]

Despite the activism of Comandini and his followers, and despite the bureaucratic jugglings that led to endless changes in the bodies responsible for Supplies and Consumption – first entrusted to two different ministries, then brought together under a General Secretariat – the problem of food remained critical up to the explosion of the riots in Milan and Turin in the summer of 1917. These caused the resignation of the person in charge, the social reformist Canepa. He was first replaced by a general and then, under the new Orlando government, by the Lombard industrialist Silvio Crespi.

With the transformation of the Secretariat into an immense sales department, Crespi introduced into the management of the civil service an air of efficiency which, in the state of shock following the defeat at Caporetto, broke down the liberalists' final attempts at resistance. In this struggle, Crespi, with the support of the new minister of the Treasury, Nitti, questioned the very foundation of liberalism, free trade, considering it inapplicable in the economic situation created by the war and proposing in its place the nationalization of the purchase and sale of all goods of prime necessity, and at the same time put it partially into practice.

Price fixing was of no use, controls were counterproductive. Crespi wrote on 27 February: 'in wartime the buyer and seller of all goods of absolute necessity must be one and one only: the State'.[25] From that time on, despite the pressure of serious problems of a personal nature, Crespi dedicated his time and efforts to the task of preparing by April the presentation of 'a series of legislative measures the likes of which have never been promulgated in any country, and which are to be found only in the early legislation of the Roman Republic', as he wrote in his diary, revealing at the same time, and with the same lack of modesty, that he had by then become 'definitely the czar of foodstuffs'.[26]

Presented to the Chamber of Deputies in April 1918 in response to innumerable interpolations and questions advanced by deputies of all political persuasions concerning the food situation, the new decrees on consumption obtained, roughly speaking, a good reception, and gained for Crespi the long-awaited title of Minister.[27]

Following Crespi's measures during the last six months of war, practically all foodstuffs of prime necessity were placed under State control, but the forms that these controls assumed were not equally rigid for all products and, with the exception of meat, no new monopolies were introduced. Thus, rather than nationalization, we should speak of semi-nationalization or a consortial regime, and even in this Crespi did nothing but continue, by generalizing it, a procedure inaugurated by the previous administrations.

The sectors in which Crespi met with the greatest operational difficulties were the meat and milk markets. Meat, which enjoyed only limited distribution among the people,[28] and was thus considered not essential, had been subjected to controls only starting from January 1917 as a part of the policy of limiting the consumption of luxury items.

Sober by necessity rather than by nature, as observers of the economy of the time loved to repeat, the Italian people, between March 1909, the date of the last general census of livestock, and the beginning of the war, had not only maintained, but had even managed to increase the country's wealth in livestock, consuming only the natural surplus in production while at the same time maintaining an active foreign trade balance.[29]

With the war, and the passage of millions of people from a substantially vegetarian to a meat-based diet,[30] the forty to fifty thousand tons of meat consumed in the pre-war period had increased by about 50 per cent and began to represent a serious threat to the future of the nation's livestock and, therefore, to the country's entire farm economy. The importation of large amounts of frozen meat was unthinkable owing to a lack of merchant vessels, but this solution was also inadvisable from the financial standpoint. The only possible solution appeared to be that of limiting civilian and military meat consumption. The weekly ration of meat for the army was cut by 50 per cent, with a decrease of 125 grams per day even for the troops at the front.[31] At the same time, in December of 1916, the number of cattle and sheep that could be butchered was set at no more than 50 per cent of the number butchered the year before; butchers' shops were ordered to close for two days a week, Thursdays and Fridays, instead of just one.

For cattle in particular, since a spontaneous decrease of about 25 per cent had taken place in 1915 compared to the pre-war period – from 1,850,000 to about 1,400,000 head – in 1917 no more than 700,000 were to be butchered, with a theoretical saving of 75 per cent as compared to the pre-war period.[32] In reality, disregard for the decree, in the form of clandestine butchering, together with the necessity of restoring a full meat ration for the soldiers following Caporetto,[33] upset all predictions on savings; from a quick, rough census carried out on 6 April 1918, it was discovered that livestock, especially cattle, had undergone a sharp decline,[34] thus making more drastic measures necessary.

By dismissing the possibility of a total suspension of meat consumption by civilians, Decree no. 496, dated 18 April 1918, proposed by Crespi, put an end to the free market for meat and established that military requisitioning commissions would be responsible for supplying the municipalities with the predetermined number of animals that could be butchered. The butchering of animals not supplied by municipal authorities was forbidden; the sale of butchered meat required a licence from the prefecture; and the number of days that meat could be sold was limited.

The decree established the obligatory closure of butchers' shops from Tuesday to Friday, but the scantiness of the quotas made available, amounting to 30 per cent of that of the pre-war period,[35] meant that the meat was bought up in the space of a few hours between Saturday and Sunday morning. Only the innards and pork sausages were exempt from control, while for poultry the prefects were to establish, province by province, the days of sale, which had to be three consecutive days.

As far as dairy products were concerned, together with the six food rationing decrees promulgated on 18 April 1918, Crespi announced before the Chamber of Deputies a new decree which in practice placed the buying and selling of milk for industrial purposes, which up to then had been free, under state control.[36] Crespi had decided to give short shrift to the demands of the dairy farmers of the three most important milk-producing regions, Lombardy, Emilia and Piedmont, who refused to renew contracts except at much higher prices, even double those of the previous year,[37] and for no more than three months at a time. With Decree no. 493 of 21 April 1918, he extended *ex officio* for another year the contracts that had not yet been renewed, with prices to be established on the basis of those of the controlled market.

Wherever agreement was lacking between the parties to the contract, specific arbitration committees were to set the price, favouring the party willing to agree, i.e. the party 'obeying not only the decrees, but also the moral precepts', in the words of Crespi who, on referring to the recalcitrant dairy farmers in a speech before Parliament, spoke of the fight against the 'sharks' and of food distribution as not only a technical matter but also as a political one: a defence 'against selfishness in time of war'.[38]

As in the case of the technical aspects, even the moralization of food rationing, presented as a corollary to nationalization, was certainly not Crespi's invention. His was the merit, however – or the courage – of not trying to hide the clearly pre-modern character of all the restrictive measures required by an operation of this kind.

In substance, we can say that Crespi was not afraid to acknowledge the country's 'degree of senility';[39] on the contrary, he was convinced that he could continue the modern war in which Italy was involved only by exploiting the tenacity that was a characteristic of the *ancien régime*. In reality he did nothing but use to best advantage a creeping design underlying all government measures: in fact, the loud declarations in defence of the market economy could not conceal the fact that although price fixing on the national level dated from January 1915, in periods prior to the war the laws allowed a departure from economic doctrine represented by price fixing at the municipal level.[40]

The 'transience of the boundaries that could be traced between industrial and pre-industrial attitudes'[41] was not produced by the existence *per se* of price fixing, but by the paternalistic design on the basis of which the adoption of the measure was justified and by the fact that price fixing was fundamentally a means for keeping the masses quiet and away from outbreaks of 'sedition'.[42] It is this view of price fixing as a police measure, that reveals 'the inexorable tragedy of historical persever-ance', as Mayer calls it,[43] nor can this statement be considered at all exaggerated when we consider that, just as happened during the French *Guerre des Farines* in 1775,[44] the supervision of supplies was entrusted to the Italian Ministry of the Interior in 1917, following a debate over the disorders in Turin.

Exploiting all possible connotations – economic, social, moral – of the term 'moralization', Crespi succeeded in transforming the question of price fixing from the difficult problem it had been up to then into the patriotic fulcrum behind the policies of the country at war.

At first, the meaning of the term price fixing required moral purification, thus inaugurating the crusade against those infesting the food market, i.e., the speculators, hoarders and sharks. In line with this first, immediate meaning, Crespi gradually proposed a long series of penalties, distinguishing between those who hoarded food and other goods 'in such a way as to cause an increase in price' and those who were guilty of the more serious offence of 'leaving their goods to rot or throwing them away rather than selling them at the proper time for a fair profit' or, in the case of producers rather than merchants, of 'voluntarily destroying their produce when an abundant crop may have led to a lowering of prices on the market'.[45]

This kind of legislation had a strong moral characteristic; in substance it denied that the normal laws of the marketplace applied, on the basis of which the merchant's job is to subtract goods from immediate consumption in view of future consumption, as was continually stated by the various liberalist economists such as Ricci, Einaudi and Pantaleoni: they also brought into play the authority of the ancients, from Adam Smith to our own Luigi Cossa.[46]

'Merchants are the precious ants of society', Ricci wrote,[47] pointing out that normally, in the course of free trade, the merchant always acts as a hoarder, in the sense that he gathers up the goods of which there is an abundance and sells them in times of scarcity. The merchant 'is no saint', but '. . . what is important is that although he acts out of self-interest, he still acts for the benefit of society'.[48] On the other hand, besides being unscientific, the use of moral judgements in political economy is also of limited utility: 'Political economy is completely independent of morals', as the liberalists pointed out, citing a text by Cossa written in 1892, 'because it explains phenomena that it has not created and cannot modify. The propositions of economic science can be only *true or false*, never *good or bad, useful or dangerous* . . .'.[49]

Crespi's 'moralization' also acted on these economic laws by refusing to acknowledge their existence and, to accomplish this, he used the second meaning of the term, the appeal on historical grounds, as it were, to the moral economy of the *ancien régime*, which obliged the baron, the 'good lord', to take care of the needs of his serfs in times of calamity.

Crespi's decrees appeared to inaugurate a new style in the conduct of the war economy: to a large degree, it was the philosophy behind them that was successful, the fight against the selfishness of single individuals, dubbed 'sharks'. Great efforts were made by the State to ensure the well-being of the many, in the sense of the overall citizenry, putting soldiers and civilians on the same plane as far as their needs were concerned, something which had never before been done.

Furthermore, the fact that it was Crespi, an industrialist who in the past had been a rabid liberalist,[50] who championed nationalization, was for many, especially among the socialist opposition, the sign of a change of course representing a good omen for reforms to come in the post-war period. Citing Rathenau,[51] Crespi himself considered his policies of government as belonging to the school of the new economy of declared 'war socialism' which, perhaps for too brief a season, was to involve the most up-to-date thinkers of the time in new forms of productive and political interaction.[52]

Convinced he had laid the foundations for a perfect organization for dealing with the food situation of the country at war,[53] Crespi was betrayed by the coming of peace: the enormous amounts of food set aside during the summer – to be dumped on the market at the beginning of winter to cause sharp decreases in prices during the crucial season – had to be used to supply the four or five million inhabitants of the newly 'freed lands', the four hundred thousand enemy prisoners of war as well as Austria itself, which Crespi strongly intended to save from hunger and disorder.[54]

In a short time, peace led to what Crespi had wished to avoid at all costs – the dismembering of inter-allied organizations of all kinds, transportation, finance, food distribution – and the return to the normal, but for Italy quite burdensome, pre-war economy.[55]

Crespi's later promotion to plenipotentiary minister of peace deprived Italy of perhaps its most important force of the time. The office of Supplies and Consumption was once again downgraded, first to an under-secretaryship and then to a General Commission, in the mistaken conviction that the coming of peace would automatically make food problems less urgent. This quickly led to the worst days of its existence, culminating in the food riots of July 1919.

Notes

1. For studies on the period between the two wars, cf., R. Bachi, *L'alimentazione e la politica annonaria in Italia*, Laterza, Bari 1926; V. Giuffrida, G. Pietra, *Provital. Gli Approvvigionamenti alimentari durante la guerra*, Cedam, Padova 1936; U. Ricci, *La politica annonaria dell'Italia durante la guerra*, Laterza, Bari 1939 (2nd edn).
2. Refer to the position of Luisa Accati concerning the historiography of the peasants' struggle in the 'Biennio Rosso' in the 'Introduzione' to P. Bois, *Contadini dell'Ovest*, Rosemberg & Sellier, Torino 1975, pp. XVIII–XIX.
3. Cf., E.P. Thompson, 'L'economia morale delle classi popolari inglesi nel sec. XVIII', in *Società pastrizia e cultura plebea*, Einaudi, Torino 1981, p. 59.
4. Ibid.
5. Cf., A.M. Pult Quaglia, 'Sistemi annonari e commercio dei prodotti agricoli: riflessioni su alcuni temi di ricerca', in *Società e Storia*, 1982, no. 15, pp. 181–98.

6. Cf., R. Bachi, *L'alimentazione*, cit., pp. 486–88; U. Picci, *La politica annonaria*, cit., pp. 22–3, concerning the disappearance of goods. The most glaring example of the discouragement of production was to take place following the lowering of prices fixed for wheat decided by the Boselli government in June of 1916.

7. Concerning this whole dispute, cf., M.C. Dentoni, 'La politica degli approvvigionamenti alimentari in Italia durante la grande guerra', in *Studi e ricerche in onore di Paolo Spriano*, Annali Facoltà di Magistero, Cagliari, quaderno no. 30, 1988, p. 352 on.

8. Cf., V. Giuffrida, 'La corsa alla rovina (A proposito della propaganda di Einaudi)', in *Critica Sociale*, XXX, 1920, pp. 6 on; Atti Parlamentari, Camera, 24 Legislatura, Discussioni, sitting of 13 June 1918, speech by Nitti, p. 16780 on. See also 'Introduzione' by Lucio Villari to W. Rathenau, *L'economia nuova*, Einaudi, Torino 1976, pp. XX–XXI.

9. The reference to Weimar Germany is found in G. Mori, 'Le guerre parallele. L'industria elettrica in Italia nel periodo della grande guerra', in *Studi Storici*, 1973, no. 2, p. 351; on this subject see also C.S. Maier, *La rifondazione dell'Europa borghese, Francia, Germania e Italia nel decennio successivo alla prima grande guerra mondiale*, Bari, De Donato 1979, p. 29 on.

10. E.P. Thompson, 'L'economia morale', cit., p. 59 and p. 122.

11. Cf., G.D. Feldman, 'Contadini e piccoli commercianti di fronte all'inflazione: il conflitto sulla Zwangwirtschaft nel dopoguerra tedesco', in *La transizione dall'economia di guerra all'economia di pace in Italia e in Germania dopo la prima guerra mondiale*, a cura di P. Hertner and G. Mori, Il Mulino, Bologna 1983, pp. 350–51, and V. Hunecke, *Introduzione alla terza sezione*, ibid., pp. 342–5.

12. Cf., M.C. Dentoni, 'Questione alimentare e questione sociale durante la Prima Guerra Mondiale in Italia', *Società e Storia*, 1987, n. 37, pp. 611–18.

13. On the positions, especially of the British, cf. the reports sent from London to Salandra and Sonnino between January and March of 1916 by Italian officials, in the Archivio Centrale dello Stato, Roma (ACS), PCM, Prima Guerra Mondiale, 17.1.8, f. 2.

14. Cf., Report by Mayor to Sonnino, n. 1141, 8 March 1916 and, for Salandra's entirely opposite position, Salandra's personal letter to Sonnino, 11 March 1916, in ibidem.

15. Cf., M.C. Dentoni, 'Questione alimentare e questione sociale', cit., pp. 624–5.

16. Decree Law no. 1709, 12 September 1916; no. 1364, 19 October 1916; no. 1681, 3 December 1916; no. 14, 7 January 1917; no. 371, 8 March 1917.

17. Cf., L. Einaudi *La condotta economica e gli effetti sociali della guerra*, Laterza, Bari 1933, pp. 179–81; S. Somogyi, 'L'alimentazione nell'Italia unita', in *Storia d'Italia*, vol. I, Torino, Einaudi 1973; G. Zingali, *La bilancia alimentare prebellica, bellica e postbellica di alcuni stati in Europa*, Stab. Poligrafico dello Stato, Roma 1925/6.

18. See, for example, the '. . . pane, pane, pane', indicated by Salvemini (*L'Unità*, March 1917) as the only food of Apulian peasants.

19. ACS, PCM. b. 40, f. 22, Unione Generale Insegnanti, Comitato Lombardo, *Collaborazione di Medici e Insegnanti alla guerra*.

20. Cf., L. Bruti Recuperati, *Il clero italiano nella grande guerra*, Editori Riuniti, Roma 1982, p. 41. On propaganda, see in particular, L. Tosi, *La propaganda italiana all'estero nella prima guerra mondiale*, Del Bianco Editore, Udine 1977.

21. Without wishing to reopen the dispute concerning the spontaneity and organization of the mass protests of 1916 and 1917, it is, however, impossible not to point out that police files indicated with growing insistence the accentuation of socialist propaganda in the rural areas: see, on this topic, the documents contained in R. De Felice, 'Ordine pubblico e orientamento delle masse popolari nella prima metà del '17', in *Rivista Storica del Socialismo*, 1963, n. 20, on pp. 478, 484, 486, 488, 489 and 493. See also, P. Spriano, *Storia di Torino operaia e socialista*, Einaudi, Torino 1972, p. 355, where a 'leftist' tendency among Italian socialists after the return of Serrati from Kiental in May 1916 is discussed.

22. Cf., letter from Nitti to Sonnino dated 23 July 1917, ACS, Carte Boselli, b. 4, f. 51, now in A. Monticone, *Nitti e la grande guerra*, Giuffrè, Milano 1961, p. 366.

23. Cf., letter of the Prefect of Bari dated 29 January 1917. See also the telegram of the Executive Council of Brescia dated 21 February 1917; Report of the Superintendent of Schools of Bergamo dated 2 June 1917; the letter of the Royal Commissioner of Spaccoforno, province of Syracuse, dated 29 June 1917, with enclosed leaflet, etc., all addressed to Boselli, in ACS, PCM, 17.2., Fasc. gen., s/f. 12.

24. Letter from Countess Spalletti Rasponi to Boselli, dated 18 January 1917, containing the Manifesto of the League and membership cards, in ACS, PCM, 17.2, cit.; on this subject, see also M.C. Dentoni, *L'arte di viver bene mangiando poco. signore e Contadine di fronte ai problemi alimentari*, paper presented to the Convegno di Ravenna, June 1990, in press (no. 12 of the 'Annali Istituto Cervi').

25. S. Crespi, *Alla difesa d'Italia in guerra e a Versailles*, Mondadori, Milano 1937, p. 58.

26. Ibid., p. 83.

27. Cf., Orlando's confidential remark about 'this obsession' of Crespi's, in O. Malagodi, *Conversazioni della guerra*, Ricciardi (ed.), Milano/Napoli 1960, v. II, p. 346.

28. There are no exact and reliable data on meat consumption in Italy in the pre-war period. The different criteria used in collecting data lead to results that even double the amounts calculated, from a minimum of 12 kg to a maximum of 25 kg per capita per year. It is possible to state, however, that meat consumption in Italy was among the lowest in Europe. Cf., P. Sorcinelli, 'Note sull'alimentazione nell'età giolittiana', in *Italia Contemporanea*, March 1985, n. 150, pp. 89–94; S. Somogyi, *L'alimentazione*, cit.; G. Zingali, *La bilancia alimentare*, cit.

29. Cf., N. Fotticchia, 'La produzione zootecnica italiana', in *Nuovi annali del Ministero per l'Agricoltura*, anno II, giugno 1922. For imports and exports, c.f., R. Bachi, Annuario 1916, *Italia Economica*, Lapi, Città di Castello, p. 46.

30. Data on meat consumption by the army are not homogeneous. See, in any case, G. Zingali, 'Il rifornimento dei viveri dell'esercito italiano durante la

guerra', Appendix to R. Bachi, *L'alimentazione*, cit., pp. 423–4. Concerning the general increase in meat consumption during the war years, cf., ISTAT, *Sommario di statistiche storiche italiane*, Roma 1958, p. 226, where an average availability of 500,128 metric tons for the decade from 1901 to 1910 is given against the average of 701,700 metric tons for the four war years.

31. Besides difficulties in supplies, it was the advice of two illustrious physiologists, Baglioni and Rho – the latter in particular the leader of a crusade against the 'luxury' food budget of the Italian army – that determined the reduction in the meat and bread rations of the frontline troops. On this subject, cf., G. Zingali, *Il rifornimento dei viveri*, cit., p. 530 on, where we find Bottazzi's critical observations on the scarcity of proteins in such a reduced diet, which was the principal, although not the only cause, as he later attenuated his position, of the feeble physical and moral resistance of the troops at Caporetto.

32. Cf., R. Bachi, *L'alimentazione*, cit., p. 429.

33. Rations were increased in two stages: an extra 50 grams of meat, but with the abolition of 50 grams of cheese, on 19 November 1917; the reinstatement of the 50 grams of cheese, an increase of 10 grams of sugar and another 50-gram increase in meat on 11 December 1917. Cf., G. Zingali, *Il rifornimento dei viveri*, cit., p. 540 and pp. 548–9.

34. Differences in the numbers of animals present in 1914 and 1918: horses: –10,214; donkeys: +19,162; mules and hinnies: +80,555; cattle: –660,659; swine: –441,074; sheep: –246,090; goats: +82,558. From R. Bachi, *L'alimentazione*, cit., p. 430.

35. Cf., R. Bachi, Annuario 1918, Lapi, Città di Castello, 1919, p. 230; Atti Parlamentari, Senato, sitting 14 March 1918, speech by Crespi, p. 4241.

36. The decree of the Ministry of Agriculture dated 15 September 1916 had placed fixed prices on cow's milk (as food), butter and cheese. Subsequently, and at different times, price fixing was replaced by total control over the butter and cheese markets by different authorities, both consortial and military; in April 1918, fixed prices were still in effect for sheep's cheese and cottage cheese ('ricotta') as well as for milk for food; the market for industrial milk was still completely open.

37. Prices for industrial milk showed the following trend (prices in Italian lire per 100 kg.): 1914: 17–18; 1915: 14–15; 1916: 20–21; 1917: 30–32. From R. Bachi, Annuario 1917, cit., p. 100. For the new contracts producers were asking ITL 68 per hectoliter, cf., R. Bachi, *L'alimentazione*, cit., p. 448.

38. Cf., Atti Parlamentari, Camera, cit., sitting of 21 April 1918, pp. 16384–5.

39. Cf., A.J. Mayer, *Il potere dell'ancien régime fino alla Prima Guerra Mondiale*, Laterza, Bari 1983, p. 4.

40. See, in particular, Art. 109 of the rules for the application of the Municipal and Provincial Act, approved with Royal Decree no. 297 of 12 February 1911.

41. Cf., G.D. Feldman, *Contadini e piccoli commercianti*, cit., p. 350.

42. Cf., A. Canaletti Gaudenti, 'Il sistema annonario e le sue basi', in *La vita italiana*, 1915, vol. VI, fasc. XXXV.

43. Cf., A.J. Mayer, *Il potere dell'ancien régime*, cit., p. 2.

44. Cf., C. Tilly, 'Approvvigionamenti alimentari e ordine pubblico nell'Europa

Moderna', in C. Tilly (ed.), *La formazione degli stati nazionali nell'Europa occidentale*, Il Mulino, Bologna 1984, p. 229 and, for the Italian situation, M.C. Dentoni, 'La politica degli approvvigionamenti', cit., pp. 22–3.

45. For hoarding, penalties were stiffened from the maximum of six months' imprisonment and a fine from 500 to 3,000 lire established by Decree no. 94 of 20 January 1918, to up to two years in prison and a fine from 500 to 5,000 lire in September. The destruction of goods and produce called for imprisonment up to two years and an astronomical fine of 20,000 lire (Decree no. 1464 of 23 September 1918 and Memorandum of the Ministry of Supplies and Consumption dated 26 November 1918, in R. Bachi, *L'alimentazione*, cit., p. 342). Fines from 100 to 300 lire per 100 kg, and the obvious confiscation of the goods, were also levied for placing on sale goods of poor quality.

46. Alberto Canaletti Gaudenti ('Il prezzo di stato', in *La Voce*, 1915, no. 12, p. 11 on), reporting on a dispute in the pages of the *Giornale d'Italia* which continued through the months of August and September 1915 – a dispute during which Maffeo Pantaleoni had defined as 'economia sporca' the price fixing policy, listed in favour of Pantaleoni's arguments the different economists who, from the eighteenth century on, had expressed criticism of price regulations, especially if they originated from 'un'iprocrita morale di stato', from 'motivi di ordine pubblico o da principi di falsa umanità o di falso morale', as Canaletti Gaudenti commented.

47. U. Ricci, *La politica annonaria*, cit., p. 16.

48. Ibid.

49. Cf., L. Cossa, *Introduzione allo studio dell'economia politica*, Milano 1892, p. 32 on, referred by A. Canaletti Gaudenti, *Il prezzo di stato*, cit.

50. Elected to Parliament as a deputy from the district of Caprino Bergamasco, Silvio Crespi was a staunch asserter of liberalism in the Chamber of Deputies. Contrary to all state intervention in economic activities, he opposed the nationalization of the railroads in 1905. In 1911 he had a memorable dispute with Nitti, who proposed a state monopoly in the sector of life insurance. Presenting the overall lines of his war programme before the Senate on 4 March 1918, Crespi reminded the senators of his battles in the past, consequently defining himself as 'una voce non sospetta e tantomeno interessata'. He repeated these concepts before the Chamber of Deputies on 21 April explaining that it had been 'la necessità diversa da quella del tempo di pace' that had made him change his attitude. Responding to a deputy who had interrupted him by defining his speech a 'mea culpa', Crespi said: 'No, non è una "mea culpa", ma la ricognizione di due stati economici assolutamente diversi'. Cf., Atti Parlamentari, Camera, p. 16368.

51. Ibid, p. 16364.

52. Cf., F. Barbagallo, *Nitti*, Utet, Torino 1984, p. 268 on.

53. 'L'immenso lavoro (of the Ministry) si svolge ora tranquillamente su binari ben stabiliti, verso scopi precisi . . . Nessuna derrata alimentare sfugge al controllo di questo ministero di guerra, che ha poteri dittatoriali e ha persino la sua propria milizia. E così la restrizione dei consumi, che meglio si deve chiamare equa distribuzione degli approvvigionamenti, si opera

sistematicamente ed è accettata dalla immensa maggioranza dei cittadini, si può dire *in laetitia*'. Cf., S. Crespi, *Alla difesa d'Italia*, cit., p. 117.

54. 'Lavoro tutta la mattina per regolare gli invii nei paesi redenti ed anche in quelli ancora irredenti. Preparo treni di derrate anche per l'Austria; mi pare buona politica salvarla dalla fame e dai disordini atroci che ne possono sequire', wrote Crespi on the day of the armistice; the next day he wrote: 'Devo nutrire, oltre tutta la Venezia, l'Istria, la Dalmazia, la Jugoslavia, l'Albania. Secondo un rapido calcolo devo provvedere a una nuova popolazione affamata di sette milioni di persone. Mobilito tutte le mie risorse. Da Genova, dove si lavora giorno e notte a caricare migliaia di vagoni, partono treni su treni di vettovaglie. Quale fortuna', he commented in closing, 'aver accumulato così abbondanti riserve in vista del progettato colpo al ribasso'. Cf., ibid., p. 195.

55. Cf., P. Frascani, *Politica economica e finanza pubblica in Italia nel primo dopoguerra*, Napoli, Giannini ed., pp. 111 on.

3 The rationing system in Bohemia during the First World War

Lydia Petránová

Sources and literature

The records of the central Austrian authorities concerning the administration of the Czech lands were transferred to Czechoslovakia as part of the Czechoslovak-Austrian separation of archives and record offices in 1920. They are kept in the State Central Archives in Prague where the documents of the authorities of the Czech lands may also be examined. Of special importance are the resources of the Presidium of the Czech Governor's Office, the Prague Police Directorate, the Provincial School Board and the Board for the Administration of Mines (due to the specific situation involved in supplying the mining districts). A rich source of information about the supply and sustenance of the inhabitants of Prague exists in the Archives of Prague, the capital city.

When investigating the printed papers of that period it is necessary to take into consideration the war regulations on censorship, issued in 1915, which were later tightened several times due to the deterioration of supplies.[1] For instance, it was strictly forbidden to publish information concerning exports from Bohemia to Germany or relating to the increase of poverty. The unreliability of statistical data about war agriculture is dealt with by R. Franěk.[2] The Austrian authorities themselves were aware of the fact that the data concerning the harvests, which were compiled by informants who were teachers, gendarmes and members of the Czech local authorities, were purposely lowered as a defence against the requirements of increasing war supplies. Therefore, the authorities automatically increased the supplied figures by a quarter when determining the amount of supplies.[3] Also, the price lists, compiled in full for Prague and fragmentarily for the countryside, can only be a partial index due to the differences between the officially set prices and the black-market prices, especially from 1916 when practically all foodstuffs disappeared from open sale and were restricted under the rationing scheme. Information from diaries, memoirs and the numerous entries in parish records are valuable, if unsystematic.[4]

The subject has yet to be investigated in full. The records of supplies for Prague during the period 1914–1922, compiled by the officials of the so-called 'Provisioning Institutes' which were responsible for allocating food to inhabitants under the extreme conditions of the war and the formation of the new Czech state, present many valuable resources.[5] They have been interpreted by P. Scheufler who makes an attempt to place them in a wider context, though he underrates the effect of human factors, the role of which is increased in totalitarian regimes under extreme situations (e.g. charity, self-help and community aid on the one hand and fraudulent trade practices etc., on the other).[6] The dependence of food supplies on the agriculture of a state at war has recently been dealt with by R. Franěk.[7] War criminality – where the most frequent crimes were thefts, concealment or reserves of foodstuffs and economic swindles (forgery of food coupons etc.) – has been investigated by V. Solnař.[8]

The existence of hunger riots, strikes and demonstrations against extortionate prices and shortage of food supplies was researched in detail by the Marxist historians of the 1950s and 1960s. Their papers mostly overrate the extent of the class struggle to the detriment of objective evaluation.[9]

The position of the Czech lands during the war economy of the Empire

For the war economy of the Austro-Hungarian Empire, the Czech lands, because of their heavy industry, arms manufacture and agricultural production, represented the principal resource of the Cisleithan Regions. In spite of this fact, the central Austrian authorities underrated the problem of supplying the inhabitants of the Czech lands (both the Czechs and the Germans) with later deplorable consequences. Perhaps expecting a quick victory, the bureaucratic war machine employed a harsh, predatory political line against the Czech lands which did not change as the war became prolonged. The export of Hungarian corn to the Cisleithan Regions was stopped; Bohemia had formerly received about 40 per cent to 50 per cent of it. The industry-oriented Czech lands were to be not only self-supporting as regards agricultural products but they were to contribute to the supplies going to Vienna as well (e.g., potatoes from the most productive potato-growing regions near Havlickuv Brod, Pelhrimov and Chotebor were sent there). In addition, though the export of corn from Austria-Hungary was forbidden, barley, malt, bran and eggs were continuously exported from Bohemia to Germany. The data relating to the amounts are only known for 1914, since later they were declared a war secret, but the export continued throughout the course of the war. At the same time, the extent of imports was negligible with regard to total consumption (potatoes from the Netherlands, corn from Romania and eggs requisitioned in the occupied Russian part of Poland) or, in some cases, imports simply failed (e.g., the import of cattle from Denmark in 1915).

Agricultural production itself was decreasing during the war due to a decrease in the work-force and available work animals, changes in the structure of produce, a decrease in the area of arable land and, finally, the unfavourable weather of the years 1917 and 1918. R. Franěk made an attempt to present an objective survey of war harvests in comparison with pre-war ones[10] and a survey of the number of cattle.[11] The food industry suffered as well. For instance, the production of beer was decreased from 7,382,000 hecto-litres (1 hecto-litre is about 22 gallons) in the season 1914–15 to 1,315,000 hecto-litres in 1917–18. The production of sugar was decreased from 40.8 million quintals (1 quintal is about 2 hundredweights) in 1914 to 18.3 million quintals in 1917.[12]

The total volume of war supplies was not increased during the war but the share of the supplies from the total harvest was increased. The highest volumes were those of barley (up to 70 per cent) and wheat; relatively low were those of rye and oats. The supplies were calculated in such a way that the self-sufficient farmer could retain just the necessary amount of corn for sowing, and for feeding the members of his family and his horses, according to a set norm. The rest of his production was bought by the state at the prices set by the War Corn Office, which in Bohemia had separate branches for the Czech and German areas. The first norm (240 grams of flour per person per day), set after the introduction of the corn monopoly in February 1915, was higher in Bohemia than in, for example, Germany (225 grams) but much smaller than in Hungary (428 grams). It was, however, gradually decreased.

Requisitioning

For understandable reasons, the farmers fulfilled the compulsory supply quotas unwillingly since the purchasing prices set by the state were lower than the prices in the black market. On the other hand, the local commissioners compiling the lists of stocks and estimates of harvests were not interested in hard norms and usually favoured the farmers. On the farms where the supplies were gathered, no requisitions took place; they were only carried out in the case of supplies being unfulfilled or if a farmer was denounced to the police. The requisitioning committees were civic at first, composed of the officials of the state administration, members of local boards of representatives and teachers. Usually, the commissioners were delegated to operate outside the districts where they lived. From 1917, the activities of the committees were supported by military and police assistance. From that time, there occurred a number of complaints about the conduct of German and Hungarian soldiers who behaved as if they were in a conquered country and not in their own state (it is, however, possible that the Czechs assisting requisitions in Hungarian villages could act similarly). In any case, it was a symptom of increased national antagonism and the absence of 'Austrian patriotism', both amongst civilians and in the army. The committees were mostly assisted by soldiers unfit for active service, convalescents, etc.

The officially authorized rations (4 kg of corn per person a week for hard-working persons and 3 kg for others) were not sufficient for farmers. The only defence against requisitions was to hide stocks. The recollections of both commissioners and farmers concerning the ingenious hiding places used, would make an amusing commentary on human wit and indomitable inventiveness, were they not related to the harsh reality of war.[13] From the viewpoint of ethnographic studies, a return to the primitive methods of clandestine home milling and the use of a number of folk recipes for simple meals made from this low quality flour are of interest. They apparently seem archaic but, in essence, they are a sign of regression to a more primitive domestic economy.

Provisioning for the Army

The state made the whole economy subordinate to the armament of the army as well as to its food supply. The system of provisioning for the Austro-Hungarian Army was theoretically elaborated in great detail and, in its nutritional expertise it was, for that period, highly professional in its ability to differentiate between the so-called full (strengthening), normal (maintaining) and reserve rations (for short-time survival).[14] In practice, however, everything was different.

In the first months of the war, the war machine worked in such a way that soldiers even wasted foodstuffs. Even later, when in 1916 the situation got worse, the army was still well supplied by comparison with the rationing system for civilians. This is shown by demonstrations of miners and workers at the militarized plants who voluntarily asked to join the army in order to get enough food for themselves and to secure regular support for their families.[15] As the war dragged on, supplies started to diminish and the morale of the provisions officers deteriorated. In addition, sabotage by civilians and thefts from trains occurred. In the summer of 1918, the generals informed the Crown Prince that generally only half the supplies for the army reached their destination.[16]

Supplies for the reserve troops in particular worsened, even resulting in mutinies. A typical example was the famous Rumburk mutiny where the immediate issue was decaying sauerkraut in the food. The monarchy, nevertheless, attempted to meet the demands of the front-line troops almost until the last moment of its existence, and military historians agree that the troops at the Italian front were best supplied. The present author has gathered many testimonies about the food of Czech soldiers who took part in the catastrophic battle at the river Piave in June 1918.[17] This offensive was the last great effort of the Austrian forces, in provisioning as well as military terms: under dense artillery fire at regular intervals, the field kitchens hourly produced substantial meals which the soldiers, in the stress of the human slaughter, were unable to eat. They, nevertheless, gratefully accepted the increased rations of cigarettes and rum (as much as 0.5 litres a day!).

When the offensive failed, the supplies to these troops also completely collapsed. Then the soldiers spent most of the time during the tactical stalemate that followed searching for food. They bought eggs and milk from Italian farmers or exchanged them for tobacco. During the summer, they stole from fields and gardens: mulberries, green Indian ears of corn, wheat, beans, grapes, pumpkins, ripe Indian corn. In the trenches they cooked over fires, ground coffee, cooked in kettles – all with the silent consent of the officers: 'As we are not issued with anything, they send us to the fields to steal pods ("if anybody comes, run away!(f)' (31 August 1918, Codogne).[18] In September 1918, Italian aeroplanes dropped leaflets with a somewhat mocking message, saying that Italians did not want to shoot in vain since the Austrian soldiers were seen only when satisfying their hunger in the vineyards and in the Italian cornfields and, that after eating everything, they would withdraw – in no longer than 14 days. Their estimate was quite correct.

The rank-and-file Austrian soldiers were convinced that the allied German army was getting better provisions. This belief would require an objective evaluation. In the soldiers' slang, the German soldiers were termed 'Marmeladebruder' (marmalade brothers) because the Austrian soldiers envied their rations of sweet jam.

Illicit ways of obtaining food and cooking were a matter of sheer survival for Austrian soldiers on the Italian front at the end of the war. To complete the picture, it must be mentioned that the common cooking in kettles, as a social activity, was carried out during the whole course of the war by well-fed troops as well as in the prisoners-of-war camps. After demobilization, the soldiers brought the recipes and names of foreign meals back to their homes and some of them caught on even in Czech folk cuisine.

Provisioning for Civilians

Separate legislation for the two parts of Austria-Hungary, which was already well developed by the end of the nineteenth century, existed regarding foodstuffs and there was also a system of food control (these were taken over, unchanged, by Czechoslovakia in 1918). Consequently, at that time, there existed different food legislation in Bohemia and in Slovakia. The Austrian *Codex Alimentarius Austriacus* of 1896 was valid until the middle of the 1930s and both state institutes (Czech and German) for the control of food, established at Charles University in 1897, continued working as well. Food control during the war concentrated primarily on two main categories: bread and milk. The imperial, provincial and local laws, regulations and by-laws regulating provisions for the inhabitants during the war are summed up in the older literature.[19]

The attempt at rationing the economy by means of a state monopoly was the first of its kind in Austria-Hungary. Perhaps it was a lack of experience that produced grave mistakes in the very beginning: import duties were abolished too late; the maximum price of corn was declared late; and the stock-taking of the reserves, etc., was carried out incompetently, which diminished the hope that the measure would be successful. The selected method of state monopoly did not have any hope of long-term success, primarily because it lacked sufficient resources of raw materials. Therefore, the regulations about milling and mixing 80 per cent of the flour, the introduction of zones for selling, etc., as well as the manufacturing of substitutes (though some of them achieved popularity with consumers, e.g., artificial honey, goats milk, oatmeal, etc.) could produce only limited results.

The state monopoly first included corn and then, on the basis of the Provincial Act No. 20 of 29 March 1915, bread and flour began to be sold in exchange for food coupons. From 1916, potatoes, fats, meat, milk, sugar and eggs, and from 1917, fruit, vegetables and coffee, were distributed with the use of a food coupon system. The survey of prices (see Appendix) demonstrates the situation in the market and shows goods in short supply. The prices of flour and bread are not shown; they were regulated by the state as follows:

Bread

April 1915	1400g	66 hellers
October 1917	1260g	1.3 crowns (70 hellers for the inhabitants of Category I – 'the poor')

The official rations were gradually decreased:

	a non-self-supplier – 7 days	a self-supplier farmer – 7 days
1915	1400g of flour or 1960g of bread	1680g of flour (from July 2240g of flour) + 35 kg of oats per horse
1917	1260g of bread + 500 g of flour	2100g of flour + 7 kg of oats per horse
1918	1260 g of bread	1575 g of flour + 7 kg of oats per horse

The rationing system was in practice organized by local authorities and the rations conformed to available supplies. From 1916, food coupons were frequently not covered by supplies, which resulted in demonstrations and hunger riots. In mining and industrial regions, they occurred in the spring of 1915 (the Ore Mountains, the region of Ostrava); in Prague the first ones took place in the middle of 1917. In July of 1918 the hardships reached a head – in Prague, at that time, bread was not baked for 3 weeks. The weekly ration was quite insufficient (0.25 kg of flour, 0.25 kg of meat, 1.5 kg of potatoes, 1260 g of bread, i.e., 774 calories per day) and in addition, it was not available. Only wealthy people could shop on the black market. The wage of a qualified miner was increased by 50 per cent during the war but in order for him to continue eating the same food as before, it would have had to have been increased by 500 per cent.[20] A rescue network for the starving people should have been the State Auxiliary Sustenance Action of 1917, but with the Viennese authorities behaving in a step-motherly way (they preferred Vienna) this further stirred the anti-Austrian sentiments of the intelligentsia. There was, however, some outcome at least in Prague: nearly a quarter of the 40,000 inhabitants classed into the category 'poor' (I: the poor; II: the means-tested; III: the others) received free lunches in March of 1917.

The efforts of local authorities to secure provisions for the inhabitants deserve positive evaluation. Though they were in theory merely the distributors of the supplies allotted by the state, in most cases they made all efforts to secure additional supplies. One odd situation was the purchase of two wagon-loads of high quality fresh seafood, which, together with cooking instructions, were sold very cheaply by provisioning authorities in the November of 1916 to relieve hunger. Though there was a shortage of food at that time, the fish remained unsold. They were bought only by a small number of wealthy people who were accustomed to eating them. The working-class people, for whom they were destined, did not have confidence in them.

The increased number of tuberculosis and influenza patients at that time was related to undernourishment, and various intestinal diseases to the bad quality of flour. The first ailments resulting from hunger were reported as late as the summer of 1918. How was it possible that people did not die of hunger when 'the system of war sustenance, which the government took on itself and was not able to manage properly, failed completely?' Here I quote the words addressed from Prague's City Hall to the Institute for Sustenance of the People in Vienna in May 1918.[21]

Unofficial Parallel Systems of Provisioning

The starving front-line soldiers, who officially received only thin coffee substitute and a distasteful mixture of dried vegetables (mockingly nicknamed 'Hindenburg' or 'Drahtverhaue' – barbed-wire blocks), survived only thanks to their trading, stealing and mutual sharing amongst friends of parcels sent from home, i.e., due to an informal and spontaneously developed rationing system. Similarly, there originated 'alternative' ways of provisioning among the civilians. These semi-official or unofficial means of obtaining supplies were organized by political parties, workers' trade unions (e.g., the workers of 33 Prague machine works exacted direct deliveries and exemption from the monopoly system), self-help associations and charities. The most important of the latter was the Czech Heart (Ceske srdce), which from 1917 arranged for town children to stay in farmers' households and for help from countryside families to urban ones.[22] There existed in Prague 44 war auxiliary associations altogether which provided limited aid for some age-groups (i.e., school children) and professional groups.

The black market and the prosecutable trips to the countryside to obtain provisions were the principal unofficial parallel systems of supply. As late as the autumn of 1918, the government allowed legal purchases of potatoes 'into knapsacks' direct from the growers; previously, only official help from relatives was allowed. A considerable part of the supplies passing through the unofficial supplying system came from the concealed reserves of farmers, sabotage, and thefts from state reserves. It was, in fact, a spontaneous redistribution of reserves. Because of the anti-war and anti-Austrian sentiments at the end of the war, stealing from the Austrian state was considered almost a patriotic act, although the motive was often speculation in foodstuffs.

As in any totalitarian system, the Austro-Hungarian centrally planned and managed system of supply during the war failed due to the human factor, the strength of which increases, both in the positive and negative sense, in extreme situations.

Conclusion

At the very last moment, in October 1918, the Viennese government ordered the removal of the remaining reserves of corn and coal from Bohemia, an act which intensified anti-Austrian sentiments. Out of all possible solutions to the domestic post-war situation, this act contributed to the victory of the concept of an independent Czechoslovakia. The first act of the National Committee (the revolutionary government) was to take over the branches of the War Corn Institute and to immediately ban any export of foodstuffs. An improvement in provisioning was already evident in the first post-war winter and, by 1921, the Czech foodstuffs market had almost completely recovered from the war catastrophe.

Notes

1. Státní ústřední archiv (SÚA) Praha, sign. pp. 1916–20, p 57/1, čj. 6851/17; ad 9412/17.
2. Franěk 1965, p. 22.
3. Zemědělské zprávy, ústřední věstník českého odboru zemědělské rady v král. Českém. Praha 1915, pp. 591–2; SÚA Praha, sign. MZ/R 1916–17.
4. See, Domov za války 1914–1918.
5. Aprovisace obce pražské za války a po válce 1914–1922, pp. 3–5.
6. Scheufler 1977, pp. 146–7.
7. See Franěk 1965, Koloušek 1914, Stoklasa 1916, Viškovský 1914, Viškovský 1915.
8. Solnař 1931.
9. See, Beránek 1955, Kolejka 1957, Křížek 1958, Otáhal 1957, Otáhalová 1964, Pichlík 1958, Šolle 1952.
10. *Crops in Bohemia,*

in 1000 q	1905–14	1914	1915	1916	1917	1918
Wheat	4092	4093	3036	2410	1782	1976
Rye	8673	8447	5050	4205	3478	4211
Barley	5906	5871	2210	3024	1509	1646
Oats	7452	9559	2744	4500	1656	3068
Potatoes	31261	32218	21288	11162	13024	10478
Sugarbeet	38866	40962	29184	28174	19038	28654
Peas	197	193	36	66	19	16
Lentils	21	16	1,3	1,6	0,3	0,5
Clover	12185	16134	12981	12753	5705	5492

Source: Franěk 1965, p.22

11. *Number of Horned Cattle in Bohemia,*

Year	in all	Cows	Oxen	Heifers
1910	2 290 587	1 122 152	341 675	826 760
1914	2 600 000	1 250 500	408 500	941 000
1916	2 192 608	1 026 753	246 186	919 669
1917, 31.5	2 223 228	1 000 423	280 323	942 573
31.10	2 018 223	975 962	242 827	799 434
1918, 30.4	1 753 609	938 051	203 875	611 683

Source: Franěk 1965, p. 28

12. Zprávy Zemského statistického úřadu království Českého 25, 1923, p. 208.
13. Kozák 1929, pp. 246–53.
14. See, *Vorschrift für die Verpflegung im Kriege,* 1,1914, pp. 3–8. The following nutritional evaluation was made in 1991 by Stanislav Hejda:

Full ration
The so-called full ration was the most ample ration as regards energy value and nutrient content. On average the soldier received 3230 kcal (13530 kJ), 101 g protein, 114 g fat, 380 g carbohydrates, 155 mg calcium, 15 mg iron, several mg vitamin C. The energy allowance was obviously adequate even for moderately heavy physical activity. It is, however, not clear that this allowance met the needs of the soldiers' lifestyle. From the documents, it is obvious that catering was not much related to lifestyle, and in particular to physical activity, but depended rather on the possibilities of ensuring supplies. The protein allowance was adequate or excessive due to the relatively high beef ration (400 mg/day). It is, however, possible that the actual protein intake was lower as it is not clear whether gross weight, i.e., meat on bone, was given from which inedible parts (bone, skin, tendons etc.) have to be subtracted. But even then the protein intake was probably adequate, provided the listed amounts were actually issued. Obviously at the end of the war this was not the case and in the records the amount of meat for the midday meal is described as 'the size of a nut' or 'the size of the little finger' etc.

The fat allowance was adequate and probably higher than the actual requirement. Here again the same reservations apply as for proteins. If tins contained fatty meat, the actual fat consumption could be even higher and the protein consumption lower. However, this cannot be ascertained.

The carbohydrate allowance was adequate and consisted mainly of flour, and to a small extent of sugar. It contained also foods from the group listed as 'vegetables': pearl barley, groats, millet, buckwheat, pulses, rice, pasta, potatoes, dried vegetables.

The calcium consumption was very low and averaged 155 mg/day instead of the required 800 mg/day. This was due to the fact that the ration did not contain cream cheese, and because cheese and milk were substitute foods for coffee and sugar. On days when the soldier was issued with 500 ml milk instead of 20 g roasted coffee and 25 g sugar, the calcium intake would increase by 600 mg/day, i.e. to a reasonable level, close to the contemporary recommended allowance. Although cheese and cream cheese are not listed in the allowances, they are found occasionally in the soldiers' menus and were obviously obtained from local resources.

The vitamin B_1 and B_2 allowances were low and inadequate. The intake of vitamin C was alarmingly low; in the full ration it was 1 mg per head per day. The actual intake should be 70 mg. It is possible that those who drew up the allowances took it for granted that the soldiers themselves would procure some sources of vitamin C (fruit and vegetables). Potatoes as an important source of vitamin C are listed in the allowance only as a possible substitute, e.g., instead of 100 g beef 1000 g potatoes, instead of 100 g tinned vegetables 1000 g potatoes, etc. If the potatoes were actually consumed, an allowance of 1000 g/day – which is rather unlikely – would represent an intake of 50 mg vitamin C, 700 g potatoes about 35 mg. It was, however, possible – and obviously this was not exceptional – to comply with the standard and not serve any sources of vitamin C except 1 g dried leafy vegetables and 5 g dried onions/day.

Such profound vitamin C deficiency leads to rapid exhaustion of bodily reserves and reduced resistance to various diseases. It is quite likely that after several weeks clinical symptoms associated with scurvy would develop, e.g., bleeding gums, haemorrhage into joints, skin, liability to develop infectious diseases etc. As a matter of fact the soldiers supplemented the issued rations with vegetables and fruit they bought or more likely stole – obviously only when the season permitted, in summer and autumn.

Normal ration
This ration differed from the full one only by the removal of 500 ml wine per head per day. On average this allowance provides 2930 kcal. (12,265 kJ), the intake of main nutrients and accessory food factors being equal. The evaluation is similar to that of the full ration. Instead of 500 ml wine: 750 ml beer, 100 ml schnaps, 100 ml brandy or rum could be issued.

Substitute ration
The substitute ration differed from the previous one markedly, having a considerably lower energy and nutrient content. The mean energy intake was 1625 kcal (6800 kJ), the protein content 61 g, fat 56 g, carbohydrate 210 g. The calcium intake was extremely low, only 80 mg/day, i.e., about one-tenth of the requirement. The iron intake was 7.6 mg, i.e. just above half the required amount. The intake of vitamins of the B group was even lower than in the previous rations and the vitamin C intake close to zero. This allowance was more or less feasible during inactivity if supplemented with vitamin C, vitamin A and calcium. It is, however, quite likely that this ration was used during battles, troop movements etc., i.e. at a time when the physical activity of the soldiers was high.

15. SÚA praha, sign.PM 1911–20, 8/1/52/27, č.9316/17; MVP/R 1908–18, 276b/ 1914–18, čj.29254-XVb; pres.mor.místodr.1, čj.21677/2047/16 k.407.
16. Domov za války 5, pp. 246–7.
17. L. Petráňová and S. Hejda, Catering for the Austrian Army at the End of the First World War, in print. *Conclusions*:

1. The food allowances of soldiers, i.e. full and normal rations were adequate as regards energy, protein, fat, carbohydrate and iron.
2. Calcium, vitamin B group and probably also vitamin A were low.
3. The vitamin C consumption was alarmingly low, and this increased the risk of disease.
4. The energy (calorie) and nutritional value of the diet deteriorated with time and during the last two months of war it was deficient. The soldiers must have shown signs of malnutrition.
5. Soldiers improved the standard of their diet by purchasing, collecting or stealing agricultural products and foods. This increased in particular their carbohydrate intake, the intake of vitamin C and carotenes from which the body produces vitamin A.
6. The level of food consumption during the last two months of war would not be feasible for a prolonged period and would have manifested itself by the increased incidence of disease, by greater vulnerability to minor ailments, haemorrhage and finally a reduced ability to fight.
7. Frequently used exchanges (substitutions of foods) were not based on nutritionally equivalent substances but rather on lay evaluation.

18. Deník vojína Fučíka z roku 1918. Private Archives of Family Fučík.
19. Scheufler 1977, pp. 148–82.
20. Otáhalová 1964, p. 59.
21. Věstník obecní 1918, p. 149.
22. Domov za války 5, p. 424.

Bibliography

Beránek, J., *Rakouský militarismus a boj proti němu v Čechách*, Praha 1955.
Domov za války 1–5 /1914–1918/. Svědectví účastníků. Praha 1929–1931.
Frieberger, K. *Die österreichischen Ernährungsvorschriften*. Wien 1917.
Franěk R., *Důsledky válečného hospodářství pro české ze-mědělství (1914–1918)*, *Sociologie a historie zemědělství* 2, 1965, 21–22.
Koloušek J., *Výživa českých zemí vlastními plodinami*. Hospodářský stav českých zemí přirovnán k ostatním zemím rakouským. Naše doba 21 (20.9 1914), pp. 1079 af.
Kolejka J., *Revoluční dělnické hnutí na Moravě a ve Slezsku v letech 1917–1921*. Praha 1957.
Kozák V., 'Vzpomínky na válečnou výživu a rekvizice', *Boleslavan*, Vladtivědný sborník Mladoboleslavska a Benátecka 3, 1928–29, pp. 52–6, 116–17, 246–53, 311–17.
Křížek J., *Příspěvek k dějinám rozpadu Rakouska-Uherska a vzniku Československa*, Příspěvky k dějinám KSČ 5, 1958.
Opočenský J., *Konec monarchie rakousko-uherské*, Praha 1928.
Otáhal M., *Dělnické hnutí na Ostravsku 1917–21*, Ostrava 1957.
Otáhalová L., *Příspěvek k národně osvobozeneckému boji lidu v českých zemích, srpen 1914-březen 1917*, Rozpravy ČSAV, řada společenských věd, seš. 3. Praha 1964.

Pech, L., Kremlička, L., Marek, A. Eds *Aprovisace obce pražské za války a po válce 1914–1922*. Praha 1922.

Pichlík K., *Čeští vojáci proti válce 1914–1915*. Praha 1961.

Sellner K., 'Vojenská strava v době válečné', *Boleslavan* 3, 1928–29, pp. 87–93.

Scheufler P., 'Zásobování potravinami v Praze v letech l.světové války', *Etnografie dělnictva* 9. Praha, 1977, pp. 143–97.

Solnař V., *Zločinnost v zemích českých v letech 1914–1922 s hlediska kriminální etiologie a reformy trestního práva*. Praha 1931.

Stoklasa J., *Výživa obyvatelstva ve válce*, Praha 1916.

Šolle Z., *Dělnické hnutí v českých zemích za imp. světové války*. Praha 1952.

Viškovský K., *Válka a obilí. Příspěvek k časové otázce*, Praha 1914.

Viškovský K., *Boj o chléb*, Praha 1915.

Viškovský K., *Válečný obilní ústav a zemědělci*, Praha 1915.

Viškovský K., *Rekvisice obilí dle zákona o válečných úkonech*, Praha 1915.

Vorschrift für die Verpflegung im Kriege, 1 Heft, Allgemeine Grundsätze, Leitung des Verpflegsdienstes bei den höheren Kommandos, Verpflegsdienst bei den Truppen, Wien 1914.

Appendix:

The Rationing System in Bohemia during the First World War

Year	Month		Beef 100g	Pork 10000g	Fat 1000g	Butter 1000g	Vegetable oil 1000g	Milk 1 l	Eggs each	Potatoes 1000g
						Prices of foodstuffs 1914–19 (–) not on sale				
1914	July		2.20	2.20	1.84	2.50	1.85	0.30	0.08	0.16
	Aug		2.20	2.25	2.30	3.00	1.85	0.30	0.09	0.14
	Sept		2.16	2.25	2.20	3.20	1.85	0.30	0.10	0.14
	Oct		2.14	2.35	2.20	3.00	1.85	0.30	0.12	0.14
	Nov		2.14	2.25	2.46	3.10	1.85	0.30	0.12	0.16
	Dec		2.14	2.25	2.58	3.70	1.85	0.30	0.16	0.16
1915	Jan		2.24	2.35	2.84	3.30	1.98	0.32	0.16	0.16
	Feb		2.50	3.20	3.56	3.60	2.50	0.32	0.14	0.16
	Mar		2.73	3.70	4.00	4.20	2.70	0.33	0.13	0.18
	Apr		3.40	4.10	4.70	4.60	3.40	0.34	0.13	0.20
	May		4.14	4.40	5.33	5.00	3.60	0.34	0.14	0.22
	June		5.60	5.70	5.60	4.90	3.60	0.38	0.15	0.21
	July		5.00	5.20	4.70	5.10	3.50	0.38	0.15	0.22
	Aug		4.40	5.10	4.90	5.40	3.40	0.38	0.16	0.25
	Sept		4.60	5.40	6.60	5.50	3.60	0.38	0.17	0.20
	Oct		4.60	5.80	7.80	5.90	4.10	0.39	0.20	0.17
	Nov		4.60	6.20	8.20	6.20	4.40	0.41	0.21	0.16
	Dec		4.60	6.10	8.00	6.20	4.40	0.42	0.21	0.16

	Month								
1916	Jan	4.60	6.00	7.60	6.20	4.40	0.42	0.20	0.16
	Feb	4.80	5.80	7.02	6.20	4.40	0.42	0.17	0.16
	Mar	5.00	5.96	6.57	6.20	5.35	0.42	0.16	0.17
	Apr	5.98	6.40	6.02	6.40	5.35	0.42	0.16	0.18
	May	7.40	7.80	5.98	6.90	5.35	0.42	0.19	0.19
	June	7.70	8.40	5.98	9.50	–	0.50	0.24	0.19
	July	7.40	8.40	5.98	9.50	–	0.50	0.24	0.27
	Aug	7.40	8.20	8.60	9.50	–	0.50	0.24	0.27
	Sept	(7.40)	(8.20)	(9.60)	(11.20)	–	(0.50)	–	(0.30)
	Oct	(7.40)	(8.20)	(8.60)	(10.20)	–	(0.50)	(0.31)	(0.25)
	Nov	(7.20)	(8.20)	(8.60)	(11.50)	–	(0.50)	(0.50)	(0.20)
	Dec	(7.20)	(8.20)	(8.60)	(11.50)	–	(0.50)	(0.50)	(0.16)
1917	Jan	(7.20)	(8.20)	(8.60)	(11.50)	–	(0.50)	(0.43)	(0.14)
	Feb	(7.20)	(8.20)	(8.60)	(11.50)	–	(0.50)	(0.43)	(0.16)
	Mar	(7.10)	(8.20)	(8.60)	(11.50)	–	(0.50)	(0.39)	(0.20)
	Apr	–	(9.80)	(8.60)	(13.50)	–	(0.50)	(0.35)	(0.22)
	May	(6.70)	(8.20)	(8.60)	–	–	(0.59)	(0.36)	(0.22)
	June	(6.70)	(8.20)	–	(10.80)	–	(0.59)	(0.40)	–
	July	(6.70)	(8.20)	(8.60)	(10.80)	–	(0.78)	(0.64)	(0.40)
	Aug	(6.70)	(8.20)	(8.60)	(10.80)	–	(0.78)	(0.67)	(0.30)
	Sept	(6.70)	(8.20)	(8.60)	(10.80)	–	(0.80)	(0.73)	(0.28)
	Oct	(6.70)	(8.20)	(8.60)	(10.80)	–	(0.80)	(0.75)	(0.30)
	Nov	(6.70)	(8.20)	(8.60)	(10.80)	–	(0.80)	(0.81)	(0.28)
	Dec	(6.70)	(8.20)	(8.60)	(10.80)	–	(1.00)	(0.92)	(0.28)
1918	Jan	(6.70)	(8.20)	(8.60)	(10.80)	–	(1.08)	(0.91)	(0.28)
	Feb	(6.70)	(8.20)	(14.50)	(16.50)	(13.40)	(1.68)	(0.78)	(0.28)
	Mar	(6.70)	(8.20)	(14.50)	(16.50)	(13.40)	(1.68)	(0.72)	(0.28)
	Apr	(6.70)	(8.20)	(14.50)	(16.50)	(13.40)	(2.14)	(0.72)	(0.28)

Prices of foodstuffs 1914–19
(–) not on sale

Year	Month	Beef 100g	Pork 10000g	Fat 1000g	Butter 1000g	Vegetable oil 1000g	Milk 1 l	Eggs each	Potatoes 1000g
1918	May	(6.80)	(8.20)	(14.50)	(16.50)	–	(2.16)	(0.95)	(0.28)
	June	(6.80)	(14.60)	(26.00)	(16.50)	–	(2.16)	(1.11)	(0.28)
	July	(9.10)	32.00	–	–	–	–	–	(0.92)
	Aug	(10.10)	40.00	–	–	–	–	–	(0.92)
	Sept	(11.00)	48.00	–	–	–	–	–	(1.60)
	Oct	–	48.00	–	–	–	–	–	(1.80)
	Nov	(7.0)	32.00	–	–	–	–	–	–
	Dec	(7.0)	28.00	–	–	–	–	–	–
1919	Jan	(8.00)	27.00	–	–	–	2.36	1.50	–
	Feb	(8.00)	21.50	–	–	–	2.36	1.40	–
	Mar	(8.00)	21.50	(21.50)	(23.50)	(12.00)	3.00	1.15	–
	Apr	(7.60)	33.50	–	–	(12.00)	2.54	0.82	–
	May	(7.60)	34.00	(21.50)	–	–	2.54	0.85	1.80
	June	(7.60)	27.00	–	–	–	2.50	0.80	2.25
	July	(7.80)	29.00	–	–	–	2.50	0.85	2.25
	Aug	(7.80)	31.00	–	–	–	2.20	0.85	–
	Sept	(7.80)	29.00	–	–	–	1.92	1.25	–
	Oct	(7.80)	28.50	37.00	49.00	–	2.12	1.45	3.70
	Nov	(7.80)	29.00	37.00	49.00	–	2.32	1.75	3.70
	Dec	(7.80)	35.00	38.00	49.50	–	2.60	2.15	3.70

Source: Lydia Petránová

4 The policy of survival: food, the state and social relations in Belgium, 1914–1921

Peter Scholliers

In August 1914 Belgium was invaded by Germany and remained occupied until November 1918. Economic, social, political and cultural life was totally disrupted. Undoubtedly the most urgent difficulty was the disruption of the production, trade and distribution of food. Already in October 1914, the country faced insuperable nutritional problems. In the course of the Winter 1914–15, international help was organized and a rigidly directed, national system of food distribution came into being. Occupied Belgium got through the war years at a high cost, with increasing mortality as the final consequence.

It is relevant to consider Belgium and its nutritional problems in order to contribute to general questions with regard to the reactions of people and the state when confronted with huge nutritional shortcomings. Exceptional circumstances can reveal much about the nature of social policy and society in general. Also, it is important to consider the medium term: did the shortcomings during the war lead to social outbursts and/or radical changes immediately after the war?[1]

The establishment of the 'Comité National': a state within the state

A difficult question with regard to Belgium during the war is to know precisely what is meant by the 'state'. Belgian ministers moved to France hoping to continue the fight, and King Albert I stayed in a small unoccupied part of Belgium. The ministers and the king were cut off almost completely from their country and their administration.

The occupation involved the setting-up of a German government in Brussels (the 'Zivil-und Militärverwaltung') and all existing official bodies (ministries, central bank, railroad) were put under German control. Only municipalities were able to keep a relative degree of autonomy. Obviously, the actual government of occupied Belgium was in German hands. One of the main aims was to use Belgian production capacities in order to help Germany's war effort. Next to the many requisitions of food, cattle and coal, the invader simply moved whole factories to Germany.[2]

When the German government was confronted with the very first signs of nutritional problems, it did not want to help in any way although international legislation foresaw this. It claimed that since the British had organized a blockade against Germany, it was relieved of any obligation.[3] A total lack of organization of food distribution or public charity occurred.

From September 1914 the need among the poor of large cities and the Walloon industrial areas was increasing. Alarmed by this, some members of the Brussels bourgeoisie called upon the social feelings of E. Solvay, a wealthy industrialist who was known for his sympathy towards the labouring classes. He agreed to become the chairman of the 'Comité central de secours et d'alimentation'. This 'Comité' was supported by the Brussels mayor, by bankers and industrialists. So, a remarkable group of people was formed in the best tradition of nineteenth century paternalism. The Comité dealt only with the Brussels area, providing soup to the poorest parts of the population.

The Brussels Comité was asked to co-ordinate the many small-scale initiatives that emerged in other cities as well. In October 1914, it changed its name to 'Comité National de secours et d'alimentation' and took on national responsibility. It became necessary gradually to enlarge the committee and alongside the original group of 18 members, 21 new members joined the committee. Again, there were many bankers and industrialists but also politicians of all parties, including the Belgian Labour Party. The enlargement of the committee was not without political significance. It was clearly the intention of the leaders to represent 'the nation'. They wanted to gather representatives of all social and political forces in a spirit of close collaboration in order to obtain moral and political authority.[4] In fact, the Comité National considered itself as the substitute for the absent legal Belgian government.

The committee had taken over a specific, traditional function of the state. So, what had started as a local initiative with rather limited aims, gradually became a national body with a relatively high degree of autonomy, not controlled by parliament or other Belgian institutions. The Comité National directed provincial committees and these controlled the municipal organizations: a Belgian administrative network existed all over the occupied country.

The Germans were pleased with the existence of the Comité

National.[5] This was easily understandable: in this way, Germany was relieved of the heavy burden of organizing food aid and, moreover, social protest by the Belgian working class could be limited. The latter pleased leading Belgian circles too, who were happy with the efforts made to maintain the labour force: 'Il fallait sauvegarder . . . les sources d'énérgie, les forces du travail de demain'.[6] Thus, the Comité National was not only guided by sentimental feelings or by pity, but also by the preservation of Belgium's economic future.

Organizing aid amidst immense difficulties

Belgium had become highly dependent on the import of bread grains, the Belgians' most important food item. By 1913, imports accounted for no less than 80 per cent of the wants, whereas the country was able to provide most of its needs for potatoes, meat and dairy products.[7] In August 1914, all trade stopped abruptly: neither food nor raw materials were imported, no finished products were exported. The first consequence was the stoppage of all activity in heavy industry, leading to large unemployment and diminishing incomes. The second consequence was the increase of wholesale and retail prices.[8] The ensuing fall in purchasing power led to the setting up of the Brussels Comité Central in the first months of the war. Purchasing power dropped dramatically throughout the war years due to ever-increasing food prices and ever-increasing unemployment.[9]

The war activities in Belgium (there was an 'Operationsgebiet' in Flanders) prevented both harvesting and tilling over large areas of land. Moreover, thousands of land labourers were away (being soldiers, refugees or working in Germany) and finally, there was a general lack of fertilizers. All this resulted in diminishing agricultural yields, not just in 1914 but during the whole war.[10]

Due to failing imports and domestic production, the food supply diminished dramatically. But the situation became even worse at the distribution level. The German occupier interfered with food distribution at various levels (food rationing, price maxima), which also involved the partition of Belgium into production and consumption areas, between which no movement of food products was allowed. This led to a situation where sufficient food was available in one region whereas deficiencies occurred in an adjacent region.[11]

So pre-war conditions of food production and distribution were totally disrupted, leading to significantly lower yields, almost empty shops, a huge black market and sharply increasing prices. It became impossible to obtain food in a normal way and more and more people were forced to depend on public charity.

The Comité National saw just one solution: the immediate organization of mass imports of food. The Germans were prepared to allow this but the British were not, fearing that the food might be sent to Germany. In the winter of 1914, negotiations between the Belgian government in France, the British government, the Comité National and the Germans resulted in the guarantee that the food would end up in Belgian stomachs. Administratively, nothing prevented the sending of food.

With the help of the Commission for Relief in Belgium (CRB), the first mass import of food was shipped to the port of Antwerp in December 1914. The help was paid for by rich Belgians, a consortium of Belgian banks, the British government but especially by the Belgian government in France, under guarantee of the gold reserve of the Belgian central bank.[12]

However, it soon became clear that organizing food aid during war was extremely difficult. The programme of the Comité National and the CRB, initially intended as merely providing additional rations for those who needed it most, was never achieved. There were shortfalls of 26 per cent in 1915, 15 per cent in 1916, no less than 44 per cent in 1917 and 31 per cent in 1918 with regard to the total intended imported quantities.[13] Still, a respectable total of 3,177,428 tons of food products were sent to Belgium between January 1915 and December 1918. The difficulties faced by ships bound for Belgium was, of course, the main reason for the shortcomings.[14] The disastrous figure of 1917 is explained by the U-boat campaign against the Allies' ships as follows: 1915: 5; 1916: 8; 1917: 14; and 1918: 5 sinkings.[15]

Considering the fact that the programme of the Comité National was only meant to provide additional food rations and that this minimum programme was never achieved, it will become clear that the Belgians suffered greatly during the 50 months of occupation. It will be shown below that an ever-increasing part of the Belgian population had nothing else but the food supplied by the CRB and the Comité National. The ups and downs of this food aid determined the degree of well-being or suffering of most Belgian families.

The work of the Comité National

The main task of the Comité National was organizing food distribution. This took many forms. The main activity was providing the daily meal for thousands of people: a simple meal (mostly 1/2 litre of soup and bread) was prepared and sold in the *cantine*, at a price according to the income of the family. Families with less than the minimum income,[16] were not charged. Gradually, more and more families fell beneath this minimum. In March 1915, 23 per cent of the inhabitants of the Brussels area benefited from the soup distribution, a number increasing to 41 per cent by the end of the war![17] There is other evidence, however, of the growing extent of the food aid. In February 1917, for example, it appeared that the inhabitants of villages near Mons 'ne subsistaient qu'au moyen des rations de la CRB, et n'avaient que peu de nourriture provenant des produits indigènes'.[18] Generally, industrialized regions were worse off than rural ones: from 1917 onwards in some industrial villages 80 to 90 per cent of the inhabitants queued daily for the soup distribution, against only 5 to 10 per cent in rural areas.[19] A clear-cut division of Belgium between relatively well-fed regions and under-nourished regions came into being. This led to huge black-market activities[20] and to keen bitterness from the city-dwellers who accused farmers and shopkeepers of getting rich by exploiting the misery of other people.

From the beginning of 1915, it became obvious that not just the working class and the poor were in great need, but that clerks, teachers, small independent artisans, shopkeepers or rentiers also faced nutritional difficulties. The testimony of M. Castiau (in March 1915) is of great relevance here. He pointed to the increasing number of people supported by poor relief,[21] stressing that 'les inscrits récents sont les plus intéressants: ce sont presque tous des bourgeois, ayant toujours joui d'une certaine aisance'.[22] The severe drop in the income of the *petite bourgeoisie* made the dole accessible for this class. Gradually, poor relief was extended to all social classes. This had never occurred before.

Alongside the food aid to all Belgians, the Comité National organized medical and clothing help, as well as the traditional poor relief and help to the unemployed. This latter type of help, however, was abolished in November 1917, since the misery by then was so extensive that there was barely a distinction between the unemployed and employed poor.[23] The Comité National also aimed to help specific categories of the population and in particular, the children. Again, this policy was not guided by mere charity but by dictates of political economy: 'Il fallait faire oeuvre, non de bienfaisance, mais de prévoyance sociale, comme d'ailleurs dans tous les domaines des secours'.[24]

The specific food aid was organized at different levels. First, special canteens were opened for pregnant women. In the *cantines maternelles* meals of some 1,300 kcal were served, consisting of bacon, eggs, bread and potatoes or macaroni.[25] However, the actual energy value often fell to 700 kcal per meal.[26] This resulted in a lower birth-weight, especially for babies in the big cities and the industrial regions.[27] Arrears were not made up during the first months of life, because most young mothers, when breast-feeding their babies, were weak: 'L'allaitement maternel laisse à désirer et le gain des nouveaux-nés qui devrait être en moyenne de 180 gr. par semaine, n'est actuellement que de 50 gr. par semaine'.[28] Yet, young mothers were urged to breast-feed their babies. If they did not (and many were unable to breast-feed their babies longer than six months), both mother and baby were closely watched in the *consultations maternelles*, known by contemporaries as the *goutte de lait*. These *consultations* were organized throughout the country and were the responsibility of physicians. Before the war, 97 such offices had been opened but in December 1918, 768 centres were in existence. In this month alone 86,332 children were helped by the *goutte de lait*.[29] Children between 4 and 18 months were relatively well fed, and in the case of working-class children, in a more hygienic way than before the war.

Children between 2 and 13 years old also benefited from food aid. This took the form of the *repas scolaire*, which was distributed from July 1916 onwards in every school. In the beginning, this meal varied but in the course of 1917 the meal was nothing more than a biscuit with a caloric value of some 200 kcal, and a cup of cocoa. In November 1918, 1,174,100 children received a biscuit every day. Sick children were given special care. The *colonies d'enfants débiles*, where weak, undernourished children were able to spend some weeks, were organized in February 1917. In November of the same year, some 5,000 children were transported from the cities to the 'grand air des campagnes'. The children were 'suralimentés sous la forme de quatre à cinq repas par jour'.[30] Here again, the help provided by the bourgeoisie and aristocracy in lending villas and even castles is not without political significance for the image of a united nation facing a common enemy and aiming at social peace once the war was over.

Another initiative of the Comité National was the help given to the 'Ligue nationale Belge contre la tuberculose', which was not only meant for children. Initially, only working-class families were considered for help, but in the course of 1917 members of the *petite bourgeoisie* were admitted too.[31]

Finally, it should be mentioned that the Comité National helped in organizing many initiatives with regard to the 'nouvelle cuisine' imposed by war conditions. The 'Union patriotique des femmes belges' (helped by the Comité National) published books, organized conferences and acted as an employment agency. For the first time, many women of various social classes were given the opportunity to learn about cooking techniques. The aim was to teach women how to cook with restricted means and how to use unfamiliar foodstuffs.[32] Advice was given on how to boil macaroni, how to prepare vegetables, how to bake wafers of potato flour and even how to chew . . ..[33]

Exhausted Belgians

The effectiveness of social policy

'Sans doute le Comité National intervient-il dans une certaine mesure. Mais cette intervention est loin d'être suffisante'.[34] This is how the aid effort during the war and the living conditions were judged by contemporaries. We will examine the extent of the food crisis in order to evaluate the effectiveness of the aid and the social policy in general.

Physicians made inquiries into the food consumption of the Brussels unemployed depending entirely upon public charity[35] and the results are summarized in Table 4.1.

Table 4.1 Total energy intake of Brussels unemployed, in kcal/day/head.

	December 1915	April 1916	September 1917
soup and bread	962 (49.9%)	1003 (55.9%)	824 (61.2%)
'2nd meal'	⇦ 378 ⇨		266.1 (19.7%)
'aliments Comité'	⇦ 500 ⇨		256.5 (19.0%)
total	1928	1793	1347

Source: J. Demoor and A. Slosse, *L'alimentation des Belges*, 464.

The daily energy intake of the unemployed dropped from 1928 kcal in December 1915 to 1347 kcal in September 1917. Brussels workers who were not on the dole had an intake of 1500 kcal in 1917.[36] The difference between being unemployed and employed – in terms of calorie intake – became extremely narrow and was represented by some 'conserves alimentaires'.

In December 1915, the main meal (consisting of 1/2 litre soup and bread) provided 962 kcal and 25.3 gr of proteins; in April 1916 the portion of bread and soup supplied 1003 kcal and 26.8 gr of proteins, and in September 1917, the *repas* provided only 824 kcal, or some 18 per cent less than in 1916. Despite the drop in energy in 1917, the importance of the *repas* in the total calorie intake increased from 50 to 61.2 per cent, clearly indicating the deterioration of the daily diet. The 'second meal', consisting of small portions of potatoes, *torréaline*, bread and sugar – food of domestic origin – provided less calories in 1917 than in 1915/1916 (–30 per cent). But the *aliments Comité*, consisting of foodstuffs such as rice, bacon and macaroni – or imported products – provided many fewer calories in 1917 than in 1915/1916 (–48 per cent).

This report mentioned results of other inquiries too. Adult male (employed) workers in the city of Liège had 1508 kcal in April 1916, whereas they had 1831 kcal in Namur,[37] quantities that confirm the very low average energy intake, as well as regional differences. The investigator's conclusions were obvious: more people became dependent on food aid, and the food aid provided less and less calories. So, 'la famine était générale'. H. Hoover mentioned an average of 1552 kcal per day and per person between November 1916 and November 1917, which was 'about 50 per cent below the normal consumption of the Belgians and about 50 per cent below what was being consumed by the British at the time'.[38]

Huge calorie shortfalls must have had an impact on illness and mortality. In a letter from E. Franqui to H. Hoover, dated 2 July 1917, this relationship was clearly indicated: 'In certain comparative graphs, the curve of mortality rises on the same proportion as the curve of the importations descends!'.[39] I have checked this at the Brussels level.[40] There seems little or no direct relationship between food imports and mortality in 1915, but a direct relationship was established from the second half of 1916 onwards and became quite obvious in 1917. In the first trimester of 1917, corn imports fell by some 30 per cent and the number of deaths increased by some 70 per cent. But the disastrous imports of 1918 did not result in an equally wretched increase in the number of deaths (although a second mortality peak then occurred). In October–December 1918, there was a third mortality peak, which had no immediate origin in food imports but was caused by the influenza epidemic. So, there seems indeed to have occurred a relationship, but one which was subject to changes during the war years: fluctuations in food aid only had a tragic impact from the end of 1916 onwards.

Information on mortality during the war can be refined by introducing age cohorts. This is done by examining national mortality statistics and the results are given in Table 4.2.

Considering the total number of deaths during the war, it appears that the pre-war trend of decreasing mortality was continued in 1915 and 1916. In fact till the end of 1916, reports were relatively optimistic about the health situation in Belgium. The physician W.P. Lucas wrote in August 1916 that 'la population adulte est dans un état tel qu'elle pourra revenir promptement à l'état normal; la sollicitude générale pour les enfants a eu pour conséquence une amélioration réelle de la santé infantile jusqu'à un niveau supérieur au niveau normal'.[41] This can be explained by the fact that food imports were not yet disastrous, but also by high emigration, the declining number of births and incomplete mortality statistics.[42] But the trend turned radically in 1917, which can of course be related to deteriorating nutritional conditions.

Looking at the age cohorts, it is striking that mortality of the newly

Table 4.2 Index numbers of deaths by age cohort, Belgium, 1910–19
(1910 = 100).

	< 12 months	1 to 4 years	> 5 years	total
1910/13	101	90	100	102
1914	86	68	103	96
1915	66	81	97	89
1916	49	79	103	90
1917	51	87	131	111
1918	48	115	170	139
1919	52	71	119	101

Source: P. Scholliers and F. Daelemans, *Standards of living*, 150.

born diminished more rapidly than that of the other age cohorts. This
conclusion certainly is valid when comparisons are made between the
mortality by age cohort; but if the child mortality is related to the
number of living births, then it appears that mortality did not decrease in
such a spectacular degree: 130 children died per 1,000 live births
between 1910 and 1913, a number that decreased in 1915 (125) and
1916 (116), but increased in 1917 (140). Finally, in 1918 the pre-war
level was again reached. Apart from 1917, the mortality of children under
one year of age fell below the pre-war level. Undoubtedly, considering
the disastrous living conditions during the war, this can be regarded as a
success.

Positive consequences of the activities of the Comité National can also
be noted in 1914–16 with regard to children between one and four years
old, indicating that there was a marked fall of mortality in 1914, followed
by a small increase (in 1915) and stagnation (in 1916–17). But 1918
witnessed a steep rise, which outnumbered the mortality rate of the other
age cohorts: 'C'étaient les malheureux enfants de guerre, qui étaient nés
dans des circonstances les plus douloureuses peut-être que le pays ait
jamais traversées'.[43] As for the remaining age cohort (above five years
old) mortality stagnated from 1913 to 1916, but climbed in 1917 and
especially 1918.

When looking at the causes of death, the relationship between illness,
death and malnutrition clearly appears. Tuberculosis, despite great efforts
by the Comité National, was responsible for an increasing number of
deaths. In Antwerp, deaths caused by tuberculosis amounted to 8.4 per
cent of the pre-war total number of deaths but reached 13.2 per cent in
1916;[44] in the city of Brussels these figures amounted to 11 per cent in
1913–14 and to 16.5 per cent in 1917;[45] in the Brussels suburbs, 10.9
per cent of deaths were caused by tuberculosis in 1913–14 but 17.8 per
cent in 1917.[46]

Food aid and social relations

According to inquiries and reports, social unrest was non-existent in the first two years of the war but became clearly apparent after the end of 1916. With the debacle of food imports in the beginning of 1917, social unrest in the form of strikes, demonstrations and riots occurred.[47] There are no statistics of labour protest during the war. One can assume that social unrest was related to living conditions and, in the end, to the fluctuations of food imports. This would suggest that social unrest was significant in the winter and summer of 1917 and in spring and summer 1918.

How did the ruling circles in and outside Belgium perceive such unrest? They were aware of the possibility of huge social conflict, which was immediately related to shortfalls in the food supply. E. Franqui (of the 'executive committee' of the Comité National) wrote in May 1917 to Ch. de Broqueville, the Belgian premier in France, in the following way: 'Je suis effrayé de la situation qui se présente à nous tant au point de vue matériel qu'au point de vue politique'.[48] To H. Hoover, Franqui wrote in July 1917 that 'the population is beginning to lose the patience and proud stoicism . . .. We are perhaps on the eve of more serious outbreaks'.[49] Was this fear justified? In order to evaluate the social and political climate in occupied Belgium, a report was written in May 1918. Conclusions were rather reassuring: 'Aussi ne doit-on pas craindre des troubles de la part des 6,000,000 d'habitants restés au pays . . .. Des difficultés politiques ne nous semblent pas à craindre. D'autres questions plus pressantes que la lutte des partis ou des classes préoccuperont les esprits'.[50] These 'autres questions' were the desire to relieve misery, to reconstruct and to rebuild. Also, extremely strong feelings of solidarity, nationalism and royalism 'cimentent l'Union des Belges'. This may be true, but nevertheless fear of serious social outbreaks existed.

This fear became acute in November 1918 when the war ended. In a letter of 16 November 1918 to King Albert, J. Wauters sounded a warning note: 'la lecon de la guerre, les réformes pratiquées à l'étranger, les évenements de Russie et d'Allemagne, ont sussité l'assaut des travailleurs'.[51] Indeed, between November 1918 and December 1920 there were huge movements of social protest, riots and especially strikes all over the country (and all over Europe). However, the fact that there were no major outbreaks (nor a revolution) is of importance here (although the ruling classes had never feared a revolution more than between November 1918 and January 1919).

Food aid during the war had a very large impact on the way social and political tensions evolved in the immediate aftermath of war. The collaboration between bankers, industrialists and representatives of the Labour Party in the Comité National established an example for the post-war government: 'Tous lui [the king] conseillèrent de construire un ministère de l'Union Nationale ou fût consacré le principe qui avait fait la force du Comité National pendant l'occupation'.[52] A tripartite government was formed in November 1918, with three influential social-democrats in important ministries. The spirit of this *Union sacrée* was strongly inspired by that of the Comité National. From 1919 to 1921, this government launched numerous initiatives dealing with rents, the control of food prices, the one-man-one-vote principle, the control of food imports and exports, a new tax system and the linking of wages to the official price index number. Such radical initiatives would never have occurred so rapidly without the impact of war and occupation. The background of this new policy was the low standard of living of the Belgians during the war; the aim was the immediate improvement of living conditions. But in the end, the primary goal was the reconstruction of the productive capacities of Belgium's industry.

Evaluations by contemporaries of food aid and the general social policy during the war were concurrent. Although changes in political and social life occurred, Belgium was not faced with revolution: 'la Belgique à papa' was saved although a price had to be paid. Some considered changes as revolutionary, but in fact the 'new' Belgium was largely shaped by those who were in charge of the Comité National, namely bankers and industrialists.[53] In the words of G. Rency: 'Cette tutelle de guerre . . . a tari une source de conflits possibles . . ., on peut affirmer qu'elle a joué un grand rôle et contribué efficacement au rapprochement social'.[54] In the words of H. Hoover: 'These American labors [i.e. the food aid] not only saved human lives, they saved civilization for the Western world. They erected dams against the spread of communism'.[55]

Next to these more general implications, living conditions and social policy during the occupation led to the continuation of some of the initiatives taken by the Comité National. One of the most important was the organization of the *oeuvre nationale de l'enfance* (law of 5 September 1919).[56] This may come as no surprise since the *goutte de lait* probably was the most successful of the initiatives of the Comité National during the war. But other initiatives, such as the *restaurants économiques*, disappeared immediately.

Conclusion

This contribution aimed at considering the living conditions of the Belgians and the internationally organized aid during the war. The Belgian people survived 50 months of occupation thanks to the organization of large-scale help by the CRB and the Comité National. It goes without saying that living conditions deteriorated. Decreasing per capita calorie intake and increasing mortality rates prove this point. Judging from mortality figures, 1915 and 1916 were not disastrous but 1917 and 1918 were. Although the relief effort was enormous, an increasing number of people of all social classes starved during the war. Nevertheless, the activities of the Comité National made an important contribution to the decreasing mortality rate of infants.

If the effect of aid on living conditions was ambiguous, it can be accepted that the influence on post-war class relations was quite important. The collaboration within the Comité National was continued in the tripartite government in November 1918. This took several initiatives leading to the beginning of social security on a more significant scale. Some right-wing circles considered this as a defeat. Therefore, when the government fell in 1921 and social- and Christian democrats left, some laws and new initiatives were abolished. But actually, Belgium was modernizing in many respects between 1918 and 1921 and arrears of social policy compared with, for example, Great Britain and France, were made up.[57]

The title of this contribution mentions 'The policy of survival': it is clear that this not only refers to survival of the people, but also – and above all – to survival of the economic system and the state. Social policy, and food aid in particular, has always had such ambiguous aims.

Notes

1. In this respect, see the volume edited by R. Wall and J. Winter, *The upheaval of war. Family, work and welfare in Europe, 1914–1918* (Cambridge, Cambridge University Press, 1988) and especially p. 2.
2. F. Baudhuin, *Histoire économique de la Belgique 1914–1939*, vol. 1. Brussels, Bruylant, 1946, p. 68.
3. *Rapport général sur le fonctionnement et les opérations du Comité National de secours et d'alimentation. Première partie. Le Comité National,* Brussels, Vromant, 1919, p. 24.
4. M. Liebman, *Les socialistes belges 1914–1918. Le P.O.B. face à la guerre,* Brussels, Vie Ouvrière, 1986, pp. 17–22.
5. A. Henry, *Le ravitaillement de la Belgique pendant l'occupation allemande,* Paris, Presses Universitaires de France, 1924, p. 37.
6. *Rapport général sur le fonctionnement,* op. cit., Troisième partie. Tome 1. Rapport. Brussels, sd., 21.
7. G. I. Gray, *The Commission for relief in Belgium. Statistical review of relief operations,* Stanford, Stanford University Press, 1925, p. 4.
8. Ch. De Lannoy, 'Quelques données rétrospectives sur les prix de détail à Bruxelles de août 1914 à octobre 1918', in: *Revue du travail,* 1919, 642–62.
9. The real wages of Brussels workers evolved as follows (1914=100): 1915=84, 1916=59, 1917=34, 1918=26, 1919=39, 1920=67; P. Scholliers, 'Koopkracht

en indexkoppeling. De Brusselse levensstandaard tijdens en na de eerste wereldoorlog, 1914–1925', in: *Revue belge d'histoire contemporaine*, 1978, 3/4, p. 366.

10. Algemeen rijksarchief Brussel, *Papieren A. Henry*, no. 4, 'Situation en Belgique durant le mois d'août 1918'. The agricultural development during the war was described by A. Henry, *L'agriculture belge et la guerre*, Brussels, Goemare, 1919. Figures for agricultural yields during the war are non-existent.

11. *Rapport spécial sur le fonctionnement et les opérations de la section agricole du Comité national de secours et d'alimentation. Section agricole, 1914–1918*, Brussels, Vromant, 1920, p. 102.

12. A (personal) history of the international aspects of the relief of Belgium can be found in: H. Hoover, *An American epic. Volume 1. The relief of Belgium and Northern France, 1914–1930*, Chicago, H. Regnery Co., 1959. See also A. Henry, *L'oeuvre du Comité National de Secours et d'Alimentation pendant la guerre*, Brussels, J. Lebègue, 1920.

13. A. Henry, *Le ravitaillement*, op. cit., p. 192.

14. E.g., ships were not allowed to use the Channel; they had to sail around the Shetland Islands!

15. A. Henry, *Le ravitaillement*, op. cit., p. 72.

16. This minimum income was adapted to changing circumstances during the war, e.g., in January 1915, the minimum reached 14.20 Frs. per week for a family of four; *Rapport général sur le fonctionnement*, op. cit., Troisième partie, vol. 1, p. 28.

17. *Rapport général sur le fonctionnement*, op. cit., Deuxième partie, vol. 1, pp. 214–5.

18. 'Choses de Belgique. La crise alimentaire en Belgique envahie (par A. Jane)', in: *La libre parole*, 16.9.1917, p. 3.

19. *Rapport général sur les opérations*, op. cit., Troisième partie, vol. 1, pp. 32–4.

20. See the testimony by Brand Whitlock, *Belgium under the German occupation. A personal narrative*, London, W. Heinemann, 1919, vol. 2, 161–63.

21. This does not refer to the people attending the soup distribution, but to the 'traditional' aid to the poor. In the Brussels area, 16.2 per cent of the inhabitants were on the dole in September 1914, but 25.9 per cent in February 1915. See the week-to-week development of the official figures in: P. Scholliers and F. Daelemans, 'Standards of living and standards of health in wartime Belgium', in: R. Wall and J. Winter (eds), *The Upheaval of war*, op. cit., p. 148.

22. Archief koninklijk paleis, *Archief kabinet Koning Albert, 1914–1918*, no. 606, manuscript, M. Castiau, Comment Bruxelles fut nourri, 306.

23. *Rapport général sur les opérations*, op. cit., Troisième partie. vol. 1, pp. 40–44.

24. *Rapport général sur les opérations*, op. cit., Troisième partie. vol. 1, p. 73.

25. Archief koninklijk paleis, *Archief kabinet koning Albert (1914–1918)*, no. 615, 'Rapport de E. Franqui (?) à M. van den Steen de Jehay (chef du cabinet du Roi), 16 novembre 1917', p. 9.

26. J. Demoor and A. Slosse, 'L'alimentation des Belges pendant la guerre et ses conséquences', in: *Bulletin de l'Académie royale de médecine de Belgique*, XXX, 1920, p. 477.

27. Archief koninklijk paleis, *Archief kabinet Koning Albert (1914–1918)*, no. 609, 'CRB Considérations générales de l'hygiène en Belgique. Rapport de W. P. Lucas, dr. en médicine, 14.8.1916', p. 14.
28. Ibid., pp. 14–5.
29. G. Rency, *La Belgique et la guerre. Volume 1. La vie matérielle de la Belgique pendant la première guerre mondiale.* Brussels, H. Bertels, 1920, pp. 75–6.
30. Archief koninklijk paleis, *Archief kabinet koning Albert (1914–1918)*, no. 615, 'Rapport E. Franqui (?) à M. van den Steen de Jehay', doc. cit., pp. 12–13.
31. *Rapport sur l'activité de la Ligue nationale Belge contre la tuberculose pendant la guerre*, Brussels, Imprimerie Ministère des Travaux publics, 1920, p. 93.
32. Tante Claire, *Un trésor alimentaire: le riz*, Soignies, F. Guilmot, 1915; Tante Claire, *La viande nous est-elle indispensable?* Brussels, 1916.
33. A brochure of the 'Union patriotique des femmes belges', written by M. Parent, *Recettes de guerre*, (Brussels, C. Bulens, 1916) ends by giving advice on the way in which one should breathe and eat.
34. Archief koninklijk paleis, *Archief kabinet koning Albert (1914–1918)*, no. 341, 'Copie du rapport de M. Oliviers au tribunal de première instance à Bruxelles. Rapport fait à la demande de M. le secrétaire général du service spécial de recrutement à Folkestone, 28.5.1918', p. 2.
35. J. Demoor and A. Slosse, 'L'alimentation des Belges', op. cit., pp. 463–5.
36. Ibid, pp. 464–6.
37. Ibid, pp. 468, 472.
38. H. Hoover, *An American epic*, op. cit., vol. 1, p. 215.
39. Quoted in H. Hoover, *An American epic*, op. cit., vol. 1, p. 350.
40. By comparing the imported grain with mortality, both in the Brussels area; see P. Scholliers and F. Daelemans, 'Standard of living', op. cit., p. 153. The correlation coefficient between the two variables for the whole period was calculated as -0.525, suggesting that one half of the trend in the death series could be explained by changes in imports.
41. Archief koninklijk paleis, *Archief kabinet koning Albert (1914–1918)*, no. 609, doc. cit., p. 21.
42. P. Scholliers and F. Daelemans, 'Standard of living', op. cit., p. 152.
43. C. Jacquart, *La population et la guerre*, Leuven, Nova et Vetera, 1922, p. 12.
44. Archief koninklijk paleis, *Archief kabinet koning Albert (1914–1918)*, no. 609, doc. cit., p. 9.
45. *Bulletin communal de la ville de Bruxelles, 1919. Rapport annuel.* Brussels, 1920, p. 509.
46. J. Demoor and A. Slosse, 'L'alimentation des Belges', op. cit., p. 505.
47. 'Choses de Belgique. La crise alimentaire en Belgique envahie', in: *La libre parole*, 16 September 1917, p. 3.
48. Algemeen rijksarchief Brussel, *Papieren A. Henry*, no. 7.
49. H. Hoover, *An American epic*, op. cit., p. 350.
50. Archief Koninlkijk paleis, *Archief kabinet koning Albert (1914–1918)*, no. 341, 'Copie du rapport de M. Oliviers', doc. cit., 28.5.1918, pp. 4–5.
51. Algemeen rijksarchief Brussel, *Papieren J. Wauters*, III-aanwinsten no. 596, doc. no. 266, 'Lettre de J. Wauters à Albert I', 16 November 1918.
52. G. Rency, *La Belgique et la guerre*, op. cit., p. 354.

53. E. Witte, J. Craeybeckx and A. Meynen, *Politieke geschiedenis van België. Van 1830 tot heden*, Antwerpen, Standaard, 1990, pp. 173–4.
54. G. Rency, *La Belgique et la guerre*, op. cit., p. 112.
55. H. Hoover, *An American epic*, vol. 1, xv.
56. See for the activities from 1915 onwards: H. Velge, *L'activité de l'Oeuvre nationale de l'enfance pendant vingt-cinq ans (1915–1940)*, Brussels, Oeuvre Nationale de l'Enfance, 1941.
57. This refers, for example, to the voting system and the system of collective bargaining.

PART 2: STATE POLICY AND GROUPS AT RISK

5 The rise and decline of school meals in Britain, 1860–1990

John Burnett

Introduction

In the dark days of October 1941, Lord Woolton, the wartime Minister of Food, was reported in *The Times* as saying: 'I want to see elementary school children as well fed as children going to Eton and Harrow. I am determined that we shall organise our food front that at the end of the war . . . we shall have preserved and even improved the health and physique of the nation'.[1] By 1945, 40 per cent of schoolchildren in England and Wales were eating school dinners, either free or subsidised, which provided around 1,000 kcals, at least one-third of their energy requirements, while a similar proportion was also benefiting from the Milk in Schools scheme. The wartime expansion of these services, both of which had existed on a smaller scale previously, provides a striking example of Richard Titmuss's theory about the effects of wars on social policy – that as twentieth century wars became more 'total', with a higher participation ratio involving civilian as well as military personnel, so the state's commitment to social welfare increased in order to sustain the nation's physical and moral strength and to compensate for the sacrifices demanded.[2] War, the fear of it and the retreat of the danger of it, has been a major influence throughout the history of school meals. The introduction of a publicly funded service in 1906 came about largely because of fears of a national deterioration of physique which Britain's poor military performance in the South African War had seemingly revealed, while its expansion in the late 1930s was associated with preparations for the coming conflict as well as with increased anxiety about malnutrition of children in the depressed areas. But to view the rise and fall of school meals as principally militarily determined would be much too simplistic. The issue of whether certain children attending school should be fed at public expense had strong moral and political overtones and has been hotly, even passionately, debated throughout its hundred years' history because it raises fundamental questions about the responsibility of the state as against that of parents. While in the later nineteenth century the state was prepared to protect the consumer against the adulteration of food, to encourage local authorities to build homes for the working classes and to make elementary (but not secondary) education compulsory and free, it held back persistently even from permitting councils to provide meals for schoolchildren who were so hungry that they were unable to profit fully from their lessons. The main objection was a deep, ideological one – that for public bodies to feed children was to take away the proper responsibility of parents to maintain their offspring, and that to invade this was to weaken, and, perhaps, ultimately destroy, the family as the basic unit of society. Feeding was regarded by many as in a different category from housing, clothing or educating: it was the most fundamental responsibility of parenthood, and the family meal, however simple, was akin to a sacrament which only socialists and atheists would wish to desecrate.

It is for these reasons that the passing of the Education (Provision of Meals) Act in 1906, which allowed (but not required) local authorities to levy a special rate for providing free meals to 'necessitous' children, without penalty to their parents, has been hailed by historians of social policy as having a significance far beyond its limited provisions. Charles Pipkin in 1931 considered that 'It would be difficult to place too much emphasis on the new principle of state action . . . for in a nation jealous of individual rights and proud of its conservative instincts it was nothing less than a revolutionary principle'.[3] And Professor Bentley Gilbert has gone so far as to claim that the Act 'marked the beginning of the construction of the welfare state',[4] in that, for the first time, a benefit was given by the state without a corresponding disbenefit to the recipient.

What makes school meals also of contemporary interest to observers of social policy is the debate which has accompanied the reduction of the service in the 1970s and 1980s. From the 1940s onwards, school meals became a normal, integral part of the education system and few people even questioned whether, in a period of rising standards of living and improving health, there continued to be a justification for heavily subsidised meals for the children of parents who – the great majority at least – could afford to feed them adequately and to pay the market price. As at the beginning of the century, the debate again evoked issues about family responsibility as politicians of the New Right sought to 'roll back the frontiers of the state' and reinstate individual choice. The history of school meals therefore provides an excellent example of the underlying ideological influences on food policies, as well as more immediate military, political and economic pressures.

The voluntary movement

In common with many other areas of social policy, the initiative for the provision of school meals came from philanthropic individuals and groups concerned at the evident poverty and hunger of some children attending schools in the great cities. At the beginning, therefore, there was an essentially charitable element which, in the context of the mid-nineteenth century, almost inevitably went together with religious zeal – religious teaching and food being seen as complementary weapons in the process of conversion. Appropriately, the earliest school meals (in day-schools as opposed to boarding schools for the children of wealthy parents) were given in Ragged Schools, institutions specifically designed for the poorest children whose behaviour, dress and manners made them unacceptable in normal schools. Such children were the products of slum life, of drunken parents and broken marriages; some were actual or incipient delinquents, for whom it was hoped that the strict discipline of the school would act as a reformatory. The Ragged School movement began as a charitable effort in the 1840s under the leadership of Lord Ashley, the champion of many causes for the welfare of children. The Ragged School Union was founded in 1844, and by 1861 had 176 schools under its control, maintained by the voluntary subscriptions of the wealthier classes.[5] First started in London, such schools quickly spread to other towns, particularly the new industrial cities of the north where extreme poverty existed in the residuum of casual and unemployed workers. These local efforts to provide some nourishment for the poorest of all school pupils were put on a more organised basis by the foundation of The Destitute Children's Dinner Society in 1864: by 1870 there were 58 dining-rooms open in London.[6]

That year marked a turning-point in the early history of school feeding, since the new Elementary Education Act required local School Boards to provide sufficient school places for all children in their districts up to the age of 10: attendance was in effect made compulsory in 1876. Now, for the first time, teachers confronted working-class children *en masse*, including those from poorer families who had previously evaded formal education. They were alarmed to see the extent of stunted growth, physical defects such as rickets, defective eyesight, teeth and hearing which were especially prevalent in the inner cities, and quickly concluded that such children's concentration and learning capacity were inhibited by hunger and malnutrition. Under the Revised Code, introduced in 1862, a school's grant was dependent on the proportion of pupils who passed annual examinations in 'the three R's' set by Her Majesty's Inspectors, and teachers complained that this system of 'payment by results' put excessive pressure on them – and, hence, on their pupils – to succeed in the required tests which depended largely on rote learning.

Teachers themselves began to take a lead in organising free breakfasts and dinners for the more obviously hungry children, and in the early 1880s Mrs E.M. Burgwin, headmistress of a school in a poor area of Southwark, enlisted the support of George R. Sims, a journalist much concerned with social issues, who wrote for *The Referee*. The outcome of this and other publicity was the formation of a voluntary body, the London Schools Dinner Association, in 1889, to raise subscriptions for school feeding on an organised scale. Another contributory factor had been the growing anxiety about the effects of forced learning on hungry children, accompanied as it often was by harsh discipline and punishment. In 1884 a Medical Officer, Dr Crichton-Browne, published a *Report on the Alleged Over-Pressure of Work in Public Elementary Schools*, which pointed to ' a larger question than dullness – perhaps the largest and most important of all is that of starvation'. The report coincided with a period of industrial depression in the 1880s when unemployment increased considerably, reaching almost 10 per cent even in some of the skilled trades; significantly, it was in 1886 that Charles Booth began his influential study of the *Life and Labour of the People of London* (1886–1902) which was to conclude that 30.7 per cent of the population of the capital were living below the poverty line. A little later, Seebohm Rowntree's identification of the 'poverty cycle' showed that household resources were at their lowest in the early stages of family formation when children were liabilities rather than contributors to family income.[7]

The effect of these increasing anxieties about child health and poverty was to expand the voluntary provision of school meals between 1880 and 1900, and several of the debates which were to characterize the history of the service now began to emerge. With the establishment of socialist organizations such as the Social Democratic Federation (1884) the issue quickly took on political dimensions when they also entered the field as meal providers: Socialist Dinners were organised by the SDF and also by the Independent Labour Party (1893) which, it was hoped, would develop fraternal 'social feeling' as well as sounder bodies. Their demand was for publicly provided free meals each day for all children as part of the education system, as H.M. Hyndman argued: 'in order to enable them to take full advantage of the free teaching at their disposal'.

By the end of the century the issue had become strongly politicized. The idea of free meals, or of publicly provided meals whether free or not, ran counter to much contemporary ideology, including that of some of the bodies engaged in voluntary provision who regarded themselves as genuinely humane and philanthropic. For example, the Charity Organisation Society, founded in 1869, was itself sponsoring a Penny Dinner movement in many towns, by which children were expected to contribute 1d. towards the cost of hot meals which were normally served only on three or four days a week in winter: it was felt that this preserved family responsibility, a cardinal principle of COS policy, without undermining existing social ideals and institutions. Commenting on the Crichton-Browne Report, J.G. Fitch wrote: 'If it once becomes understood that the state will provide food for all the children in public schools who seem to require it, the influence of a large number of parents in diminishing their sense of responsibility may become a serious public danger'. There was even a revival of Malthusian fears about improvident marriages and over-population, given a new focus by the belief that it was the least responsible and socially desirable classes who were reproducing themselves most rapidly. 'If, then, it is recognised as the duty of the state to feed the starving child, one more check upon population will be removed.'

At a time when most charity was still associated with religion, another powerful argument against free school meals was that they would be contrary to the moral teaching of the Church, which, especially in its evangelical wing, stressed individualism and parental responsibility. But, for many late Victorians, the greatest objection was political – that freely-provided meals would be an extension of socialism which could eventually replace a family-based social structure. The idea that a few bowls of soup to hungry children would have such disastrous consequences, however risible, has to be seen in the context of a deep-seated fear of the advance of socialism at the end of the century, now that the working class was enfranchised and organizing itself industrially and politically. The warning by Sir Arthur Clay in 1905 would have been received with much approval: 'To the socialistic school of thought . . . the duties of parents ought to be confined to producing and handing over their infants to the state'.[8] Sir Arthur further argued that the problem of malnutrition was 'not quantitative, but qualitative. The mischief begins at birth, and the only effectual cure is the better instruction of mothers in the judicious feeding of their children'. This widely held view, that the problem of underfeeding was caused by ignorance rather than lack of means, provided yet another argument against school meals; they would only tempt lazy mothers to neglect their children still further when what was needed was instruction in cheap, nutritious cooking and lessons in household management.

The Education (Provision of Meals) Act 1906

By the end of the nineteenth century, charitable agencies for feeding hungry schoolchildren had reached their peak of endeavour. In 1889 the London School Board estimated that 44,000 children, or 12.8 per cent of those attending London schools, were habitually in want of food, but that less than half of these were receiving meals.[9] By then, there were some 300 voluntary feeding bodies in the United Kingdom, but the process of selection of the children deemed to be 'necessitous' varied greatly. In some towns, mothers had to apply for their children's meals; in others, the children were selected by teachers or doctors, and their homes then visited by members of the voluntary committee. If, after such investigation of home circumstances, permission was given, it was sometimes granted only for two or four weeks, after which reapplication was required. Meals were usually provided only between December and March, the coldest months of the year and the period of highest unemployment, and only on three or four days in the week – on the ground that on Mondays children could be fed at home on the 'leftovers' from the Sunday meal. Food was not provided at weekends or during school holidays. The Independent Labour Party, which was itself providing free meals in the 1890s, commented that the system of investigation was 'calculated to deter all self-respecting parents from making an application'.[10]

Between 1900 and 1906, however, attitudes towards school feeding changed radically, resulting in the latter year in the first legislation permitting public funding for school meals. The reasons for this awakened concern for the welfare of children were various and complex, but have been summarised as 'a blend of humanitarianism and self-interest'.[11] In the late nineteenth and early twentieth centuries there was renewed anxiety about the state of public health and, particularly, that of children. Although the general mortality rate had shown progressive improvement and had been reduced to less than 20 per thousand – Edwin Chadwick's target of the mid-century – infant mortality (deaths under 1 year per thousand live births) and child mortality (deaths under 5 years) had not responded similarly. Indeed, the infant death-rate, which had averaged 154 per thousand in 1855–59 stood at 158 per thousand in 1895–99, and in one district of Sheffield in 1901 reached the alarming figure of 234 per thousand.[12] Even when babies survived the early, hazardous months of life, subsequent growth-rates clearly reflected their social class origins, such that in 1908 boys aged 13 from upper-class homes averaged 58.6 inches, while those from the lower class reached only 54.9 inches.[13]

These fears about the degeneration of the urban populations were voiced as early as 1885 by James Cantlie, who portrayed the typical, third-generation adult male Londoner as only 5 feet 1 inch tall and with a chest measurement of 28 inches,[14] but around the turn of the century they escalated into a major national scare, and a campaign for remedial action. In *The Heart of the Empire* (1901) C.F.G. Masterman argued that the effect of unprecedented urban growth during the previous half-century had been to produce a typical 'City type' – stunted, narrow-chested, easily wearied, yet voluble, excitable, with little ballast, stamina or endurance, seeking stimulus in drink, in betting, in any unaccustomed conflicts at home or abroad'.[15] Much of this anxiety about physical degeneration focused on the ability of a small nation to defend her vast empire against the territorial ambitions of other European countries: faced with an already declining birth-rate, Britain must make up for her small numbers by greater National Efficiency, which would include better standards of education, greater industrial productivity and, above all, improved national health. As Arnold White wrote in *Efficiency and Empire* (1901):

The first element of efficiency, is health . . .. Nothing less than the downfall of the Anglo-Saxon is assured unless improved stamina and greater physical fitness of our city folk are assured . . . . Our species is being propagated by, and continued increasingly from, undersized, street-bred people. . . . Unless our town-dwellers take heed, and recognise that we have begun to rot, our position as a World Power is doomed. . . .[16]

For many people, these gloomy prognostications seemed to be confirmed by Britain's poor military performance in the South African War (1899–1902) when the cream of the British army was hard pressed to defeat the amateur battalions of Boer farmers. Even more disturbing, it had been found necessary to reject a high proportion of the young volunteers, supposedly in the prime of life, on grounds of medical unfitness. At the end of the war, the Inspector-General of Army Recruiting reported that in the period 1894–1902 of 679,700 men who had enlisted and been medically examined, 234,900 had been rejected as unfit (34.6 per cent) and a further 3.0 per cent discharged as invalids within 2 years, making a total of 37.6 per cent; he also observed that even this high figure did not represent anything like the full extent of unfitness since recruiters were instructed not to submit men for medical examination unless they had a reasonable expectation of passing: the true rejection rate, he estimated, was therefore nearer to 60 per cent. 'The one subject that causes anxiety in the future as regards recruiting is the gradual deterioration of the physique of the working classes from whence the bulk of recruits must always be drawn . . . .'[17]

In this atmosphere of national anxiety, Imperialism became strongly mixed with social reform, particularly, though not exclusively, in the

Liberal party which was already undergoing conversion from Gladstonian individualism and self-help towards a collectivist ideology which recognised the state's responsibility to protect groups in genuine need. The revelations of the Boer War spurred on this process. In his theory about the influence of wars on social policy, R.M. Titmuss wrote of 'the ferment of inquiry' which followed after 1902, and argued that publicly funded school meals, together with other social reforms affecting children, 'stemmed directly from the Boer War, and show how, in modern times, our concern for communal fitness has followed closely upon the course of our military fortunes'.[18] With the present state of unfitness of the adult population little, perhaps, could be done, but there was still time to improve the health of children – 'the next generation of recruits for the army'. Two influential official enquiries followed closely in the wake of the ending of hostilities. In 1903 a Royal Commission on Physical Training in Scotland recommended that education authorities be empowered to co-operate with voluntary bodies to provide food for needy schoolchildren, though without cost to public funds. The intention was that reimbursement of the cost should be obtained from the parents – an unlikely expectation since the need arose principally because of family poverty.[19]

The following year, an Inter-Departmental Committee on Physical Deterioration reported, the very title of which suggested the degree of public alarm over recent revelations. In fact, the Committee was unable to establish evidence of national deterioration, simply because there had been no earlier, comparable investigation, but it did produce abundant evidence of low standards of health and physique. Much attention was given by medical witnesses to the feeding of infants and children, including those in school. Some blamed the decline of home cooking, the use of tinned foods and excessive dependence on white bread, tea and cheap jam, while one witness believed that the root of the problem lay in the fact that ' a large proportion of British housewives are tainted with incurable laziness and distaste for the obligations of domestic life'.[20] Expert witnesses disagreed about the actual extent of underfeeding and malnutrition since there was no scientific definition of such terms, but the Committee favoured the opinion of Dr Eichholz, one of Her Majesty's Inspectors of Schools, who estimated that 122,000 children, or 16 per cent of the elementary school population of London, and 15 per cent of that of Manchester, were in need of school meals.[21] In its final recommendations, which included systematic medical inspection of children and the inclusion of games and physical exercise in the curriculum, the Committee proposed that 'definite provision should be made by the various Local Authorities for dealing with the question of underfed children',[22] suggesting that this would be best achieved by co-operation between the Local Authorities and voluntary agencies.

In January 1906 the Liberals were elected to power after a General Election which also returned 29 Labour MPs, the first time that this new party had had any significant success. Social reform had not figured prominently in the election, and the school meals issue not at all, but in the same year the Labour MP for Lancaster, William T. Wilson, Chairman of the Amalgamated Society of Carpenters and Joiners, introduced a Bill for education authorities to supply school meals with funding from local rates: school feeding would be regarded as an education service, outside the Poor Law and free from any taint of pauperism. The Liberal government gave time for the Bill in the parliamentary programme, and thereby in effect adopted it as their own, but in Select Committee the original proposals were considerably amended. The Education (Provision of Meals) Act which passed in 1906 allowed, but did not require, local education authorities to provide meals for children 'unable by reason of lack of food to take full advantage of the education provided for them'. The costs were to be met by the existing voluntary bodies, which it was hoped would now increase their efforts, by parents' contributions, and as a last resort, by a local rate which was not to exceed a halfpenny in the pound. Payment by the parent was normally expected 'unless the Education Authority is satisfied that the parent is unable by reason of circumstances other than his own default'. The important point was that no punitive consequences would follow from inability to pay – in effect, meals were to be provided free for necessitous children and, as Bentley Gilbert suggests, 'with this mild proposal the welfare state began'.[23]

When the Act came into operation in 1907, the number of users quickly increased, so that by 1909 the 27,000 London children who had previously received meals had doubled. In 1908 Sir Charles Elliott observed with satisfaction that it had not been necessary to levy a rate in London since voluntary contributions had much increased: the Council had drawn up menus under medical advice, costing 1½d., and the children found these much more palatable than the former soup and bread – 'The increased supply has created the increased demand'.[24] By 1909 five out of every six London schools were serving meals, and the cost went well beyond voluntary contributions, which were now beginning to fall. The Education Committee reluctantly levied the ¹/2d rate, most of which went towards the costs of equipment and staff. Elsewhere the resort to unpopular rating was even slower, having been adopted by only 95 out of the 322 local education authorities in England and Wales by 1911/12. Nevertheless, by 1912/13 100,000 children were being fed in London, and 258,000 in the rest of the country,[25] suggesting a large pent-up demand which was previously unsatisfied.

From 1914 to the Education Act, 1944

The introduction of conscription in 1917 again demonstrated the low levels of national fitness, when only 36 per cent of recruits were graded A1 by the army medical authorities, and 41 per cent were rejected for service when classified in Grades C and D. Clearly, the limited extent of school feeding before the War had had no general effect on the physical fitness of the young men who were now required to offer themselves for military service. It is surprising, however, that the disclosures of the poor state of health of recruits were not followed by a policy of nutritional reform. The 'C3 Nation' of the popular slogan was put down principally to bad, overcrowded and insanitary housing, not to inadequate diet, and post-war governments set in motion large-scale housing programmes. This was no doubt due to the fact that standards of living of the working classes had improved during the war years with virtually full employment, increased wages and the recruitment of women into relatively well-paid munitions work. Despite shortages of some foods, more families could afford to feed their children adequately, with the surprising result that the provision of free school meals fell dramatically. The official *Report on the Working Classes' Cost of Living* in 1918 quoted evidence from the School Medical Officers that the percentage of children in a poorly nourished condition was now considerably less than half that in 1913, and that in most cities, including London, the provision of meals to 'necessitous' children had declined by around four-fifths.[26]

The 20 years between the two World Wars present stark contrasts and difficulties of interpretation. On one hand, standards of living of the employed population continued to rise by around 30 per cent over the period as Britain enjoyed falling prices of imported food: the population as a whole ate a more varied and nutritious diet than before 1914, and many were better housed in new, sanitary homes of modern design. On the other hand, inter-war social policy was dominated by the spectre of unemployment, which averaged 14.4 per cent of insured workers, and rose to 22 per cent in 1932, when more than 3 million were out of work. Malnutrition again became the subject of public debate in the 1930s, reinforced by the new knowledge of the importance of vitamins and 'health protective' foods in which the poorer classes were heavily deficient. John Boyd Orr in 1936 claimed that half the population was unable to afford a nutritionally perfect diet, and that a quarter of the nation's children fell into the lowest income group which failed to satisfy every one of the required nutrients.[27] Again, the 'Hungry England' debate became highly politicized, both within the medical profession and the general public.

Although medical inspections of schoolchildren in the 1930s showed

10 per cent – 11 per cent to have a 'slightly subnormal' nutritional assessment, and 0.5 per cent – 1 per cent to be graded as 'bad', there was no significant development of the school meals service. In so far as there was any change in policy, it was towards targeting school meals to children in the depressed areas of high unemployment, since medical inspections demonstrated that in such places the proportions of undernourished children rose well above the national average – in Pontypridd, South Wales, to 24.2 per cent and in Jarrow to 29.6 per cent.[28] As part of the government's economies in public expenditure in 1921 the Board of Education set a limit of £300,000 to the rate support grant to local authorities, and at the same time introduced a rationing system based on the regional unemployment index.[29] In 1938 only 160,000 children were receiving school meals, or 4 per cent of the elementary school population; of these, 110,000 were free, only half the number fed in 1914. The one success which has been claimed for inter-war nutritional policies was the Milk Act of 1934 which provided a third of a pint of milk a day for all children in elementary schools at the subsidised price of ½d.: some were resistant to an unfamiliar drink but by 1939 54 per cent of the eligible children were benefiting from it.

The Milk in Schools scheme provided an important precedent for the major expansion of school meals during World War II. In rationed Britain, school meals were seen as part of the communal feeding programme which included British Restaurants and works canteens: not only had the large-scale evacuation of children from the cities disrupted normal feeding arrangements, but it was feared that even the children of well-to-do parents might suffer from food shortages. In the wartime climate of egalitarianism, the whole concept of school meals shifted from a mainly free service to a small number of very poor children towards a universal provision for all children in school, the great majority of whom would pay a nominal amount for a heavily subsidised midday meal. School meals were to be an important source of supplementary feeding for children at large, providing 1,000 kcals a day for older pupils, around one-third of their energy requirement. By the end of the war in 1945, 1,650,000 children, 40 per cent of the school population, were taking school dinners and 46 per cent drinking school milk, the supplies of which had recovered after an initial fall.

There was no inherent reason why the expansion of the school meals service should have survived the end of the war, or, at least, the end of food rationing in the early 1950s. In 1944, however, as part of the plan for social reconstruction after the war, R.A. Butler's Education Act, as well as raising the school leaving age and introducing secondary education for all children, made it a duty on all local education authorities to provide a school meals service as an integral part of the educational provision. No longer was it to be a special service for the relief of need, but an ordinary social service conceived as part of a comprehensive Welfare State for all citizens.

1944–90, The decline of school meals

From the Education Act of 1944 onwards local education authorities were obliged to provide school meals either free or paid, for all children who wished to take them. Free meals were dependent on a 'means test' of the parents, available for those receiving Supplementary Benefit or Income Support. The Act prescribed that the meal should be 'suitable in all respects as the main meal of the day': it normally consisted of a meat course followed by a pudding or sweet, and later regulations required that the meal should provide 42 per cent of daily protein and 33 per cent of energy needs. For paying children there was a fixed price set by the Ministry of Education which met approximately half the total cost, and also under the 1944 Act the daily third of a pint of milk became free to all pupils. These provisions made up a comprehensive nutritional policy for schoolchildren accepted by all political parties, which remained inviolate until the 1970s.

The take-up of school meals after 1944 never approached totality, substantial numbers of children preferring to return home at midday or to bring a packed lunch to be eaten at school. At their height, in 1975, school meals provided for 70 per cent of all children, the proportion receiving free meals having risen from only 4 per cent in 1954 to 12 per cent in 1979. By then, rapid inflation had raised the charges for paying pupils substantially, and the numbers taking paid meals began to fall while the proportion of free meals increased. Free milk in secondary schools had already been withdrawn by the Labour government in 1968, to be followed in 1971 by its withdrawal for children over the age of seven in primary schools, the controversial decision of Margaret Thatcher as Minister of Education in the Conservative government. This reduction in the school milk programme seemed to be justified by a Report on *Nutrition in Schools* in 1975 which stated that 'The nutritional status of children . . . is generally good' and that there was no need on grounds of health to restore free milk to older pupils.[30]

These relatively minor changes presaged the fundamental revision of the school meals service made by the Education Act of 1980. This made the provision of meals by local education authorities optional rather than compulsory; it abolished the requirement that meals should conform to prescribed nutritional standards, and allowed authorities to determine the form, content and price of meals. The Act proceeded from the Thatcherite philosophy of reducing the extent of control by central government and returning autonomy and choice to the individual consumer: it also reflected the fact that eating habits of children were changing, away from the traditional two-course meal and towards more varied patterns. Anxieties were shared by some leading nutritionists, and were expressed, particularly, in The Black Report on *Inequalities in Health* (1980) which argued that undernutrition existed in Britain and would increase unless school meals and milk were restored and extended as a free service for all children.[31] The Conservative government preferred the more optimistic conclusions of the 1975 Report and saw no reason to change the policies set out in the Education Act.

Under the terms of the 1980 Act it was agreed that the diets of schoolchildren would in future be monitored in order to detect whether the change had any detrimental nutritional effects. A major Report by the Committee on Medical Aspects of Food Policy was published in 1989, though the fieldwork on which the research was based related to 1983, arguably too soon for any long-term effects to be evident. But in comparing the nutritional value of the different meals now being provided in schools the Report was confident that the changes had not been harmful: school meals, when taken, still contributed between 30 per cent and 43 per cent of average daily energy intakes, and there were no significant differences between the energy and nutrient intakes of children using a 'free choice' cafeteria service and those eating a fixed price/fixed meal.[32]

Since 1980 two important changes in school meals have occurred. The proportion of children taking a school meal, whether free or paid, has fallen from the peak of 70 per cent in 1975 to around 43 per cent in 1988; second, the proportion of all children receiving a free meal first increased to a peak of 19.6 per cent in 1986 and thereafter fell to 12.5 per cent in 1989.[33] The welfare concept of a universal meal service has been abandoned for one which attempts to restore family responsibility and consumer choice while retaining a selectivity element for those who, a century ago, were described as 'necessitous' children. The difficulty now, as then, is to identify precisely who these are, but also it is important to know whether the recent changes in policy are having any substantial effects on the nutritional status of more than half the school population who are not now eating school meals.

Notes

1. *The Times*, 3 October 1941.
2. R.M. Titmuss, *Essays on the Welfare State*, Ch. 4, 3rd edn, George Allen and Unwin, 1976.

3. Charles W. Pipkin, *Social Politics and Modern Democracies*, vol. 1, New York, 1931, pp. 72–3.
4. Bentley B. Gilbert, *The Evolution of National Insurance in Great Britain*, Michael Joseph, 1973, p. 102.
5. David Owen, *English Philanthropy, 1660–1960*, Harvard University Press, Cambridge, Massachusetts, 1964, pp. 147–8.
6. M.E. Buckley, *The Feeding of School Children*, G. Bell and Sons, 1914, p. 4.
7. B. Seebohm Rowntree, *Poverty: A Study of Town Life*, Macmillan and Co. 1901, ch. 5.
8. Sir Arthur Clay, *Free Meals for Underfed Children*, Monthly Review, 1905, p. 94.
9. Buckley, op. cit., p. 16.
10. Margaret McMillan and A.C. Sanderson, *London's Children. How to Feed Them and How Not to Feed Them*, ILP, 1909, p. 1.
11. Ivy Pinchbeck and Margaret Hewitt, *Children in English Society*, vol. 2, Routledge and Kegan Paul, 1973, p. 637.
12. Gilbert Slater, *Poverty and the State*, Constable and Co., 1930, pp. 173, 176.
13. D.J. Oddy, 'The Health of the People'. in Theo Barker and Michael Drake (eds), *Population and Society in Britain, 1850-1980*, Batsford, 1982, Table 1, p. 123.
14. James Cantlie, *Degeneration Amongst Londoners*, 1885, cited in G. Stedman Jones, *Outcast London*, Peregrine, 1976, p. 127.
15. C.F.G. Masterman, *The Heart of the Empire*, 1901, Harvester ed. 1973, p. 8.
16. Arnold White, *Efficiency and Empire*, 1901, Harvester ed. 1973, pp. 95, 99, 100, 121.
17. *Report of the Inter-Departmental Committee on Physical Deterioration*, vol. I, Report and Appendix Cd. 2175, 1904, p. 96.
18. Titmuss, op. cit., p. 81.
19. *Report of the Royal Commission on Physical Training (Scotland)*. Cd. 1507, 1903.
20. *Inter-Departmental Committee*, op. cit., p. 40.
21. Ibid., 66.
22. Ibid., Summary of Recommendations, p. 91.
23. Gilbert, op. cit., p. 112.
24. Sir Charles Elliott, 'State feeding of school children in London', *The Nineteenth Century and After*, vol. LXV, Jan–June, 1909, pp. 864–5.
25. Pat Thane, *The Foundations of the Welfare State*, Longman, 1982, pp. 75–6.
26. *Report of the Sumner Committee on the Working Classes' Cost of Living*, Cmd. 8980, 1918, para. 51.
27. John Boyd Orr, *Food, Health and Income. A Survey of Adequacy of Diet in Relation to Income*, Macmillan, 1936.
28. Oddy, op. cit., p. 131, citing *The Health of the School Child, 1935*, 1936.
29. John Hurt, 'Feeding the Hungry Schoolchild in the First Half of the Twentieth Century', in *Diet and Health in Modern Britain*, eds Derek J. Oddy and Derek S. Miller, Croom Helm, 1985, p. 182.
30. *Nutrition in Schools. Report of the Working Party on the Nutritional Aspects of School Meals*, Department of Education and Science, 1975, pp. 11, 18.

31. Sir Douglas Black, *Inequalities in Health*, Report of a Working Group, Department of Health and Social Security, 1980.
32. *The Diets of British Schoolchildren.* Report on Health and Social Subjects 36, Department of Health, Sub-Committee on Nutritional Surveillance, HMSO, 1989, pp. XI–XII.
33. *Social Trends*, 21, 1991 Edn: HMSO, Table 3.10, p. 51.

6 Feeding schoolchildren in the Netherlands: conflict between state and family responsibilities

Adel P. den Hartog

Introduction*

The aim of this paper is to give an analysis of school feeding as a policy measure to improve the nutrition or health and well-being of primary schoolchildren. The paper is focused on the following issues:

- The social and nutritional rationale behind various forms of school feeding programmes and changes in concept, why and how to feed children at school.
- Why is school feeding in the Netherlands not accepted as part of the school system as compared with other European countries?
- The early success of milk-in-school programmes compared with school meals.

School feeding is defined as the provision of meals, snacks or milk to children during their school attendance, designed to improve their nutrition and/or well-being. In the literature so far, limited attention has been given to the sociological and social-historical aspects of the development of school feeding. This study is a first analysis on the origin and development of feeding children in primary schools in the Netherlands and covers the period 1900–90.[1]

Compulsory education and school feeding

The debate on whether or not to introduce feeding in primary schools started with the introduction of the Schools Act in 1900 which made education compulsory. The Schools Act of 1900 had only a limited impact on participation, as a relatively high level of enrolment had already been attained.[2] Some qualifications, however, have to be made: more boys than girls participated in primary education; and school attendance varied according to season. In rural areas, in particular, attendance was much higher in winter than in summer because of seasonal labour in agriculture.

At the end of the nineteenth century, advocates of non-denominational education brought forward the idea of providing basic needs such as food and clothing for primary schoolchildren as a means to reduce non-attendance.[3] In a brochure, the physician H. de Vries pointed out the vicious circle of bad nutrition, limited school performance, less employment opportunities and poverty.[4] In major cities at this time, private child-feeding associations (*Vereeniging Kindervoeding*) were active in the provision of school feeding to destitute children.[5] Feeding was mainly given during the winter period from November to April. The kind of foods given varied from slices of bread with lard to bean and vegetable soup.[6] Another typical meal for mass feeding was hotch-potch (*hutspot*) which consisted of mashed potatoes, carrots and onions with a little bit of meat.

The idea of providing food and clothing for schoolchildren was widely accepted by the social democrats. This view, however, was opposed by both liberal and religious parties who saw the state as not responsible for the physical well-being of children. In other countries too, social democrats favoured school feeding programmes by the state. In Germany in 1897, for example, the social democrats introduced a Bill before the Reichstag authorizing school feeding in all cities. The Bill was defeated on the plea it would have resulted in increasing migration of families from the countryside to the city. It nevertheless aroused public interest among municipal councils to support school feeding services.[7]

When in March 1900 the Schools Act was debated in the Second Chamber of the Dutch Parliament, a fierce discussion flared up. The leader of the social democrats, P.J. Troelstra, pointed out that shabby and hungry children should be clothed and fed by the state. Opponents of school feeding, like the Calvinist A. Kuyper, said that the school should not become a free boarding house, and that responsibilities for children remained with the parents.[8] With a narrow majority of one vote only, compulsory education was accepted by the Second Chamber.

As far as school feeding was concerned, Article 6 of the Schools Act stated that food and clothing could be supplied to needy children only when, without these provisions, regular school attendance would be impossible.

The Schools Act of 1900 associated school feeding with poor relief. Its execution came under the responsibilities of the local councils. Only when parents were not in a position to feed their children, were children entitled to free meals during school hours. So only the very poorest children received school meals and were placed in isolation from the rest of the children who went home for lunch. Eating at school rather than at home became a social stigma. Together with the concept that feeding and clothing was a primary family responsibility, it prevented the development of school feeding as a positive means of improving the well-being of children.

When we look at school feeding in a wider European context, the situation in the Netherlands is divergent from other countries such as France and the United Kingdom. As in the Netherlands, concern for health and school attendance led to the introduction of school feeding. However, in these countries school feeding was not considered to be poor relief. In France, the Schools Act of 1882 obliged the municipalities to establish the so-called *caisse des écoles* with the aim to set up school canteens where children could get a hot meal. Depending on family income their meals were free or at reduced costs. School feeding was administered by the board of the *caisse des écoles*, detached from poor relief organizations.[9]

In the UK in the second half of the nineteenth century school feeding to 'destitute children' by various charity organizations was already widespread; a well-known example was the London Schools Dinner Association, which was established in 1889.[10] However, school feeding became gradually integrated in the school system. The Education (Provision of Meals) Act of 1906 permitted local authorities to provide school meals during school hours, free of charge for the poor or at a reduced price for the better-off children.[11]

In France, the UK, Switzerland and Italy, school feeding was considered to be an integral part of the school system. Its ultimate goal was not only to diminish the rate of non-attendance but also to improve school performance.[12]

In the Netherlands, as a result of the Schools Act of 1900, a number of municipalities appointed school medical officers and thus created school health services for the surveillance of health and hygiene of school-children.[13] School medical officers played an important role in referring children, on medical recommendations, to school feeding programmes.[14] The number of municipalities supplying food and clothing to children increased from 3 in 1901 to 58 in 1916. It comprised major cities and towns of the western part of the Netherlands but not of the Catholic provinces of North-Brabant and Limburg.[15]

Nutrition as a family responsibility

Views and ideas regarding the extent to which nutrition was part of family responsibility may be obtained from two different sources:

1. discussions on school feeding published by the various teacher organizations; and
2. health and nutrition studies which have been carried out during the critical periods of World War I and the economic depression of the 1930s.

The Association of Dutch Teachers (Bond van Nederlandsche Onderwijzers), an organization closely affiliated with the social democrats, was very active in trying to get government support for school feeding and clothing. That the state should remove impediments to school attendance and development in general by providing meals is the tenor of the discussions.[16] Some social democrat intellectuals supported the idea of further socialization of family tasks such as feeding and clothing as, in their view, the first step to a removal of the traditional family. However most of the social democrat leaders considered school feeding and other communal support as a means to alleviate depressed households.[17]

On the other hand, the problem of school feeding and clothing was not much discussed in the periodicals of the teachers' organizations of the denominational schools. Interference in the internal affairs of denominational schools by the state was not considered acceptable.

The amended constitution of 1917, which settled the dispute between public and denominational education, provided the basis for a large degree of autonomy for denominational schools. Assistance to needy children was provided by charity organizations such as the Association of St Vincent de Paul (St Vincentius Vereniging) and the social welfare work of the protestant churches, known as the *diaconie*. In any case, assistance should not be provided on school premises. The preferred term for these activities was child feeding and not school feeding. School feeding was considered to be detrimental to the family structure, a threat to parental authority.[18] Among both Catholics and Protestants, the family was seen by the church as the corner-stone of society, or 'sovereignty in one's own circle' as Calvinists used to say.[19] This point of view was again stressed in a publication of 1937, at a time when the government made provisions to feed children of unemployed households.[20]

During the First World War the economic situation gradually deteriorated, resulting in rising unemployment and diminishing food supply. In major cities, feeding programmes were introduced in municipal schools and communal kitchens were established for poor households.

In Amsterdam, the city council, dominated by the social democrats, wanted to continue with these facilities after 1918, when the economic situation gradually returned to normal. However, as soon as the parents, and in particular the mother, were able to take care again of their

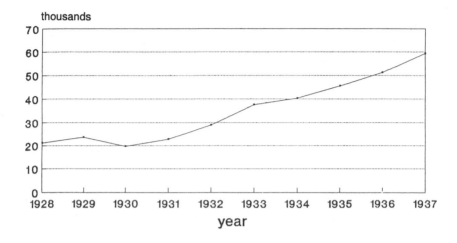

Source: CBS 1928/37.

Figure 6.1 School feeding in the Netherlands 1928–37; number of participating children.

children they turned down these communal provisions. This was the case even when they could not prepare at home a meal for such a low price.[21]

There existed a discrepancy between socialist ideals for communal facilities at household level and feelings of the working class for family responsibilities.[22] The view that the family, and in particular the mother, is primarily responsible for the care and well-being of children, was widely accepted in all segments of the Dutch society.

During the economic crisis in the 1930s, health authorities became worried that rising unemployment would lead to a deterioration of health and nutrition. Unemployment benefits were very limited. In order to avoid a decline in health standards the government issued a number of food and nutrition policy-related measures, such as distribution of cheap foods, school feeding and on a limited scale nutrition education[23] (see also Figure 6.1). Again, school feeding was conceived in the same way as in the Schools Act of 1900 – as a measure directed at the poor. In this case concern was not for school attendance, but for the health of the poor. Two nutrition studies, one carried out in Utrecht in 1935/1936 and a national survey in 1936/1937, give some data on how children and mothers of unemployed households perceived school feeding.[24]

In the city of Utrecht, school feeding consisted of winter feeding based on a hot meal and summer feeding based on bread with cheese or ginger bread together with 0.375 litre of milk. The participation rate of children eligible for school feeding was low. As to the winter feeding programme, 64 per cent of the households did not apply for school feeding; for summer feeding the applications were even lower. Households were asked why children did not make use of school feeding. A range of answers was given, such as the particular school the children attended did not supply feeding, the children did not like or could not digest the food, or children just did not want to take part in school feeding. Many parents stated they had objections against participation in school feeding and preferred to have their children at home to eat lunch.[25]

Similar reactions of parents and children were recorded during the national survey on unemployed households.[26] Food was supplied to schoolchildren solely on the basis of need and by taking part in school feeding it was obvious that a child belonged to the very poor section of society. In this way school feeding, whether it consisted of a hot meal, bread with cheese or just milk, became a means to differentiate the classroom into 'ordinary' and poor children. As a result a social stigma was attached to children and their parents, when participating in a feeding programme.

Quality of school meals

The quality of food, and thus the quality of school meals, has two dimensions: first, the taste and how people perceive their food. Is it good to eat and in accordance with the prevailing food habits and social position of the user? Second, from the hygienic and nutritional aspects, to what extent it contributes to nutritional requirements.

The tastelessness and the limited storage life of the provisions for school meals were complaints often heard.[27] This was of course not specific to the Dutch situation. In the UK, for example, Drummond and Wilbraham characterized meals in schools as monotonous and inadequate.[28] In cities such as Utrecht (1912) and Amsterdam (1919), the city council was obliged to look into these matters. In Utrecht, a commission of inquiry was established and in Amsterdam the director and deputy director of the municipal child-feeding department were dismissed because of complaints about the quality of the food.[29] Gradually municipal councils requested the food control services to take a look at the school meal programmes. This was an improvement, but food control services were more likely to look into aspects of food hygiene, than into the taste and the nutritional quality.

Meals for schoolchildren were often provided only during winter periods and would cease in spring. Long summer holidays were another point of concern. As a general rule, institutions involved in school feeding did not look into the nutritional aspects: they were more interested that children should have sufficient food.

In 1912, the physician A. van Voorthuysen carried out a study on the effect of school feeding on the health situation of schoolchildren.[30] He recommended that a meal in school should provide at least half the energy and nutrient requirements. For practical reasons, he took an 11-year-old child as reference. It is of interest to note that in 1939 the nutritionist van 't Hoog and the dietician Wittop Koning made similar recommendations: a meal in school should be based for practical reasons on half of the daily needs of a child of ten years of age – 1000 kcal, 30–35 grammes of protein and 30–35 grammes of fat.[31]

Other impediments to school feeding

Another factor which may have impeded the development of school feeding is the absence of a boarding school tradition such as existed in the UK. In the nineteenth century, generally speaking, it was not the habit of well-to-do families, with the exception of a number of Catholic families, to send their children to boarding schools. Boarding schools existed, of course, but did not develop into lasting institutions. Hence people were not used to the idea of children eating outside the family circle.

Probably a more important factor is the location of the primary schools. In a densely populated country with a relatively fast growing population, schools were located in the vicinity of residential neighbourhoods. In cities and major villages children could return home for lunch during the midday break although in rural areas this was sometimes difficult during winter.

Milk-In-School Programme

At the end of the 1930s a new approach in nutritional care for Dutch children appeared, the emergence of the Milk-in-School Programme (*schoolmelk*). The start and early development of the Milk-in-School Programme brought together economic and health interests.

The economic crisis of the 1930s confronted the Dutch dairy industry with milk surpluses. The basic causes of these milk surpluses were import restrictions from other countries, the high value of the Dutch guilder because of its linkage with the gold standard and a declining purchasing power of the home market.[32] In order to cope with the situation the government created a Crisis Dairy Bureau with the aim to deal with export problems and dairy surpluses. Until then the dairy industry in the Netherlands gave more attention to dairy export than to home consumption. Faced with increasing dairy surpluses, the Crisis Dairy Bureau started to promote local milk consumption.[33]

Dr E.G. van 't Hoog, who was also lecturer in human nutrition at the University of Amsterdam, advocated that milk supplied to schoolchildren was an excellent and relatively cheap means to improve the nutritional situation. Dr van 't Hoog like other Dutch nutritionists was well aware of similar developments in other countries such as the British Milk-in-Schools Scheme and the so-called 'Oslo-breakfast'. In Norway, children received a nutritious meal in the morning before going to the class-room.[34] The Oslo breakfast was also praised in the UK by Boyd Orr, not only because of its content but because it was given to every child who wished it, whether rich or poor.[35]

The provision of meals to schoolchildren was preferred by Dr van 't Hoog to milk in school, as milk is a supplementary food only. Because promotion of school meals was not a realistic option, he turned to milk for schoolchildren as a second-best option in marginal nutritional situations.[36] He referred to the studies by Dr Corry Mann in the UK, carried out between 1922 and 1925, on milk supplements to schoolboys living in an institution. Boys receiving a milk supplement made greater gains in weight, compared with the group of boys not receiving milk.[37] According to Dr J.C. Drummond the investigations by Dr Mann led to the scientific justification of a milk-in-schools scheme.[38]

The idea of milk in school was well received by the Crisis Dairy Bureau. Their objective was to raise milk drinkers and when it could be combined with health objectives, so much the better.[39] In other European countries such as the UK, similar developments occurred. The National Milk Publicity Council had been promoting milk in schools since 1927. Faced with milk surpluses a new Milk-in-Schools Scheme was established in 1933.[40] In the Netherlands there was awareness of these developments in both dairy and health circles.

A pilot project of a Milk-in-School Programme started among 1000 schoolchildren in Rotterdam and proved to be successful. Encouraged by these results a larger programme started in 1937 among 6000 children both in municipal and denominational schools. Children received daily a quarter of a litre of whole milk in a bottle with a straw. In the meantime, a Central Milk-in-School Committee was established by the Crisis Dairy Bureau. Necessary funds for distributing milk at a low price or even for free were supplied by the Bureau. Likewise the municipality of Rotterdam supported the programme.

The first Milk-in-School Programme was nearly jeopardized by the provincial council of South Holland. The provincial council stated that municipal subsidies for milk in schools were incompatible with the Schools Act. According to the Act, feeding could only be supplied to promote school attendance. The objections were, however, more of a financial nature than by way of principle. In the event, the Crown nullified the objections of the provincial council taking the general health considerations into account and so milk in school became in 1937 a legally accepted nutrition policy measure.[41]

The Milk-in-School Programme grew steadily in size, but events of World War II interrupted its development. In 1943 milk was short in supply and the programme had to be stopped. Likewise the provision of meals came to an end because of lack of food. After 1945, when life returned to normal, the Milk-in-School Programme regained its vigour, but nobody was interested to start again with a school meal programme.

Acceptance of milk in school

Why did milk in schools become accepted more easily by children and their parents than was the case with school meals (see Figure 6.2)?

In the first place it was the way in which the Milk-in-School Programme was set up. All children were, in principle, eligible to receive milk in school, so no distinction could be made any more between poor and better-off children. Parents and teachers were involved in the organization and distribution of milk. The general character of the programme to promote health of all schoolchildren bore no resemblance to poor relief.

Milk as a healthy food, in particular for young children, was widely accepted among all segments of society. The appreciation of fresh milk as a drink is closely connected with the rise of the modern dairy industry in the second half of the nineteenth century. Modern food technology and transportation made the distribution of safe, fresh milk possible in all regions of the country.[42] As a result of progress made in nutrition research it became apparent that milk is an excellent source of protein and also of vitamins A and D and the minerals calcium and phosphorus.[43] Taking the poor living conditions of the working classes into account, milk was indispensable for health improvement. Gradually milk and health were indissolubly connected. In other countries similar developments occurred.[44]

Milk is a drink and not a meal: therefore mothers perceived it as less of a potential threat to their responsibilities for feeding the children. However, suspicion of milk in school remained in both Catholic and Protestant circles. To get milk accepted in Catholic schools it was important that the bishops of Roermond and 's-Hertogenbosch were already in favour of these programmes in 1937.[45] On the occasion of the

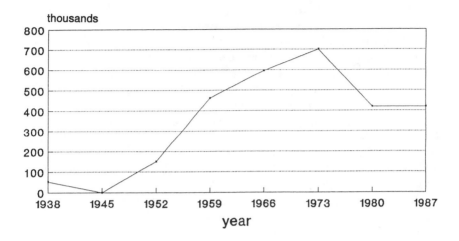

Source: Central Milk-in-School Committee.

Figure 6.2 Number of children participating in the Milk-in-School Programme in the Netherlands, 1939–88.

14th International Dairy Conference held in 1956 in Rome, Pope Pius XII made a statement on milk in school. In a special audience to the participants, the Pope stated that milk distributed in schools was a happy initiative not only in the interests of the milk industry but likewise for public health.[46] Needless to say, this statement was welcomed both in dairy and nutrition circles.[47]

Rise of a healthy drink in school

The 1950s and 1960s were the best years for the Milk-in-School Programme. Policy makers, health experts and dairy people, all shared the view that milk should be promoted in primary schools in order to improve the nutrition of schoolchildren. After the Second World War the dairy industry improved its organizational structure considerably. The Netherlands Interprofessional Organization of Dairy Products ('Produktschap voor Zuivel') was set up in 1950. This organization combined interests of dairy farmers and workers and had some legislative power. In order to promote the consumption of dairy products, the

Dutch Dairy Bureau was created in 1950. It launched large marketing campaigns in the Netherlands and abroad.[48] The Central Milk-in-School Committee became closely associated with the Dairy Bureau.

The Bureau of Nutrition Education, health superintendents, school medical officers and the Committee, all worked closely together to promote milk among schoolchildren.[49] The Dairy Bureau and its allies tried to stimulate the use of milk by means of radio programmes, articles in newspapers and magazines, diffusion of folders to parents, and discussions with municipal councils and teachers. In a letter to the boards of all non-denominational and denominational schools, the Minister of Education, Dr L.J.M. Beel, stressed the importance of the work of the Committee in providing milk for the health improvement of schoolchildren.[50] The Nutrition Council advised the government several times to continue its support to the Milk-in-School Programme.[51] However, interestingly, studies could not demonstrate a substantial nutritional effect of a milk supplement.[52]

In order to support the activities of the programme, the Committee stimulated the creation of local milk-in-school committees. The local committees were often initiated by schoolteachers. In 1952 there were 36 local committees responsible for milk distribution,[53] but these gradually disappeared because of a diminishing interest among mothers and teachers for milk as an indispensable food supplement.

Up to this point, the financial basis of milk in school came from the support of the Central Milk-in-School Committee which got its funds from the dairy industry. Municipalities likewise supported the programme. In order to secure a more solid funding, the Committee, and later the Association of Dutch Municipalities, requested the government for subsidies. The subsidy was meant for infant and primary schools only. Because of the removal of milk price control in 1953, milk prices increased and so did the milk price in school.[54] The response of the government towards subsidizing milk in schools was negative. According to the Minister of Social Affairs and Public Health, family income was generally high enough to cope with the increased price. If families could not afford to buy milk, it was a matter of wrong expenditure. Nutrition education could be the answer to such problems.[55] Nevertheless the government changed its mind under pressure from the health authorities and dairy industry. From 1958 onwards, local milk-in-school committees could receive a subsidy from the central government.[56] For budgetary reasons the government brought the subsidies to an end in 1963, but the Committee and a number of municipalities continued to subsidize milk.

Most of the activities of the programme were in the cities and major towns of the western and central part of the country. In less densely populated areas the programme was relatively difficult to carry out, as it was too expensive to supply all small schools with milk. Efforts by the Central Milk-in-School Committee to obtain a wider coverage were unsuccessful.[57]

Milk in school under pressure

In the 1950s the living standards in the Netherlands, like other West European countries, started to rise considerably. The consumption of meat, and consequently fat, sugar, fruits and vegetables, increased. On the other hand consumption of less expensive foods such as bread, potatoes and milk showed a steady decline.[58] Gradually the social and nutritional context for a milk-in-school programme changed. There was a steady decline of fresh milk consumption, from an average daily intake of 570g in 1955 to 395g in 1985. Schoolchildren also became less interested in milk because of changes in taste. Straight after the Second World War, Coca-Cola started large-scale advertisement campaigns. Coca-Cola was known before the war, but only consumed on a limited scale as a summer drink.[59] Drinking cool beverages is part of the American food culture.[60] With the acceptance of cola and other soft drinks in the Dutch food pattern, children acquired a taste for cool beverages. Milk as distributed in school, first in small bottles and later in 250 cc cartons, was not kept cool. Increasingly, schoolchildren showed a dislike for tepid milk as a drink.

In a welfare state, fewer parents saw the need for a healthy drink for their children in school. Parents became less involved in the Milk-in-School Programme. Teachers found administering milk in school an additional burden on their already heavy workload. In the changing nutritional situation, the focus shifted towards problems related to overfeeding, and the result was a loosening of the natural alliance between the dairy industry and nutritionists. Nutrition research, and later nutrition education for the general public shifted from essential nutrients to the intake of fat and cholesterol.[61] The so far unchallenged milk came under attack as one of the contributors to the undesirable high fat intake of the Dutch population. In 1977 the Milk-in-School Programme celebrated its 40 years with a conference on milk in relation to schoolchildren. One of the invited speakers, the nutritionist Dr R.J.J. Hermus, was not convinced that milk in school was essential, at least not from a nutritional point of view. Most nutrients were already covered, so there was no direct need for a supplement at school. On the other hand there might be a need for children to get a morning snack.[62] The loosening of ties between the dairy industry and nutritionists became yet more apparent when in 1981 the Bureau of Nutrition Education introduced new educational guidelines. In the period 1953–81, the general public was advised by means of a food guide to consume milk daily. In the old food guide milk was clearly depicted as a separate item. In the new food guide milk was lumped together with meat, fish and eggs as one group.[63] The dairy industry was, of course, very upset and worried about the rather obscure place of milk in nutrition education.[64]

The Dutch Dairy Bureau and in its wake the Central Milk-in-School Committee made various efforts to stop, if not reverse, the downward trend in milk consumption. The Dairy Bureau initiated nation-wide milk promoting campaigns by means of so-called collective advertisements.[65]

Educational material on dairy food and health was developed by the Committee, often in close collaboration with nutritionists. The material was free and widely distributed to teachers and schoolchildren. In order to get milk better accepted by teachers, parents and children a number of improvements were introduced. The paying system became simplified, so that instead of collecting money from the children, postal invoices for easy payment were sent to the parents.[66] The quality of the milk was improved with the introduction of electrical cool-boxes in schools in the 1970s and a wider range of products such as whole milk and semi-skimmed milk, buttermilk, semi-skimmed chocolate milk and fruit yoghurt was offered.[67]

In 1979 efforts were made to introduce cheese instead of milk to schoolchildren. A pilot project including 12 schools and 11,400 children was not successful. Children did not like cheese as a morning snack.[68] This measure was inconsistent with prevailing Dutch food habits, where cheese is mainly eaten with bread like a sandwich.

During the 1950s, the dairy industry, and with it the Central Milk-in-School committee, looked for new scientific evidence to prove that milk in school is justified. Despite the availability of food during a period of affluence, breakfast habits of schoolchildren at home were not considered to be adequate. In the period 1955–65, the Nutrition Council advised the government several times that it should support milk in school as a necessary supplement.[69] In 1969 articles appeared in the daily press pointing out the danger of fat in the Milk-in-School Programme in relation to future risks of coronary heart diseases. The Committee reacted promptly by putting more emphasis on semi-skimmed milk, so that by 1977 more than 80 per cent of the milk distributed was of a low fat content.[70]

Another argument for milk in school was a possible relationship between the consumption of milk and school performance. In 1963 the Committee supported a study based on psychological tests on the influence of milk in schools on intellectual performances.[71] The authors of the study carefully formulated their positive conclusions concerning the possible relationship between milk and intellectual performance. The Central Milk-in-School Committee and the press, however, were careful with the outcome of the study. Articles circulated in newspapers that milk enhanced intellectual performance and in particular clear thinking.[72] These reports were used in Brussels by the Minister of Agriculture, P.J. Lardinois, in his efforts to obtain from the European Community subsidies for Milk-in-School programmes.[73]

One of the objectives of the common agricultural policy of the European Community was to abolish national food subsidies. This meant a threat for the Milk-in-School Programme: in the long run milk-in-school programmes could not be supported anymore by national governments. On the other hand the European Community, faced with dairy surpluses, was very susceptible to arguments seeking to stimulate milk consumption in all member countries. In 1976 the EC proposed a 50 per cent subsidy of the price for whole milk or whole chocolate milk. National governments were asked by the EC to give a subsidy on top equivalent to half the value of the EC contribution.[74] The EC proposals were not acceptable to the Netherlands, as 75 per cent – 80 per cent of the distributed milk in its schools was semi-skimmed. At the request of the Dutch Minister of Agriculture, P.J. Lardinois, whole milk and semi-skimmed milk were put on the same level.[75] The EC subsidy included all educational institutions and not only primary schools. From 1977 on, the Milk-in-School Committee expanded its activities to secondary schools in view of EC regulations.

This expansion was, however, also due to a reconsideration of the target group of the programme. The Dutch Dairy Bureau changed its marketing philosophy at the end of the 1970s. Milk should be seen as a cool, refreshing drink, alongside other drinks, and not so much as a health drink.[76]

Conclusions

School feeding is a long-standing nutrition-oriented food policy measure. In the Netherlands during the last 100 years various efforts have been taken to provide meals, snacks or milk for children on school premises. On the whole, school feeding remained an unresolved matter with only a few short periods of success.

School feeding is an example of a food policy measure which did not take fully into account food habits and the social meaning of food. From the start it was based on wrong principles by linking school feeding with poverty. A food policy measure associated by the beneficiaries with a social stigma will have no lasting effect.

Food policy is often an area of conflicting interests between food producers and nutrition or health experts. This was very clearly the case with the setting up and further development of the milk-in-schools programmes. In a period of nutritional change, the interests of dairy producers and nutritionists ran largely along the same lines. In a modern welfare state, however, the situation is completely different. A particular food can no longer be singled out as a major contributor to nutritional improvement.

Acknowledgement

* I should like to thank Ms M.H. van Roggen-Benes, Head of the Central Milk-in-School Committee, Rijswijk, for information and material received on the Milk-in-School Programme. Likewise many thanks are due to Ms J.C.M.N. Nooij-Michels and Dr S.K. Kroes-Lie, research assistants of the Department of Human Nutrition. Finally my thanks go to Ms Ir. M. Jansen, Ir. R. Claessen and Ir. H. Vis, former students of the Department of Human Nutrition.

Notes

1. Important sources are, among others: *Statistiek van het Armenwezen* and *Armenzorg Statistiek* of the Central Bureau of Statistics; municipal reports and health statistics of major cities such as Amsterdam, The Hague, Rotterdam and Utrecht; Annual reports of the Dutch Dairy Bureau (Nederlands Zuivel-bureau), Netherlands Interprofessional Organization for Dairy Products (Produktschap voor Zuivel).
2. Knippenberg, 1986, pp. 106–10.
3. Schook, 1890.
4. Vries, de, 1894.
5. See e.g. the brochure of Hermans and van Kol, 1900.
6. Hermans, pp. 32–5; Maatschappij tot Nut van het Algemeen, 1903, pp. 98–105.
7. Scott, 1953, p. 7, the chapter on the historical development of school feeding was prepared with the help of le Gros Clark.
8. Meijsen, 1976, pp. 90–91; Oud, 1961, pp. 188–9; 1968, pp. 226–7.
9. Scott, 1953, pp. 6–7.
10. Scott, p. 8.
11. Burnett, 1979, p. 212; Scott, p. 8.
12. Scott, 1953.
13. Bergink, 1965, pp. 94–5; Loghem, van, 1948, p. 328.
14. Hartog, C. den, 1953, pp. 492–3; Loghem, van, 1948, p. 324.
15. *Kindervoeding en Kleding in Nederland,* 1918.
16. Jansen, 1981, pp. 38–9, unpublished report.
17. Regt, de, 1977, pp. 18–19; 1981, pp. 526–7.
18. Jansen, p. 42.
19. Eupen, van, 1985, pp. 24–7.

20. Duyvendijk, van, 1937.
21. Jansz, 1981, pp. 511–12; Regt, de, 1981, pp. 530–31.
22. Regt, de.
23. Hartog, den, 1983, p. 35.
24. Voedingstoestand, 1937; Voeding, gezondheid, 1940.
25. Voedingstoestand, pp. 49–50.
26. Voeding, gezondheid, p. 168.
27. Jansen, p. 75.
28. Drummond and Wilbraham, 1957, pp. 340–42.
29. Jansen, pp. 75–6.
30. Voorthuysen, van, 1912.
31. Wittop Koning and E.G. van 't Hoog, 1940.
32. Minderhoud, 1943, pp. 503–5; Zanden, van, 1985, pp. 122–3.
33. Nederlands Zuivelbureau, *Schoolmelk Express*, 1977, p. 3; Schreurs, 1991, p. 60.
34. Hoog, 't van, 1940; Wittop Koning and van 't Hoog, p. 75.
35. Boyd Orr, 1937, reprinted in 1939, p. 564.
36. Hoog, 't van, pp. 17–22.
37. Mann, 1926.
38. Drummond and Wilbraham, pp. 76–7.
39. Nederlands Zuivelbureau, *Schoolmelk Express*, p. 3.
40. Burnett, pp. 320–21; Drummond and Wilbraham, p. 447.
41. Nederlands Zuivelbureau, *Schoolmelk Express*, pp. 4–5.
42. Hartog, den, 1986, pp. 30–31, 42–3.
43. McCollum, 1957.
44. See e.g. Teuteberg, 1981.
45. Hartog, C. den, 1977, p. 18.
46. *Schweizerische Milchzeitung*, 1956, p. 571.
47. Nederlands Zuivelbureau, *Jaarverslag 1956*, p. 7; 1957, p. 16; Voeding, 1957, p. 113.
48. Schreurs, pp. 60–66, 97–101.
49. Nederlands Zuivelbureau, *Jaarverslag 1953*, p. 5.
50. Ibid., 1954, p. 7.
51. See e.g. Hartog, C. den, 1977, pp. 16–17.
52. See e.g. Lamberts, 1947 and Ornee, 1956.
53. Nederlands Zuivelbureau, *Jaarverslag 1952*, p. 6; 1954, pp. 6–7.
54. Ibid., 1953, p. 6.
55. Ibid., 1955, p. 7.
56. Ibid., 1958, p. 15.
57. Ibid., 1956, pp. 5–6; 1957, pp. 14–16.
58. Godschalk, 1985.
59. Schreurs, p. 43.
60. Root and Rochemont, de, 1981, pp. 420–21.
61. Rijneveld-van Dijk, 1981, p. 221.
62. Hermus, 1977, pp. 60–61.
63. Rijneveld-van Dijk, p. 239.
64. Produktschap voor Zuivel, *Jaarverslag 1981*, pp. 170–72.
65. Schreurs, pp. 60–66.

66. Nederlands Zuivelbureau, *Schoolmelk Express*, 1977, p. 7.
67. Ibid; Nederlands Zuivelbureau, *Jaarverslag 1975*, p. 23.
68. Produktschap voor Zuivel, 1979, p. 131.
69. The advice given by the Nutrition Council on milk in schools was also reported in the *Netherlands Journal of Nutrition*, Voeding. Important is the advice of 1957 (Standpunt).
70. Nederlands Zuivelbureau, *Jaarverslag, 1969*, pp. 16–17; Schoolmelk Express, p. 2.
71. Defares, Kema and van der Werff, 1967, Hartog C, den, 1977, p. 17–18.
72. Hartog, C. den, 1977, p. 16; Kaayk, 1968, p. 354.
73. Ibid., p. 16.
74. Produktschap voor Zuivel, *Jaarverslag 1967*, p. 38, pp. 63–4; 1977, pp. 66–7.
75. Ibid., 1977, p. 149.
76. Personal communication by Ms M.H. van Roggen-Benes, Head of the Central Milk-in-School Committee, Rijswijk, 31 January 1991.

Bibliography

Bergink, A.H., *Schoolhygiëne in Nederland in de 19ᵉ eeuw* [School hygiene in the Netherlands in the nineteenth century], Veendam, Marko Meubelen, 1965.

Boyd Orr, John, 'Nutrition in relation to education, agriculture and medicine'. Reprinted from *Health and Empire*, vol. XII, no. 3, 1937, *Rowett Research Institute Collected Papers* 4, 1939, pp. 551–66.

Burnett, John, *Plenty and Want. A Social History of Diet in England from 1815 to the Present Day*, 2nd rev. edn. London, Scolar Press, 1979.

Central Bureau of Statistics, *75 Jaar Statistiek van Nederland* [75 years statistics of the Netherlands], 's-Gravenhage, CBS, 1975.

Defares, P.B., G.N. Kema, and J.J. van der Werff, *Schoolmelk en intellectuele prestaties* [Milk in school in relation to intellectual performances], Assen, van Gorcum, 1967.

Drummond, Jack, C. and Anne Wilbraham, *The Englishman's Food. A History of Five Centuries of English Diet*. Revised and with a new chapter by Dorothy Hollingsworth, London, Jonathan Cape, 1957.

Duyvendijk, P. van, and J.B. Visser, *Schoolopvoeding en onderwijs* [Upbringing at school and education], 1937.

Eupen, T.A.G. van, 'Kerk en gezin in Nederland' [Church and family in the Netherlands], in G.A. Kooy (ed.), *Gezinsgeschiedenis. Vier eeuwen gezin in Nederland*, Assen, van Gorcum, 1985.

Godschalk, F.E., *Consumptie van voedingsmiddelen in Nederland, 1981, 1982 en 1983* [food consumption in the Netherlands, 1981, 1982 and 1983], Den Haag, LEI, 1985.

Hartog, Adel P. den, *Diffusion of Milk as a New Food to Tropical Countries: the Example of Indonesia 1880–1942*, Wageningen, Netherlands Nutrition Foundation, 1986.

Hartog, Adel P. den, 'Food habits in a situation of crisis: The unemployed and their food in the years 1930–1939 in the Netherlands', in H.J. Teuteberg (ed.), *Nutritional Behaviour as a Topic of Social Sciences*, Supplement to Ernährungsumschau, Frankfurt, 1983., pp. 33–6.

Hartog, Cornelis, den, '40 jaar schoolmelkvoorziening' [40 years of milk in school provisions], *Melk in Relatie tot de Gezondheid*, 4, 1977, no. 4, pp. 5–22.

Hartog, Cornelis, den, 'Schoolvoeding' [School feeding], *Voeding*, 14, 1953, pp. 492–504.

Hermans, L.M., H. van Kol, *Schoolvoeding. Een aansporing voor onze wetgevers* [School feeding. An incentive to our legislators], Amsterdam, 1900.

Hermus, Ruud J.J., 'De voeding van de schoolgaande jeugd: gezonde voeding of gezondheidsopvoeding' [Nutrition of schoolchildren: a healthy nutrition or a health education], *Melk in Relatie tot de Gezondheid*, 4, 1977, no. 4, pp. 35–62.

Hoog, van 't, E.G. 'Richtlijnen voor de schoolvoeding' [Guidelines for school feeding], *Voeding*, 1, 1939–40, pp. 17–22.

Hoog, van 't, E.G. 'Oslo-ontbijt of warme maaltijd op school' [Oslo-breakfast or a hot meal at school], *Voeding*, 1, 1939–40, pp. 42–6.

Jansen, Maria, *De ontwikkeling van de schoolvoeding in Nederland, 1900–1940* [Development of school feeding in the Netherlands 1900–1940], Department of Human Nutrition, Agricultural University, Wageningen, 1981.

Jansz, Ulla, 'Gemeentelijk koken en wassen in Amsterdam 1915–1939' [Municipal cooking and washing in Amsterdam 1915–1939], *Amsterdam Sociologisch Tijdschrift*, 7, 1981, pp. 501–23.

Kaayk, C.K.J., 'Schoolmelk en intellectuele prestaties' [Milk in school and intellectual performances], *Voeding*, 29, 1968, p. 349.

Kindervoeding en -kleding in Nederland. Rapport samengesteld door het Bureau voor Kinderbescherming [Child feeding and clothing in the Netherlands. Report prepared by the Child Protection Bureau], Amsterdam, Bureau voor Kinderbescherming, 1918.

Knippenberg, Hans, *Deelname aan het lager onderwijs in Nederland gedurende de negetiende eeuw* [Participation in nineteenth century primary education in the Netherlands] *Nederlandse Geografische Studies*, 9, 1986.

Lamberts, J.H. *Onderzoek naar den voedingstoestand van Rotterdamsche schoolkinderen* [Research on the nutritional status of Rotterdam Schoolchildren], Diss., Utrecht, Rotterdam, 1947.

Loghem, J.J. van. *Algemene gezondheidsleer* [General public health], Amsterdam, 1948.

Maatschappij tot Nut van het Algemeen. *Voeding en Kleeding aan schoolgaande kinderen. Een overzicht van buiten- en binnenland, met een inleiding en advies door J. Bruinwold Riedel* [Food and clothing for schoolchildren. An overview of abroad and at home, with an introduction and advice], Amsterdam, Maatschappij tot Nut van het Algemeen, 1903.

Mann, H. Corry, *Diets for Boys during school-age*. Medical Research Council Special Report Series no. 105 London, 1926.

McCollum, Elmer V., *A History of Nutrition, the Sequence of Ideas in Nutrition Investigations*, Boston, Houghton Mifflin, 1957.

Meijsen, J.H., *Lager onderwijs in de spiegel der geschiedenis. 175 jaar nationale wetgeving op lager onderwijs in Nederland* [Primary education in the mirror of history. 175 years of national legislation on primary education in the Netherlands], 's-Gravenhage, Staatsuitgeverij, 1976.

Minderhoud, G., 'Crisis en Crisiswetgeving 1930–1940' [Crisis and Crisis legislation 1930–1940] in Z.W. Sneller, *Geschiedenis van den Nederlandschen Landbouw 1795–1940*, Groningen, Wolters, 1943, pp. 498–522.

Nederlands Zuivelbureau *Schoolmelk Express* [Dutch Dairy Bureau Milk in School Express], Rijswijk, 1977.

Nederlands Zuivelbureau, *Jaarverslag 1952–1983* [Dutch Dairy Bureau, Annual Reports 1952–1983], Rijswijk.

Ornee, P.B. *Onderzoek naar de resultaten van menuverbetering door voorlichting of extra melkvoeding bij schoolkinderen* [Research on results of dietary improvement by means of education or milk supplements among school children], Diss., Amsterdam, 1956.

Oud, P.J., *Het jongste verleden. I. Parlementaire geschiedenis van Nederland 1918–1940* [The recent past. Part I. Parliamentary history of the Netherlands 1918–1940] Assen, van Gorcum, 1968.

Oud, P.J., *Honderd jaren. Een eeuw van staatkundige vormgeving in Nederland 1840–1940* [Hundred years. A century of political shaping in the Netherlands] Assen, van Gorcum, 1961.

Produktschap voor Zuivel, *Jaarverslag 1953–1990* [Netherlands Interprofessional Organization for Dairy Products 1953–1990], Rijswijk.

Regt, Ali de, 'Arbeidersgezinnen en industrialisatie: Ontwikkelingen in Nederland 1880–1918' [Working class households and industrialization: Developments in the Netherlands 1880–1918], *Amsterdams Sociologisch Tijdschrift*, 4, 1977, pp. 3–27.

Regt, Ali de, 'Repliek' [Rejoinder], *Amsterdams Sociologisch Tijdschrift*, 7, 1981, pp. 524–32.

Rijneveld- van Dijk, Heleen L.G., 'Voorlichting over voeding in Nederland' [Nutrition education in the Netherlands], in Adel P. den Hartog, *Voeding als maatschappelijk verschijnsel*, Utrecht, Bohn Scheltema Holkema, 1982, pp. 218–59.

Root, Waverley and Richard de Rochemont, *Eating in America. A history*, New York, William Morrow, 1981.

Schook, H.W.J.A. *Vragen des tijds I Schoolverzuim, II Middelen ter bestrijding* [Questions of our time I Non-school attendance II Means to control], Amsterdam, 1890.

Schreurs, Wilbert, *Collective reclame in Nederland* [Collective advertisements in the Netherlands], Leiden, Stenfert Kroese, 1991.

Schweizerische Milchzeitung. 'Ein Höhepunkt des XIV Internationalen Milchwirtschaftskongresses', *Schweizerische Milchzeitung* 82, 1956, p. 571.

Scott, Marjorie, *School Feeding. Its Contribution to Child Nutrition.* FAO Nutritional Studies, 19, 1953.

'Standpunt ten aanzien ven de verstrekking van melk op school' [Standpoint on the provision of milk in school], *Veoding*, 18, 1957, pp. 593–8.

Teuteberg, Hans J., 'The beginnings of the modern milk age in Germany', in A. Fenton and T. Owen (eds), *Food in perspective Proceedings of the Third International Conference of Ethnological Food Research*, Edinburgh, John Donald, 1981, pp. 283–311.

Voedingstoestand, De, van gezinnen van ondersteunde Utrechtsche werklozen in 1935–1936 [The nutritional situation of supported unemployed in Utrecht in 1935–1936], Utrecht, Gemeente Utrecht, 1937.

Voeding, gezondheid en financiële toestand van 700 werklozen-gezinnen verspreid over geheel Nederland [Nutrition, health and financial situation of 700 unemployed households in the Netherlands], 's-Gravenhage, Landsdrukkerij, 1940.

Voeding, Breviarium Z.H. Paus Pius XII over de verstrekking van melk op scholen [HH Pope Pius XII on the distribution of milk to schools], *Voeding*, 18, 1957, p. 113.

Voorthuysen, A. van, 'Onderzoekingen over de schoolvoeding te Groningen' [Resesearch on school feeding in Groningen], *Nederlands Tijdschrift voor Geneeskunde*, 56, 1912, pp. 165–77.

Vries, H. de, *Waarom vordt den kinderen der armen in onvoldoende mate voeding verstrekt?* [Why is food insufficiently supplied to children of the poor?], Amsterdam, 1894.

Wittop Koning, Martine and E.G. van 't Hoog, 'De warme maaltijd als type van schoolvoeding' [The hot meal as an example of school feeding], *Voeding*, 1, 1939–40, pp. 74–82.

Zanden, van, J.L., 'Modernisering en de toenemende betekenis van de overheid: 1800–1950' [Modernization and the increasing significance of the state: 1800–1950], in L. Noordegraaf (ed.), *Agrarische geschiedenis van Nederland*, 's-Gravenhage, SDU, 1986, pp. 85–140.

7 The political history of Norwegian nutrition policy[1]

Thor Øivind Jensen

Introduction

Norway is known for its institutionalised nutrition policy which takes a structural and integrated approach. Nutritional goals are taken into a broader setting of macroeconomic planning when negotiating the national food situation. A parliamentary decision of 1975 is the symbol of this policy. Positive evaluation of the policy is based on how nutrition is structured and institutionalised into politics (Winikoff 1977, Ringen 1977, Cohen 1980). Critics point to the state's inability to handle the new health problems and how co-operation with agricultural interests damages the health aspect (Jensen and Kjærnes 1986, Winkler 1987).

This chapter will analyse the background for this policy and identify different stages in its history, from the start in the 1930s and into the 1980s.

The Socialist double marriage between science and politics, workers and peasants

The strong producer forces

Agricultural interests are strong in Norwegian politics. Norway's nation-building process in the nineteenth century as well as older historical conditions made agriculture the backbone of political culture. These interests are still locked into the political system, including a finely masked negotiating system, which in many ways imposes agricultural interests on other sectors (Jacobsen 1965, 1968).

The international food industry came into Norwegian politics in the

1920s. The international margarine trust Unilever wanted access to Norwegian markets and domestic producers wanted protection. Since margarine sales influence the butter market, agricultural interests also came onto the scene. Even the fisheries had interests due to their production of processed fish-oils for the margarine industry. The result of the turmoil was that the government fell and arrangements were made to ensure butter sales (Fjær 1990, Tønneson 1979).

Margarine is a wonderful product for producers: it has a high calorie content and requires industrial processing and the use of many raw materials. Also, it can use surplus fat from many sources. Dairy industries, fisheries, whale-hunters and plant-oil importers all had strong interests in margarine.

Surplus production of milk in the late 1920s made the parliament decide that the use of butter in margarine was obligatory. Butter was added in quantities unknown to the consumers with a very favourable price arrangement for milk producers. This arrangement was the main reason for the 30 per cent rise in milk production in the 1930s (Fjær 1990). Margarine as a dumping ground for excess butter without fair notice to consumers also occurred in the late 1980s. This example indicates that producer power is a major force in shaping food policy and eating patterns. Nutrition policy tries to modify this pattern.

Emerging nutrition policy on a scientific base

The concept 'Nutrition policy' emerged from the League of Nations before the Second World War. They formulated a 'marriage of health and agriculture' to solve falling prices, surplus production and problems of malnutrition and food shortage (League of Nations, 1937).

Developments in science in the early part of this century made the general attitudes to science and progress positive (Seip 1989). The roles of vitamins and different food elements were discovered and developed into food recommendations. Better knowledge of energy demands made it possible to recommend minimum food standards. Economic depression made it natural for scientists to help governments estimate the minimum food support needed by the poor. Statistics comparing child growth and nutrition were the background for the school breakfast programmes based on 'protective foods' (whole milk, bread and cod-liver oil). Knowledge of bacteria and epidemiology pushed hygiene into administrative food control. The food control system was seen as an important part of a nutrition policy (Thorsen 1935).

Nutrition and hygiene were at the forefront of politics and developed as a science with firm links to politics. The use of scientific arguments in politics was strong both on the left and right (Seip 1989). Both sides believed that politics should have a scientific background. Fascism, social democracy and communism shared the idea of a strong and expert-based state.

New Day

In the 1930s there was a small left-wing group called 'New Day'.[2] Based almost entirely among academics, they had strong discipline and followed the way of 'scientific socialism' combining political belief with academic and organisational work. Their belief in knowledge and science showed in many areas of intense activity.[3] This small group had a lot of influence in the public debate of their time. Many of the members became leading politicians and public administrators after the war. Maybe the most influential person from this group was the late director of health (until 1972) and key person behind the modern Norwegian health system: Karl Evang. As a medical doctor, one of his tasks for New Day was to run a group called The Association of Socialist Medical Doctors. The purpose was to attract radical medical students and doctors and develop a new health policy. Evang and his colleagues soon focused on nutrition, in addition to hygiene and sex education. They conducted research on the nutrition of the lower classes. Besides documenting nutritional problems in the narrow sense, the project indicated that a lot of variables should be considered in the handling of nutrition problems (housing, education, economy). They made policy recommendations and state clearly in the report that: 'The days have passed, when the solution of nutritional problems in a population can be left to the . . . housewife. . . . [nutrition] has become a social problem . . . solved on a society level' (Evang and Hansen 1937). They made reform proposals and documents for new policies. Housing and nutrition were regarded as important welfare topics. They should be included in social policy using new forms of state regulation of economy and production. Organization plans were made for a new public health system. In the health and nutrition sectors the proposals had great impact.

Political struggles over nutrition

Nutrition was also a topic on the right wing. The owner of a big chocolate factory founded the Institute of Nutrition at the University of Oslo. He was also active in the political debate. The nutrition issue followed lines of political division and could be seen in newspapers and public meetings as well as in books.

The right-wing position used scientific results to calculate minimum food and vitamin requirements. They preferred minimum 'eating lists' of food that could fit a 'poor relief' social policy. Food should be given instead of money and the amount should take into consideration the fact that unemployed passive people have smaller needs. Public responsibility should be restricted to what was necessary to avoid deaths. This line was quite popular in the economic depression and was supported by government.

The left-wing viewpoint represented a different philosophy. Nutrition was linked to general living conditions. A minimum level of low-quality food distributed to poor people was humiliating and irrational. Standards should rather look to the food situation of the rich. The minimum list from the British Medical Association was also used for reference purposes. Good nutrition depended on housing, hygiene, education and the economic situation of families. Good nutrition would give people working ability as well as ensuring better sales for the domestic producers. The kinds of food in surplus production were regarded as good elements in the diet and an alliance was needed between workers and peasants.

This conflict was more or less solved at a meeting of The Medical Society[4] in 1935. The meeting had to be divided into several sections and lasted for days, attended by journalists. With some modifications the left won the battle.

Even if the struggle for food is a part of working-class politics, it was the experts that established nutrition policy in the political arena. On the other hand it was not only a topic reserved for experts and sector politicians. Media and the public political agenda were completely involved (Nordby 1987, 1989; Kjærnes 1990).

A new public health

Evang and his faction promoted a vision of a different health system where medical doctors used their science in a more social and preventive way. Their thoughts had obviously some parallel to what we today would call a welfare state with its macroeconomic planning system. The (traditionally conservative) Medical Association backed the basic elements in a plan for a new health system made by New Day. This support seems politically strange but the plan would give doctors a strong position, both politically and economically (Kjærnes 1990, Nordby 1987). Evang and other members of New Day joined the Workers Party (the social democratic party that has dominated Norwegian politics since the 1930s) after economic problems and external pressure on their organization. The (Social Democratic) Workers Party came into government from 1935. Evang's group produced a document on nutrition policy in 1936 and in 1937 the party integrated nutrition policy into their programme.

Social and health policy was not the most important topic in the Workers Party, but Evang's nutrition policy was accepted: it fitted with the new ideas on economy and planning. Most important was the support it represented for a strategic alliance between workers and agriculture. The policy combined the need for 'protective' foods in the working-class diet with a solution to the surplus production in agriculture. Evang was appointed Director of Health in 1939.

Nutrition and economy

Important elements from the preventive health politics were taken into a general welfare policy that later became known as Keynesianism. These new tendencies in economic science also represented left-wing politics and the strong belief in unity between science and politics.

Knut Getz Wold, a young economist, co-operated with Evang in matters of nutrition.[5] His writings integrated nutrition with national planning. He argues (Wold 1938) that a 'social policy' must mean that housing, nutrition and public health systems are essential elements. His calculations for such a total system were most detailed on nutrition. He later became the Manager of the Norwegian State Bank, a key position in macroeconomic planning. He was a member of the National Nutrition Council for many years. Also several other leading Keynesian economists, including two Nobel Prize winners, published on nutrition and food in national planning.

Macroeconomic planning according to Keynes had great impact on Norwegian politics and science. J.M. Keynes himself wrote a letter to the Norwegian parliament arguing against the conservatives. He was invited to do this by young economists in the Workers Party. These Norwegian economists later became the leaders in making Keynesianism an operational system linked to government decision making (Jensen 1990).

In the 1920s agricultural production outgrew demand, especially for meat and milk products. This was the background for putting far more emphasis on milk products as 'protective foods', than on fruit and vegetables. This priority on high-fat food was sensible in a situation where too little energy was a problem for parts of the population. A high-fat (relatively!) diet was also thought to be part of a preventive programme for tuberculosis, a major cause of death amongst the poor (Blaxter 1976). Relations between fat and heart disease were not known.

Building blocks in the new health system

The new health system under Karl Evang was built on the thoughts developed in the health section of New Day. Some inspiration for the broad and preventive strategy came from the Soviet Union but even more from the 'public health' tradition in the United States[6] and the UK. Nutrition, housing, hygiene, prevention, health controls and education are key words. Implementation should be organized at the local level: municipalities, schools, workplaces and travelling health units. This system should be ruled by the medical profession. Leading doctors at the county level were given Public Health scholarships. The emphasis on scientific/professional steering was strong. Evang demanded the unique double position of both being head of the directorate (providing the expertise) and the leader of a ministry unit (a high civil servant in the political hierarchy). He had the advantage of both preparing proposals to the parliament and controlling their implementation.[7] Evang was also active at the international level, in the plans for establishing FAO and WHO. The National Nutrition Council also had the role as the 'Norwegian FAO committee', thus further cementing the presumed harmony between agriculture and nutrition.

Evang soon became unpaid secretary of the National Nutrition Council, and chairman just before the war. He wrote an important document to the Ministry of Social Affairs just after the war (Evang 1945) on the reorganizing of nutrition policy. This document became the basis for the institutionalization of nutrition policy in Norway. Here he suggested that a number of different contributors should be represented in the Council; to include expertise, different ministries and representatives from producer groups. He emphasized the importance of integration and co-operation, and pointed to the use of pricing and production support in the nutrition policies. Both the initiative and the organization model was suggested with a reference to FAO, which aim is to 'benefit agriculture and promote public health' (Isdahl Hansen 1990). Nutrition policy gained prestige from Evang as the architect and the chairman of the Council for many years.

Political and nutritional success

In such an integrated approach, with nutrition inside the total macroeconomic planning and health system, it is difficult to be sure of cause and effects. As basic concepts became dominant, welfare increased, health improved and under- and malnutrition was difficult to find. Agriculture kept or enhanced its strong and protected position. Workplaces, schools and health stations were arenas for nutritional promotion.

Subsidies, tariffs and production support favoured foods that combined health and domestic production. Based on the problems that should be solved, politics seemed successful well into the 1960s.

The formation of this modern nutrition policy must be understood from three important elements:

- the 'scientific socialism' in left-wing health politics;
- Keynesian macroeconomic planning; and
- the negotiating 'corporate pluralist' political culture.

Many goals met in harmony: agriculture, working-class organizations and industry. Nutrition policy thus gained a role in the early phases of the up-and-coming social democratic system.

Policy problems: fat becomes unhealthy

Many parts of the system described above ran into problems from the 1960s onwards. The whole structure of the new health system developed into a strong professional expertise-based hospital system with only a slight resemblance to Evang's visionary plans. The general political system developed into an advanced system of representation, organization and negotiations. The interests of the production sector were in strong positions in this corporate pluralist system (Kvavik 1976, Olsen 1983). This is different from a more competitive system with greater tolerance for public disagreement. The position of nutrition policy in the public agenda weakened when the old nutritional problems seemed 'solved' but the National Nutrition Council was still active along the established lines.

From 1949, both newspapers and the scientific medical debate started to discuss possible links between the growing rate of heart-related deaths and saturated fats in nutrition. Heart-related deaths became the most common cause of death in the Norwegian male population, responsible for more than half the total deaths (Jensen, et al. 1986). The debate soon focused on milk fats where Norwegian consumption was high. In the 1950s the discussion could be based more on facts and from 1959 the evidence seemed rather clear. The evidence that consumption of butter was too high came at a time when this consumption still was 14 per cent lower than the 1948 food recommendations (Lien 1990). The dairy industry tried to prove the opposite and published 'research' indicating that butter actually protected against heart attacks.

High, and steeply rising, numbers of deaths, as shown in Figure 7.1, gained public interest and the topic was discussed in parliament. No interested organization pushed the topic, but Members of Parliament in co-operation with some of the nutrition experts felt the need to discuss these matters at a political level. The most significant result from these

Source: Uemura/Pisa 1988, Lien 1990.

Figure 7.1 Male heart diseases, Norway: death rate per 100 000, 1950–86.

discussions was the appointment of a committee that would look into the possible relation between nutrition and heart disease and make recommendations. The chairman, Ragnar Nicolaisen, was a long-standing and leading member of the National Nutrition Council and a leading academic in medicine. It is worth noticing that the political distance between him and the old radical builders of the health system in Norway, with Evang as a prominent example, was large.

The report from the Nicolaisen committee (1963) was clear in its conclusion regarding the link between saturated fats and heart disease and recommended a significant reduction in fat as a percentage of energy intake and a better proportion between different kinds of fat. Saturated fat from milk was the harmful kind. The recommendations were not followed by policy decisions. The relevant policy institutions took no action, in spite of attempts by experts and the public debate.

Public policy was absolutely not in congruence with the new knowledge. Discussions in parliament (Isdahl Hansen 1990) emphasized the academic disagreement that still existed and the economic interests of agriculture: several representatives also signalled a general distrust of the new knowledge, stating that 'we all know how healthy full-fat milk is'.

Rules that required producers to keep secret the contents of margarine were enforced and discussed in parliament. One occasion was when the media focused on the possible good effect of some vegetable fat acids that could be taken into margarine. Protection of agriculture and protection of the people from 'rumours' were the justifications used in parliament.

Based on interviews, we have reached the conclusion that, with some exceptions (like Nicolaisen), the role of the experts was not helpful in this period. The old actors partly distrusted the new evidence and partly felt obligations to old priorities and agreements. Some of the strong old men from New Day said that butter 'tasted good' and people should be allowed to eat it, or gave the statement that 'everything is dangerous, and our [agriculture] policy may take lives, just like our transportation system causes accidents' (Lien 1990, Isdahl Hansen 1990). The new experts in nutrition seemed passive, not seeking conflicts (Lien 1990). The nutrition policy, including politicians and experts, seems framed inside the institutionalization and integration represented by the policy patterns laid down just after World War II.

By 1966, the population felt reasonably convinced of the relation between food and heart disease. Figure 7.2 shows this and is taken from a representative poll, taken in 1966 (Alstad 1969). Fat and food were what people thought to be the most important causes, followed by stress and lack of exercise. Even by the standards of the 1990s this is not bad, and it was way ahead of the parliament and statements by many of those responsible for health and nutrition in the 1960s.

The nutrition situation

Norway is not only among the countries with the highest absolute rate of fat-related heart deaths, but absolutely in the upper league. The growth rates in the post-war years seemed frightening. In the period 1952 to 1967 male deaths from heart disease grew by 70.6 per cent, and 98.6 per cent for ischaemic heart disease. This is the steepest growth among countries where we have data (Uemura/Pîsa 1988). Average cardiovascular mortality increased by 40 per cent in a ten year period (Lien 1990). The number of deaths outgrew traffic deaths by a factor of six. There are big differences among countries both in level and changes in the rate of diseases. Nutrition is by far the best explanation of this phenomenon, and simple calculations indicate that half of the deaths among relatively young people can be avoided (Ministry of Agriculture 1975).

Norway is a country with a high level of milk-based fats in nutrition and is one of the highest milk and butter-using countries, with an

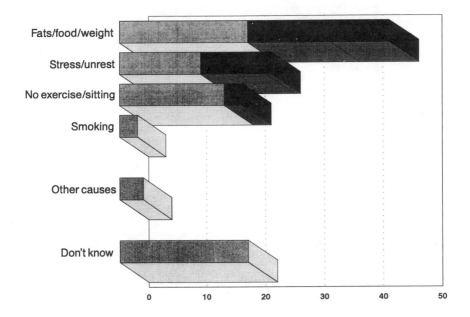

Source: Alstad (ed.) 1969.

Figure 7.2 Known causes of heart disease, Norway 1966, in per cent (total = 124).

increasing proportion of milk fats in total fat intake. (Lien 1990, Aasen et al. 1987). Figure 7.3 indicates that patterns of fat in nutrition and heart deaths follow each other with a 20-year lag for the fat to make its deadly damage, but it must be underlined that the cause and effect here is complicated, uncertain and relies on far more refined analysis! The new knowledge came in a situation of high fat consumption as well as a high, and still rising, share of milk fats in total consumption, as indicated in Figures 7.4 and 7.5.

The new approach: eat less fat, but more butter

The death toll and the new knowledge represented a pressure on the established policy and there were several initiatives for making a change. Health authorities were remarkably passive.

This changed in the mid-1970s with an initiative that emerged from both the Ministry of Agriculture and the Ministry of Social Affairs. The key actor here seems to have been the Minister of Agriculture (Isdahl

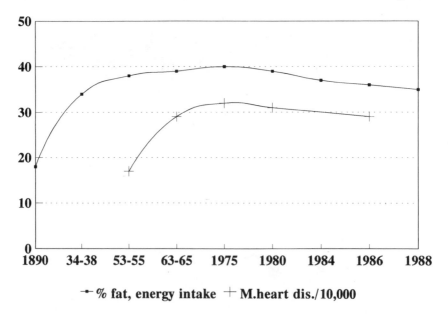

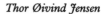

Source: Lien 1990.

Figure 7.3 Changes in nutrition and heart disease, Norway 1950–86.

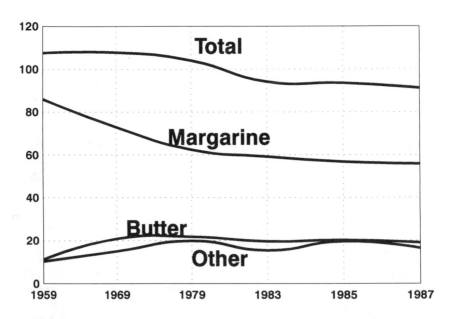

Source: Fjær 1990.

Figure 7.4 Fat consumption and composition in Norway, in mill kg., 1959–87.

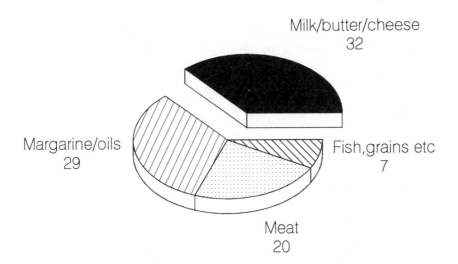

Source: Lien 1990.

Figure 7.5 Fat sources in Norway, 1987, as a percentage of total.

Hansen 1990, Lien 1990). It was argued that a new combined food and nutrition policy should be developed. The United Nations/FAO had discussed the food situation as a global problem. At the same time the economic support for agriculture came under political stress. Their political power was still strong after being well-organised on the winning 'No' side of the 1972 referendum on Norwegian EC membership. National self-sufficiency, global responsibility, nutrition, district policy and agricultural economy were taken into one integrated policy, where realistic goals and political measures should be suggested. A committee was led by the Minister of Agriculture and had representatives from three ministries and the National Nutrition Council.[8]

The resulting report to parliament was important and revitalized nutrition policy. It formulated the integrated policy that has incorporated positive international action. The document states goals in many areas with reference to both the world food situation and health problems related to nutrition. This was put into a frame that ensured several other goals, especially the agricultural interests.

The fat proportion of energy intake should be reduced, not to 30 per cent as suggested by the Nicolaisen committee, but (after negotiations) to 35 per cent. The fat composition should also be changed. On this background it is surprising that the recommendation for butter was to enlarge the usage of butter 30 per cent. Margarine usage should be reduced to 35 per cent. The composition of margarine should be changed to use more (processed and therefore saturated) Norwegian fish fats, hence further affecting the quality of the fat composition. The stated goals told people to eat less fat, but more butter. If these goals had been reached, fat usage would have gone down a little, but fat composition would be worse. A fat composition goal was set that was far from realistic given the production aims.

Both structurally and in content the philosophy behind the nutrition policy established after the war was revitalized by this document and its parliamentary backing. The key is still a Nutrition Council with broad representation, now supplemented by an Inter-ministerial Co-ordinating Committee. The policy is described by the authorities in this way:

The National Nutrition Council has been reorganized to support the nutrition and food policy more effectively. Ministries related to agriculture and food production, health, education and economy have recognised the convergence of their interests, and the administrative machinery is in place to facilitate inter-ministerial co-operation . . . The role of the Council is to advise authorities, industries, institutions and food producers . . .

An inter-ministerial co-operation committee on nutrition consisting of members from nine different ministries with interests in food and nutrition was given responsibility for long-term as well as annual policy implementation concerning nutrition and diet.

The differences from the 1930s are that this time there is no linkage to political activism or organizations outside the governmental system and no base in a strategic common interest between health values and agricultural producers. This last point is also the reason behind some internal antagonisms in the policy.

Overproduction of fat: the struggle of the century?

In the 15-year period of this new policy there is some evidence that helps us decide how public policy tried to influence the eating patterns of the Norwegian people. Even in the parliamentary debate, it was clear that most speakers regarded the nutrition policy document as a part of an agricultural debate, a way of giving more weight to the importance of agriculture. Many observers even see this whole topic as one part of the big reorganizing of agricultural support systems that came not long after the food and nutrition debate (Isdahl Hansen 1990).

Parliament (and the Nutrition Council) also took issue with the consumer authorities when they published information on health and fatty acids. This is interesting because the consumer authorities' article just repeated established facts about health effects of fat in margarine and butter. The government's critique was based on the stated goal to eat more butter and less margarine, so information from a public-supported body that could reduce butter consumption was against the nutrition policy. The debate in parliament was completely dominated by worries on behalf of agriculture. The Minister of Agriculture said that the government always gave priority to previous promises (on agricultural income and production) when there was conflict with other policies.

Institutions faced with applying the nutrition policy accept the necessity of selling the total agricultural output: 'set the prices of cheese, cream and butter so that sales of the total production are ensured' (ICC report 1981–82). Parallel formulations are found in reports from other years, thus inviting a very harsh conclusion on the character of the 'integrated policy': 'It is integrated with production so that all food produced is sold, even if people's priorities move away from the unhealthy part of production'. Parallel arguments were often heard in parliament. The Minister of Agriculture made the following remark: 'it is necessary to see the whole picture. If Representative Hagen[9] wants low-fat milk, someone else has to ensure that the surplus fat is used' (Hansen 1990).

Another angle to the implementation of nutrition policy is the pattern of food subsidizing. Nancy Milio states that fat foods are subsidised six times more heavily than the foods favoured in policy guidelines (Milio 1990). This dramatic counter-health part of the policy has been softened during recent years: there are no longer direct subsidies of butter, and milk producers are no longer paid according to fat content. On the other hand there are a lot of indirect subsidies going to support fat production. Dairy marketing is publicly supported, and in this marketing 85 per cent of recipes presented must still be classified as high fat (Aasen et al., 1987). Product development and marketing efforts for new products are of course also skewed in a way that maximizes the chance of getting rid of the surplus fat at a good price.

The story of low-fat milk is very instructive (Fjær 1990 a, b). Against the background of health considerations and experiences from other countries a test with a low-fat alternative to the rather high-fat whole milk was arranged. After some internal calculations, the dairy industry, and hence the Ministry of Agriculture, turned against such a product. They managed to arrange a testing period (1976/77) that showed total failure for the new product.[10] Much later, in 1984, as milk consumption turned slightly downwards in total, the dairy industry (after an initiative from the Nutrition Council) introduced a very successful low-fat milk. Of course they claimed guarantees for economic loss and the big problem was the surplus fat. Nutrition policy institutions were engaged in the whole process and the success of the low-fat milk starts the second part of this story. The low-fat (1.5 per cent) alternative is now the most popular milk, and this means a potential huge fat surplus. The solution was (again) margarine: after discussions with nutritional bodies a margarine was introduced where 80 per cent of the fat was butter. The marketing money backing these products is tremendous; it may be the most intensely promoted food in the late 1980s (Aasen et al., 1987). The nutritional problem here is that the fat content of modern vegetable margarine is 33 per cent–50 per cent polyunsaturated fats, while butter is the opposite. Many consumers know this and move away from butter. Selling butter as margarine is therefore much like the old food adulteration. The new 'butter-as-margarine' products, one of which is low-fat, have no clear labels explaining that they are largely butter. For the low-fat variant the consumer has to know that the brand name 'Fjords and Country' is an alias for the dairy industry or read the very small letters on the back stating the truth about the content.

On the other hand, the information campaigns from the Nutrition Council have not reflected agricultural dependence over the whole period. They have also profited from the criticisms, public debate and interest in nutritional matters, including criticisms of the food policy.

The changes from 1975 to 1987 can be summed up like this: the diet has more vegetables, fruit, skimmed milk, oils and a reduction in full-fat milk and butter. On the other hand, there is more cream, yoghurt, cheese and soft drinks. This seems to reflect an international tendency towards better nutrition within the frames of marketing pressures and arrangements to ensure that most of the total agricultural production is consumed. The proportion of fat from milk products is not much changed. Less butter and whole milk is compensated by more ice cream, cheese and new product variants.

Fat composition is better than in 1975 and better than the stated goals of nutrition policy indicate. Prices of raw materials in margarine production and consumer demands for better composition of fats have caused this change. Milk fat is still the biggest fat source. There has been a slight net change in a positive direction, followed by a small reduction in heart-related deaths. Fat content of energy intake is now under the stated goal of 35 per cent. I will leave it open whether this change is caused by or happened in spite of the public nutrition policy.

In the late 1980s there were some signs of changes in nutrition policy; information on nutrition was based more on science, but there were also signs of conflict between nutrition policy and agriculture. The National Dairy Association said in 1988 that 'reduction in the sales of milk fat is due to strong pressure from health authorities and media . . .' Agriculture was also harder pressed in the political arena and the traditional support for its unique position seemed to be weakening. It is therefore difficult to make predictions regarding nutrition policy. Maybe a change is on the way; maybe these organizations will be weaker and play a smaller role in the future. The integrated policy built on negotiating common interests was cast in the 1930s and revitalized and even more strongly institutionalized in the 1970s. The second phase stands out as less dramatic than the first. This time the common interest was not so clear; the product agriculture most wanted to sell was now the same that should be most reduced for health reasons.

Final discussion

The above-mentioned factors make it appropriate to argue that nutritional values were distorted by interest groups. Agricultural interests used (co-opted) nutritional partners to ensure support in their struggle for a better economic situation. The content of the nutritional message was changed until it no longer represented a threat. Health is a good value to have at your side as a symbol. This 'co-option' process allowed nutrition to be used as a positive symbol that strengthened agriculture.

Nutrition education is where the relative freedom for the nutrition bodies is greatest. The problem with nutrition education is that it is easily counteracted by the regular cutprice bargains in butter or promotional campaigns advertising fat cheese or the butter 'margarine'. Given the disharmony between nutrition and the achievements of the institutionalized nutrition policy in the 1970s we must both understand the character of the problem and choose between at least two causal hypotheses.

The first hypothesis is a plain and political one: the winner is the strongest political pressure group. The strong agricultural interest is the key factor. Nutrition policy is clearly successful when it is in harmony with agricultural interests, and this was the case in the first phase. If nutritional problems point against the mighty agricultural interests, nutrition policy becomes weak and full of internal problems that move it away from its goal and make it unable to carry out the tasks. This is a hypothesis derived from politics based on interest group policy, where traditional economic interests (agriculture) are stronger than a more generalized health-based interest. Nutrition politics has been a tool that agriculture has used to handle their interests, to make sure that people eat their whole output. Both money and important initiatives in nutrition came from agriculture, and many proponents of nutrition policy have their background in agriculture.

The alternative hypothesis emphasizes the force of institutionalization. The problems, values, organizational patterns and solutions that are chosen at the start form the basis of the organization and no significant change is possible until a major crisis occurs. The institutions making nutrition policy are trapped in the problem-structure they were cast in. When calories and milk-based fats are seen as unhealthy and a major cause of deaths, the institutions are unable to change basic strategies, even if they recognize the new facts.

There are some important gaps in Norwegian nutrition policy. The health system, the original base for nutrition, now seems very passive in the whole process since the initial phase. Initiative has been handed to agriculture at the political level. Compared to the visions of the architects of nutrition policy this points to a system of health that has changed greatly in the direction of repairing damage and researching causes without making the necessary connections.

The other important missing part here is the fisheries. Norway is a fishing nation and fish is generally low in fat and has a very positive fat composition. The relative absence of the fisheries in this history of nutrition may seem strange, but is caused by the tradition of nutrition policy as being in alliance with agriculture and also by the power relationship between the fishing and the agricultural sector in Norwegian politics (Jacobsen 1965). This gap makes it easier to see the institutionalized nutrition policy mainly as a policy of fat, mostly discussing and administering the fat surplus.

'People are the real heroes'

This famous saying by the late Mao Tse Tung (1967) was meant to remind the intellectuals and politicians that the masses of the people often act correctly and are well informed. Preventive health is very often paternalistic in its nature with experts advising people and seeing people's reluctance to do as the expert tells them as the main obstacle. We should consider the other hypothesis: that people within reasonable limits try to obtain good nutrition, and in this they may be helped by a sceptical attitude to experts in alliance with producers.

We should remember that most people had a sensible understanding of the causes behind heart deaths as early as 1966. Another clue is the sale of bad-tasting cod-liver oil. These sales, indicated in Figure 7.6, went significantly upwards from 1986, when it became publicly known that this product could protect against heart disease even in small doses. The downward slope before that can be interpreted as a consequence of the fact that the vitamin content is less important in today's nutrition situation.[11] There is also the fast growth in health foods and the fact that both the fat percentage of energy intake and the composition are better than we should believe from the goals in the nutrition document. In the case of butter, margarine and milk it seems clear that people's habits

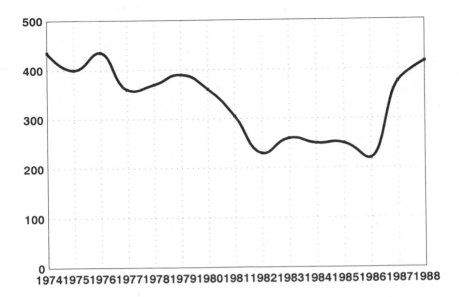

Source: Collet-Marwell Hauge 1989.

Figure 7.6 Cod liver oil, sales to consumers, in '000 litres per year.

have developed despite marketing and despite parts of the nutrition policy, all to the better of their health.

From countries without the Norwegian institutionalized nutrition policy, the evidence also supports the notion that people behave sensibly. The United States had a high mortality from heart disease, but the situation got significantly better before the Norwegian situation started to change. Many factors are behind this but the simple facts on food consumption are clear enough: butter sales per capita are down to 25 per cent of the 1910 level and were reduced by 50 per cent in the years 1950–80 (Levine 1986). Margarine sales have risen and the balance is a reduction in spread fats and a better composition. Table salt and whole milk consumption have also dropped sharply.

This all adds up to the important notion that one should not assume that the problem is unresponsive consumers who should be subjected to more massive information campaigns. Against the background of the massive marketing of high-fat products, it can be argued that people are rather shrewd in their selection of foods: if information about nutrition is available, if pricing and access is good, people tend to make quite sensible choices.

The conclusion is not that nutrition policy is unnecessary. What is required is a policy that enlightens people and forces the market to have a health-compatible price, access and marketing structure which is responsive to change. Coalitions of interests may form in response to market and policy changes: fisheries and margarine producers are reasonable partners in the 1980s and 1990s: agriculture is not. Politicians, public bureaucracies and corporate pluralism can be important targets of attack in the process of developing a sound nutrition policy.

Notes

1. The chapter is based on the results of a 3-year project that mixed competence in nutrition, political science and anthropology. The project was financed by the National board for applied social science. While I accept all criticisms arising out of the views expressed in this chapter, it is the outcome of a truly collaborative process. I am most in debt to my fellow project leader, Unni Kjærnes, but have also drawn heavily on the works of the other project colleagues: Marianne Lien, Svanaug Fjær and Ranveig Isdahl Hansen.
2. A stricter translation would be 'Towards Day'.
3. One example is their six-volume encyclopedia (1936), made in a short time to a high standard that still is admired. It is one of my general reference encyclopedias.
4. Meetings in the Medical Society were about scientific and general topics, while the Medical Association was the organization for matters regarding the doctors' well-being. These very different kinds of topic are now more or less merged within the Medical Association.
5. Knut Getz Wold was not a member of New Day, in fact he was a member of a non-socialist leftist party.
6. Evang spent time at Johns Hopkins during the war and was active both in the US and UK, learning and discussing public health.
7. This unique position gave very high power in implementing the new system. But it also opened the way for too much professional power, had problems in adjusting to new knowledge and problems, and made it difficult for politicians to have influence. After the Evang era this double system was removed and several reforms in the 1980s and 1990s have tried to reduce the position of the Director of Health and his organization. The latest reorganization plan (1991) is said to remove most administrative responsibility from the directorate.
8. It is not surprising that they did 'forget' the fisheries, given the strong agricultural influence, but the Ministry of Fisheries was added to the committee at a later stage.
9. Representative Hager belonged to 'Progress Party', which is the only party in parliament that has taken the new nutrition knowledge seriously. One reason is their opposition to the huge economic transfers to agriculture, but it is also

a coincidence that Ragnar Nicolaisen, the chairman of the committee that documented the fat problems (and one of the heroes in this story) was neighbour of a central member of this small right-wing party.

10. How this failure was 'arranged' is difficult to understand, but it helped a lot to introduce the product as suited to people 'on a special diet', to choose testing areas in strong agricultural areas and make the product appear unpleasant when it came to colours and packaging.

11. Vitamins A and D are now provided in other foodstuffs: for a long time they have been artificially added to margarine, a very early and sensible measure from the old nutrition policy.

Bibliography

Aarø L.E.: *Health Behaviour and Socioeconomic status*. Doctoral Thesis, University of Bergen, 1986.

Aasen, Edvardsen and Baugerod: *Godsmøret – ernæringsmeldinga: 1–0*, Student Essay, University of Oslo, 1987.

Alstad (red): *Norske meninger 3*, Pax forlag, Oslo, 1969.

Ashton and Seymour: *The New Public Health*, Open University Press, 1988.

Blaxter, Mildred: 'Social Class and Health Inequalities' in Carter and Peel (eds) *Equalities and Inequalities in Health*, Academic Press, London, 1976.

Bruun, K. (ed.): *Controlling Psychotropic Drugs*, Croom Helm, 1983.

Cannon, Geoffrey: *The Politics of Food*, Century Hutchinson, London, 1987.

Cohen, Marshall H.: *Norwegian Nutrition and Food Policy*, US Dept of Agriculture, report 157, Washington, 1980.

Eckhoff, T.: *Statens Styringsmuligheter*, Tanum-Norli, 1980.

Evang, K. and Galtung Hansen: *Norsk kosthold i små hjem*, Tiden, 1937.

Evang, K.: *Rekonstruksjon av Statens ernæringsråd*. Proposal from The Norwegian Director of Health to the Minister of Social Affairs, Oslo, 1945.

Esping-Andersen, G.: *Polititics against markets. The Social democratic road to power*, Princeton University Press, 1985.

Fjær, Svanaug: *Makt, Marked og margarin*, Report no. 5 from 'Nutrition and food Policy' SEFOS/SIFO, Oslo/Bergen, 1990.

Fjær, Svanaug: *Fettkabalen som ikke gikk opp. Lettmelkens historie i Norge*, Report no. 1 from 'Nutrition and food Policy' SEFOS/SIFO, Oslo/Bergen, 1990.

Held, David: *Models of Democracy*, Free Press, 1987.

Isdahl Hansen, Ranveig: *Den hensiktsmassige ernæringspolitikken*, Report no. 2 from 'Nutrition and food Policy' SEFOS/SIFO, Oslo/Bergen, 1990.

Jacobsen, K.D.: Informasjonstilgang og likebehandling, *TFS*, 1965, 147.

Jacobsen, K.D.: 'Public administration under pressure: The role of the expert in modernization of traditional agriculture', *Scandinavian Political Studies*, vol X, 1968: 1.

Jensen, T.Ø.: *Kan norsk forvaltning lære*. Mimeo, 1980.

Jensen, T.Ø.: *Kontrollpolitikk som brukerbeskyttelse*, Institute of administration, 1984.

Jensen, T.Ø.: *Application of Social Science in Scandinavia with emphasis on a* practical research method for use in public and private service, Notat 30, SEFOS 1990. Paper for the Conference on Sociology and Psychology in Economic Practice, 14–18 May, Siråva, Eastern Slovakia.

Jensen, T.Ø., Kjærnes, Unni and Klepp, Knut Inge: Health, Nutrition and Agriculture Policy: The Norwegian Experiment Paper to 1986 APHA meeting, Las Vegas. Report no. 7 from 'Nutrition and Food Policy' SEFOS/SIFO, Oslo/ Bergen, 1990.

Jensen, T.Ø. and Stø, E.: Norsk forbrukerpolitikk ved en skillevei, NST, 1987: 2

Kjærnes, U.: Velferdskrav og landbrukspolitikk. Report no. 6 from 'Nutrition and Food Policy', SEFOS/SIFO, Oslo/Bergen, 1990.

Kjærnes, U.: Ernæring, næring og forbrukerne', in SIFO (ed.) Forbruksforskning i går, i dag og i morgen, Oslo, 1989.

Kvavik, R.F.: Interest groups in Norwegian Politics, University Press, Oslo, 1976.

Levine, Janet M.: 'Hearts and Minds: The politics of diet and heart disease', in Sapolsky (ed.) Consuming Fears, Basic Books, 1986.

Lien, Marianne: The Norwegian Nutrition and Food Supply Policy. Accomplishments and Limitations of a Structural Approach. Report no. 3 from 'Nutrition and Food Policy', SEFOS/SIFO, Oslo/Bergen, 1990.

Lien, Marianne: Kunsten å gjøre alle til lags. Statens ernæringsråd i norsk ernæringspolitikk. Report no. 4 from 'Nutrition and Food Policy', SEFOS/ SIFO, Oslo/Bergen, 1990.

Lien, Marianne: Summing up Norwegian public and medical debate on cardiovascular disease and dietary fats. Unpublished project material.

March, James G. and Johan P. Olsen: Rediscovering Institutions. The organizational basis of politics, Free Press, London/NY, 1989.

Mao Tse-Tung: Quotations, Foreign Language Press, Beijing, 1967.

Milio, N.: An Analysis of the implementation of Norwegian Nutrition Policy 1981–1987. Paper prepared for WHO 1990 conference on Food and Nutrition.

Nordby, Trond: 'Profesjokratiets periode innen norsk helsevesen', Historisk Tidsskrift, 3, 1987.

Nordby, Trond: Karl Evang – en biografi, Aschehoug, Oslo, 1989.

Olsen, J.P.: Organized Democracy, Universitetsforlag, Oslo, 1983.

Ringen, K.: 'Norway's nutrition and food policy: Overview, results and future directions', in Mc Lorey (ed.) Nutrition in the Community, 163–81, John Wiley, 1977.

Segal, Mark J.: 'The politics of salt: The Sodium-Hypertension Issue', in Sapolsky (ed.) Consuming Fears. The Politics of Product Risks, Basic Books, 1986.

Seip, Anne-Lise: The influence of science on Social Policy in Norway in the 1930s. Paper presented at the conference on 'Welfare state in transition', Bergen, 1989.

Thorsen, H.: Næringsmiddelkontroll, 1935.

Tilly, Louise A.: Food entitlements, Gender and the State in France 1800–1914. Paper, New School for Social Research, New York, 1989.

Tønneson, Kåre D.: Sentraladministrasjonens historie 4: 1914–1940, Universitets-forlaget, 1979.

Winkler, J.T.: 'Nurturing nutrition the Norwegian way', Guardian 22 May 1987.

Winikoff, B.: 'Nutrition and food policy: The approach of Norway and the United States', American Journal of Public Health, 67, 552–7, 1977.

Wold, Knut Getz: *Vår Socialpolitikk*, Norges Venstrelag, 1938.

Wold, B.K., Jensen and Færden: *Mat med høyt fettinnhols Hvem spiser mye?* SIFO Report 9, Oslo, 1990.

Wood, Donna J.: 'The Strategic Use of Public Policy: Business Support for the 1906 Food and Drug Act', *Business History Review*, 1985, 59: 402–32.

Uemura/Pisa: 'Trends in cardiovascular disease mortality in industrialized countries since 1950, in *World Health-Statistics quarterly* 41: 155–78.

Governmental and other documents

Interdepartmental Co-ordinating Committee (on nutrition): unpublished reports, 1982, 1983, 1986.

Ministry of Agriculture (1975) *On Norwegian Food and Nutrition Policy.* Proposition to the Norwegian Parliament, no. 32, 1975–76 (English translation).

Ministry of Health and Social Affairs: *On the Follow-up of Norwegian Nutrition Policy.* Proposition to the Norwegian Parliament, no. 11, 1981–82 (English translation).

League of Nations: *The Relation of Nutrition to Health, Agriculture and Economic Policy*, 1937.

Collet/Marwell-Hauge: Letter regarding cod-liver oil statistics to the project, 1989.

PART 3: THE DEVELOPMENT OF QUALITY CONTROL

8 Hygiene and the control of food in Finnish towns at the turn of the century: a case study from Helsinki

Marjatta Hietala

In this chapter I explore how Helsinki and other Finnish cities and towns faced the international demand for unadulterated food and improved hygiene at the turn of the century. Of particular interest is the question of how quickly the decision-makers reacted to the problems of food control and the methods they employed in controlling the meat and milk trade. Did food control in Finland follow international developments? How far did those advocating improved standards of food succeed and how was this information utilized when developing the various aspects of hygiene in the capital, Helsinki? On the international level, hygiene was one of the key terms used by pedagogues, popular educators and medical practitioners when discussing a range of topics, from foodstuffs to personal cleanliness, from street cleaning to hygiene in factories, in restaurants, abattoirs, bakeries, private houses and schools.

Collating accurate information and compiling statistics were preconditions for combating disease, and both Sweden and Finland had long traditions in this area. Since 1749 the Central Statistical Office had gathered information on mortality and the causes of death and since 1840 doctors had been taking part, on the basis of this information, in debates on public health. During the 1840s and 1850s statistics on mortality were analysed and tables of causes of mortality according to age and gender were published by Finnish doctors. Analyses based on the Finnish statistics were compared with information from other countries.[1]

It was the advance of bacteriology, however, that in the end gave impetus to demands for the promotion of hygiene at every level. This discipline had proved how it was possible both to identify and prevent contagious diseases.[2] With pure drinking water and food one could both combat these diseases and lower the mortality rates associated with them. Medical practitioners, engineers and municipal officials made joint efforts to improve the basic health and infrastructure of their communities.[3] Finnish doctors adopted a wide concept of hygiene, considering it to form part of social hygiene, a term commonly employed elsewhere in Europe. Not only did this term embrace hygiene but also fields nowadays seen rather as social politics, health care, the welfare services, food hygiene and personal hygiene. A Finn, Akseli Koskimies, defined the individual as a member of a certain social class and economic group, 'a position which predisposed him or her to the health hazards characteristic of his social class or to be found in that class'.[4]

At the end of the nineteenth century, there emerged a substantial body of professional hygienists in European countries. A number of medical practitioners and veterinary surgeons specialized in hygiene and once stations for the control of foodstuffs had been established there was a need for chemists. A great variety of inspectorates requiring special knowledge was created.

Study abroad, study tours, organizations and periodicals as promoters of hygiene

Foreign experience has been highly valued in Finland. Over the centuries the Finnish educated upper and professional classes maintained extensive direct contacts with experts in various European countries. This influence arrived independently of Sweden or Russia, in spite of the fact that Finland was a part of the Swedish Kingdom until 1809 and after that had an autonomous status in the Russian Empire (1809–1917).

During the last century the Finnish Government could not invest in all specialized training sectors. Instead of that the government invested money in scholarships which made it possible for experts to participate in congresses and exhibitions. Approximately 500 students got their training in German universities during 1900–14.

Among those who were not able to get their training in Finland at the turn of the century were veterinary surgeons. It was not, indeed, until after the Second World War that graduation in veterinary surgery was possible in Finland. Before that time Finnish veterinary surgeons studied either in the Nordic countries or in the German veterinary universities in Berlin, Dresden and Hamburg. On the initiative of the veterinary surgeon Oskar von Hellens, matters relating to veterinary science were dealt with by the National Board of Health after 1897 and ten years later the Board established in Helsinki a veterinary medical laboratory. The first animal clinic began operation in 1892 in Helsinki.[5]

Innovations spread first through experts who had got their training in other Nordic countries or in Central Europe, or who had made study tours abroad. It was usual to take courses of advanced studies of greater length abroad, and to do circular study tours visiting various institutions as shown below.[6] Secondly, the important channels for the dissemination of the newest knowledge were scientific associations. Thirdly, the professional journals were important channels for spreading the latest information.[7] Doctors specialising in hygiene used all these channels of information.

An excellent forum for debates on the latest information and innovations was provided in Finland from 1835 onwards by meetings of the Finnish Medical Association in Helsinki and later also by meetings of doctors in Turku and in Viipuri, the second and third largest towns in Finland. The Duodecim Association, an organization specially created for Finnish-speaking doctors, was established in 1881. So far as the dissemination of innovations and the spread of foreign expertise were concerned, the central role among Finnish medical practitioners as a whole was played by the publication series *Finska Läkaresällskapets Handlingar* (1841–) issued by the Finska Läkaresällskapet, the leading body in the field throughout the whole of Finland. This society systematically increased its medical library. Its 1891 catalogue consisted of 244 pages and volumes dealing with hygiene and related subjects represented a considerable part of the collection. Among periodicals 62 out of 71 came from abroad, e.g. 18 were of Scandinavian origin and there were 13 German, 11 Russian, 9 French, 6 Belgian, 6 American, 4 Italian, 4 British and 1 Spanish journals.

In the 1880s there were two major associations in Finland whose main concern was with giving instruction in hygiene in its wider concept. Both Hälsovårdsföreningen i Finland and Suomen Terveydenhoitoyhdistys aimed at the elimination of existing health hazards in the home and in society in general and they laid a particular emphasis on preventive health care. Among the most hardworking of the chairmen of the former organization were Vilhelm Sucksdorff (1851–1934), Medical Officer in Helsinki, later a professor of hygienics at Helsinki University, and Albert Palmberg (1831–1916), District Medical Officer in Helsinki and a hygienist of international repute. Sucksdorff launched a popular health magazine *Tidskrift for Hälsovård* for the Swedish-speaking part of the Finnish population.

The most active chairman of the latter association, Suomen Terveydenhoitoyhdistys, was Konrad Relander (later ReijoWaara), the District Medical Officer in Haapajärvi, from North Finland. He launched a new Finnish-speaking magazine *Suomen Terveydenhoitolehti*, with the object of providing instruction in health care for the general public. The magazine endeavoured to change dietary habits, provide instruction for child care and encourage the following of hygiene requirements at all levels.[8]

Instruction in Hygiene

Although the idea of establishing a chair of hygiene had already been proposed at meetings of the Finska Läkaresällskapet in 1879 and 1881, it did not, however, materialize until 1890. The matter was proposed by Albert Palmberg, who suggested that a chair of public health care should be established in Finland. Similar posts had been established in German universities as early as 1865 and in some British universities it had been possible since the 1870s to graduate in public health. In Sweden, instruction in hygiene had become compulsory in 1890. Palmberg also proposed that elementary studies of health care should be made compulsory in technical colleges and teacher-training centres, and the first specialist chair in hygiene was established in Finland in 1894.

Although hygiene became a compulsory subject for medical students, the discipline itself took some time to take shape. At first, great emphasis was laid on lectures and laboratory work. But Palmberg aimed at developing the discipline to meet the requirements of its multifarious applications. Following foreign models, he was prepared to transfer part of the teaching to relevant workplaces: into waterworks, public sanitation departments, factories, abattoirs, schools and hospitals.[9] At the beginning of the 1900s this idea of Palmberg's became a reality and students completed their special projects in schools and public institutions.[10]

Health care board and the supply of pure water

The reorganization of local government in 1875 and the issuing of the 1879 Health Care Order very much resembles the equivalent statute for England and Wales and is almost a straight translation of the Swedish Health Care Order of 1874. It decreed that a special Health Care Board should be established to supervise the quality of water from wells and springs and to inspect housing, restaurants and workshops and their sanitary conditions. The order also urged the construction of sewerage systems. In addition, the Health Care Order tightened up procedures for the compiling of statistics on diseases and the responsibility of doctors to report on them. The ultimate aim was the compilation of statistics on diseases and mortality covering the whole of the country.[11] In accordance with the 1877 and 1882 regulations, the city Medical Officer had a central role in supervising health conditions in Helsinki. From 1895 until 1916 the office was held by Vilhelm Sucksdorff. In the Municipal Public Health Board, expertise from various relevant fields was also represented.

One of the main tasks of the Health Care Board was to inspect the quality of drinking water. The report of a health inspector in Helsinki indicated in 1890, that of a total of 82 wells he had inspected only six provided water suitable for drinking.[12] Two years later, samples were taken from 34 wells of which only four proved to be providing water fit for drinking. Tap water was also tested both chemically and bacteriologically. The waterworks that had been established in Helsinki in 1876 was taken over by the city in 1880. Normally the water supply was taken from the river Vantaa but occasionally it was of very bad quality. Even so, the experts could not agree on whether the chemical filtration method would produce better water than the mechanical one. In 1889 the Helsinki Municipal Water Engineer was sent abroad to investigate the developments and achievements of water-system technology as well as to collect evidence on the most modern methods of filtration. It took further study tours and comments from foreign experts before the Municipal Council of Helsinki was convinced of the need to introduce chemical filtration. In 1908 the Municipal Council of Helsinki invested money in the use of chemical and quick filtrations.[13]

The establishment of the Municipal Health Bureau

The growth of population in the capital was at a yearly rate of 3.6 per cent (in 1905 there were 100,000 inhabitants in Helsinki). The concern of its inhabitants regarding trade in foodstuffs in general and that in the market-places in particular, as well as the increasing need for qualified doctors, were all matters that had kept the Municipal Health Board busy. As early as 1888 it had begun to advocate the establishment of a general out-patient clinic and the acquisition of premises for the Board itself.[14]

The eventual establishment of a Municipal Health Bureau in 1889 marked a new step in preventive health care. The Bureau dealt with complaints and provided advice in matters related to hygiene. Most complaints were about the quality of foodstuffs and the condition of housing. The Bureau was particularly active in the 1890s when V. Sucksdorff became involved in its work. He had at his disposal a sanitary policeman and a body of junior inspectors, the number of which was greatly increased at the beginning of the 1900s and especially during epidemics of contagious diseases. Most often those selected as junior inspectors were policemen or students, but in 1908 two nurses were appointed to such posts.[15]

Table 8.1 Complaints sent to the Municipal Health Bureau in Helsinki.

Date	Total	Various diseases	Bad housing	Milk trade	Others
1891	1427				
1892	1133				
1893	1011	755	76	153	27
1894	433	268	41	99	25
1895	1021	740	35	78	12

Source: Medical Board of Finland, *Official Statistics of Finland* XI.

The trade carried on in the market-places in particular occupied both the Municipal Health Inspector himself and many of his junior inspectors. In 1894 Sucksdorff approached the Helsinki City Treasury appealing for measures to be taken to rectify the hygienically unsatisfactory conditions in the market-places caused by the selling of salted fish. Fish barrels were leaking salty water, causing unsavoury smells and contaminating the soil. The Municipal Health Board proposed that the market-place should be covered with tarmac or cement and should also be provided with a sewer.

Once established, the Municipal Health Bureau received in its first year a total of 1,427 reports and the following year 1,133 of which 1,011 led to official warnings. The main causes for complaints in these reports are given in Table 8.1.

One of the first measures taken by Sucksdorff as the head of the Municipal Health Bureau was the formulation of a proposal on meat control. The necessity for meat control, it was argued, was because of the importance of meat in the city's diet.[16] The cities of Lyons, Berlin, Paris and Munich were taken as a reference group and while the annual average consumption of meat in Helsinki was 67 kilos per person, this was compared with 73 kilos in Lyons, 79 kilos in Berlin (in 1888), 84 kilos in Paris (in 1885) and 88 kilos in Munich.

The Municipal Health Board had great expectations of their Health Inspector. The requirement that he should be a qualified doctor was suggested by the high level of mortality from tuberculosis in Helsinki: in New York 20 per cent of able-bodied adults died from tuberculosis, in Stockholm 18 per cent, Brussels 18 per cent, Paris 16 per cent and London 11 per cent, but in Helsinki the figure was 30 per cent. The more favourable situation in foreign cities, especially in England, seemed to be explained by the improvement in health conditions. An even more obvious indicator of inferior health conditions in Helsinki was the mortality from typhoid which also exceeded the Stockholm figures.[17]

Sucksdorff, the head of the Municipal Health Bureau, was himself appointed Municipal Health Inspector.

Food control

Although defective housing conditions attracted the attention of people in Helsinki, as the figures in Table 8.1 indicate, the greater concerns of private citizens related to food issues. The transportation and inspection of meat and other items of diet were defective and dust and dirt contaminated foodstuffs in the market-place.

Customers themselves were, indeed, concerned about market-place trading. A typical letter of complaint, addressed to the Municipal Health Board, demanded greater cleanliness in the market-places and listed the following defects: food was not covered but was left 'to be bathed in all kinds of dirt and dust carried by the wind', meat counters were 'positioned above the gullies near a public lavatory which spread a disgusting stench . . . . The storing of goods [was] also not practical as they [were] far too near the ground and without any cover . . . . Neither [was] their transportation all that good . . . and at the market-place the meat stalls and the fishmongers [were] placed far too near the road.'[18]

It was in 1895 that detailed regulations were eventually framed concerning such market trading. There were many proposals to ban meat trading altogether in open markets but these led nowhere. The construction of the first covered market halls produced a marked improvement in this direction.[19] Helsinki, Savonlinna and Kemi built such halls in the 1880s and Oulu, Tampere, Joensuu and Viipuri in the early 1900s. By 1920 there were already 15 Finnish towns and cities with such a hall.

The issue of food control had already been discussed in 1879 at the Municipal Health Board and investigations were made on how the matter had been resolved in Stockholm. Subsequently the Municipal Health Board made a formal proposal for the appointment of a Municipal Chemist, an appointment suggested by A.W. Forsberg while studying agricultural chemistry abroad.[20]

Later Mr Hynén, qualified dispensing chemist, played an important role in the establishment of the Food Control Station and he was appointed its first director. Compared with other countries at that time Germany was so advanced in food control that even control fees tended to follow the German model. Not surprisingly, therefore, Hynén travelled in 1883, with the support of a state grant, to Dresden and Brunswick on a fact-finding tour concerned with food control. He tried to utilise the trip to the full and even ordered necessary laboratory equipment from Germany. However, he died before he had completed the tour.[21]

The Food Control Station began to operate in 1884 under the leadership of Dr Ossian Aschan, who was aware of the underdeveloped state of the field and tried hard to collect all possible information on it, purchasing equipment as well as literature. The defining of standards and criteria for the evaluation of milk and its fat content proved at first very difficult. To define the fat content he used, initially, the Feser lactoscope and to measure the weight, the Qvennen milk scale. The numerical values used as a basis for classification of milk as good, mediocre and bad were the equivalent of those used to classify milk sold in the markets of Stockholm. These criteria differed from those used for milk sold in shops. It was difficult to distinguish between whole milk and semi-skimmed milk but fat-free milk at least could easily be distinguished. In 1886 there was an unanimous decision that the regulations valid in Stockholm should also apply in Helsinki.[22] Given the rapid progress in the field, Aschan proposed, in 1889, that the Laval lactoscope should be adopted for use.

After six years in office Aschan went to Berlin in 1890, to spend a year studying the trade in foodstuffs because he believed that there 'food control had been organised in a satisfactory manner'. He wished to learn from the highest possible authorities – to study bacteriological water and air analysis under Professor Koch in Berlin and Professor Pettenkofer in Munich.[23] As a result of this trip by Aschan, a considerable sum of money was later allocated for purchasing equipment, chemicals and books for the Food Control Station.[24]

After Aschan, Allan Zilliacus was appointed director of the Food Control Station. Zilliacus had studied agricultural chemistry and meat control abroad. The rival candidate was Mr Komppa, a civil engineer, who had also studied abroad in Zurich at the laboratories of Professor Hänzel.[25]

During the first year of its operations in 1884–85 some 4,000 inspections were carried out at the Food Control Station. In 1890, a total of 3912 investigations were carried out dealing with the quality of pork meat, milk and water as well as the arsenic content of wallpapers.[26] In subsequent years this figure decreased only to rise again during the 1900s (see Table 8.2).

At a national level, food control services were regulated by the 1879 Health Care Act and the 1908 Bakery Act passed by the Finnish Senate. In the City of Helsinki trading in meat and other foodstuffs was controlled by the regulations of 27 November 1899; trading in the market-places by the municipal regulations of 23 January 1895; and licences for carrying on the trades of bakery, patisserie and sausage-making by an even earlier regulation of 26 August 1889.

Bearing in mind foreign models, the new director of the Food Control Station, Allan Zilliacus, decided to convert the station into an Institute

Table 8.2 Investigations carried out at the Food Control Station in Helsinki.

Date	Total investigations	By private initiative	Disinfections	
			Homes	Institutions
1890	3912	–	66	59
1896	2119	1924	277	422
1902	1780	956	262	205
1908	7143	1021	725	389
1914	9083	1108	1619	335

Source: Medical Board of Finland, *Official Statistics of Finland* XI.

for Chemical and Bacteriological Research where citizens could bring samples for further investigation.[27] In 1902 he had toured Germany for a month in order to study how trading in foodstuffs was controlled in various continental cities. As a result of this journey Zilliacus took as his reference group the Hygienic Institute of Hamburg, established in 1896, and a similar institute in Berlin which had started to operate in 1901. To accord with the most up-to-date foreign laboratories the proposed Institute had also to have its own laboratories with departments dedicated to bacteriological research. In addition, more assistants were needed for taking samples.

The reformation of the Municipal Health Regulations in Helsinki

The proposal for reform of the 1879 National Health Care Act was completed in 1908 although it was not formally ratified. At the same time municipalities, including Helsinki, began actively to reorganize their health-care systems in 1907. Finally in 1915 the Municipal Health Board completed its proposal for Health Care Regulations to be discussed by a special committee appointed by the Municipal Council. In their report, published in 1916, the committee felt that some of the proposals made by the Council were too strict and they amended, for example, the regulations on the trade in foodstuffs on the outskirts of the city. In addition the committee proposed some reforms in the existing regulations on policing.[28]

Within the regulations relating to trading in foodstuffs, special attention was paid to cleanliness and hygiene. Concerning the decoration of the premises of food retail shops, for example, it was prescribed that the walls and ceilings should be painted white so that they could be cleaned easily and the same requirements were applied to shop counters and containers for storing food. It was also prescribed that 'foodstuffs for sale should not be stored in direct contact with the soil or floor but in boxes or using other methods which would ensure that neither the foodstuffs themselves nor the soil or floor would be contaminated. In addition the food should be protected in a proper manner from contamination by flies.' Also 'clean bags or wrapping paper must be used for wrapping food'. Extreme cleanliness was also expected from those involved in trading foodstuffs. They were to wear pale-coloured washable aprons with sleeves.[29] These regulations also took into account customers' earlier complaints regarding trading in market-places by prohibiting the selling in the market-places of meat, sausages and other meat products, blood, poultry, game, butter, cheese, bread, flour or cereals.

The desire to follow foreign developments also created new pressures. Thus the authorities had to prepare themselves, following examples from abroad, to take measures to counteract the adulteration of foodstuffs. The widely travelled Allan Zilliacus especially was much concerned with this possibility and believed that in many civilised countries the combating of the adulteration of food had become a real industry taking advantage of the most recent discoveries in chemistry. Consequently Zilliacus suggested that the Municipal Health Board should make a formal proposal for enactment of detailed regulations on this matter.[30]

Bacteriology

With the increase in bacteriological knowledge, the Food Control Station proved to be outdated and at their meeting on 11 November 1901 the Municipal Health Board noted that it no longer met current requirements. A sub-committee, appointed by the Board, began subsequently to deliberate on the proposed reorganization of this station and a statement on this matter was also invited from Allan Zilliacus, its director.

It was not until 1906, however, that a proposal was finally made to employ a qualified bacteriologist in the Food Control Station, which, it was proposed, should at the same time be transformed into a laboratory for health research as had happened in Stockholm. It was thought that through chemical laboratory tests it would be possible to trace the bacteria causing diptheria and tuberculosis.[31] The name of the research station was changed to the Health Laboratory and the salary of a bacteriologist was included in the 1907 municipal budget.[32] Once appointed to this post, Dr Albert de la Chapelle, Ph.D. (Med.), travelled without delay to study the working of the bacteriological laboratories of the City of Stockholm.[33] Gustaf Bergman, who was appointed to the post of assistant in the same health laboratory, had also had experience of foreign laboratories in Hamburg and Wiesbaden.[34]

Milk control

The bulk of the milk consumed by the people of Helsinki was transported from neighbouring farms and manor houses and was sold in market-places, courtyards and the streets. The first milk control measures, carried out by the inspectors of the Municipal Health Board, demonstrated that more than half of the milk offered for sale by 300 different milk distributors did not meet the required standards.[35] Already in 1886 the Municipal Health Board had proposed the establishment of milk control. Other big cities in developed countries formed the general reference group for this policy and the model adopted by the Health Board in its actual proposals was derived from the regulations enacted in Stockholm in 1885.[36]

From 1890 onwards trading in milk was regulated by a statute which was reviewed in 1898–99. This stipulated which commodities could be sold in the shops of butchers and grocers and dealt also with the arrangement and decoration of shops retailing foodstuffs. Thus the selling of milk, for example, was separated from the selling of other foods and alcohol, and the selling of milk in courtyards was forbidden. The seller also had to make his name known and indicate the quality of milk. Yet the control of the milk trade remained quite difficult, and many customers continued to buy milk directly from the producer. The situation regarding the meat trade was similar.

In 1908 the City of Helsinki prepared to implement a new Trading Act which gave municipalities the right to enact regulations on trading in foodstuffs. In 1908 the report of a sub-committee laid down regulations on the milk trade drawing on Copenhagen's regulations made in 1904. Under these, a qualified veterinary surgeon had to inspect twice a month the herd producing the milk that was on sale.[37]

The quality control of milk nevertheless remained a continuing problem and still in 1914 it was observed that one-fifth of milk samples taken were of inferior standard of purity and one-tenth sub-standard in fat content.[38] In the Municipal Health Regulations of Helsinki passed in 1915, it was stipulated that the minimum fat content of full fat milk should be at least 3 per cent and of skimmed milk 0.5 per cent, of single cream 15 per cent and whipping cream 25 per cent. Under the same regulations trading in milk was only allowed in proper dairy shops and other specially designated trading places or by selling milk directly to the customer at home. Every dairy shop was also under an obligation to give notification of the herds and dairies that were their sources of milk. If there were any doubts about the quality of milk supplied, the shopkeeper was obliged to secure a statement by a qualified veterinary surgeon on the health of the herd. In addition the regulations contained rules on the type and quality of vessels used for storing milk while the carts of the dairy proprietor had to carry the name-plate of the owner.

Meat control

The first law on abattoirs was passed in Prussia as early as 1868, making their use compulsory in all municipalities where there was a publicly established slaughterhouse. A similar act on meat control was passed in Norway in 1892. In Finland, however, there was no legislation regulating these matters because such a law, it was considered, would contravene the law concerning freedom of trade. The municipalities were therefore allowed to make their own decisions on the control of meat intended for sale. Thus compulsory meat control was only enforced in Helsinki in 1914 although in Oulu it had already been introduced as early as 1881. Municipal slaughterhouses had also already been established in smaller towns than Helsinki: in 1886 in Kuopio, in 1897 in Kotka and in 1899 in Pori. The city of Tampere had an abattoir built in 1887 but rented it to a private entrepreneur. Because such municipal slaughterhouses and meat-control stations had been established so widely in the early years of the twentieth century compulsory meat control was actually operating by 1917 in a total of 25 towns and cities.[39]

At their meeting in 1883, a powerful pressure group, the Finnish Medical Association, had already discussed compulsory meat control but ended up supporting voluntary action. Once the Food Control Station was established in 1884 it could be used for inspecting all suspect food products including meat. The services of the station could be used both by private individuals and by inspectors who had found suspect products in shops and marketplaces.

Table 8.3 demonstrates that the meat-control system mainly concentrated on inspecting the quality of pork while the inspection of beef became less and less efficient. It was believed at first that the control measures would prevent Helsinki people from buying uninspected meat directly from farmers and that the latter would not bring inferior quality meat to markets. The results from the quality checks on meat offered for sale in the market-place demonstrated, however, that this did not hold true as sub-standard meat was still available in the market-places. Consequently an increasing number of people was prepared to support a more efficient quality control of foodstuffs, though the resources of the city were not adequate to carry this out at that time.

But it was not only the transportation of meat and the cleanliness and care in its handling – however much those left to be desired – that created most concern among the population. Special anxiety was also caused by the incidence of tuberculosis in cattle. Added importance was

Table 8.3 Meat inspections carried out at the Helsinki Food Control Station.

| Date | Inspected meat | | Found |
	Pork	Beef	sub-standard
1885	1621	26	49
1886	2381	234	126
1887	2207	79	71
1888	2789	9	71
1889	3209	8	69
1890	2785	7	86
1891	2581	17	142
1892	1811	4	67
1893	1459	22	102
1894	1876	8	72
1895	1415	5	46
1896	1725	12	32
1897	2762	5	60
1898	2365	7	50
1899	3116	4	54
1900	1070	3	14

Source: Max Oker-Blom, *Yhteistoimintaan terveydenhoidon alalla I. Mietteitä lihantarkastuksesta pienemmissä kaupungeissamme*, Duodecim 1902, p. 462.

therefore given to the organization of meat control by the observation that of 2,306 animals slaughtered in the municipal abattoir, 32 proved to have been suffering from tuberculosis. This resulted in intensified attempts to create a system 'which nowadays is considered in the civilized world as the only appropriate and satisfactory one, i.e. that animals are inspected before the slaughtering and meat and offal soon after this'.[40] By the 1890s there had emerged a general opinion that abattoirs should be municipally owned. Another step forward was the 1891 decision of the Helsinki City Council that all meat slaughtered in the municipal abattoir was to be subjected to compulsory inspection.

The Finnish Medical Association again debated compulsory meat control in 1895, and decided unanimously that 'all municipalities must establish their own abattoirs in which the inspection and marking of meat should be carried out'. In addition there should next be passed another regulation extending compulsory inspection to cover all meat brought into towns and cities.[41] In 1896 the Municipal Health Board seriously discussed the organizing of meat inspection in Helsinki also. Those advocating a municipal abattoir pointed to the cost of similar establishments in Osnabruck, Tilsit, Lübeck and Essen.[42] By the 1890s many German towns and cities had, indeed, their own municipal slaughterhouses and when an architect from London County Council visited German cities he discovered the most modern of abattoirs in, for example, Halle, Frankfurt, Leipzig, Eisensee, Cologne, Strasbourg and Wiesbaden. From 1896 onwards a special sub-committee was engaged in planning a municipal abattoir for Helsinki. For their reference group they used the Nordic countries, Southern Germany, Belgium, Austria, Italy and France. In the same year the City Council decided to hire a qualified veterinary surgeon to carry out meat inspections as well as to establish a temporary meat-control station.[43] Oskar Lindström, who had studied in Sweden, was appointed to that post, and in 1897 he was able to observe that gradually even in Finland people had begun to realize the significance of meat control for general standards of health.[44]

In 1906 the Municipal Health Board accepted a proposal for compulsory meat inspection to be forwarded to the Helsinki City Council.[45] When the establishment of a municipal abattoir for Helsinki was being planned in 1906 detailed calculations on the need for a municipal abattoir and cattle market were provided by the Municipal Medical Officer, Sucksdorff, the Municipal Engineer, Idström, and the Municipal Veterinary Surgeon, Lindström. At the same time attempts were made to estimate meat consumption on the basis of examples drawn from some German cities. One of the models was Halle, which at that time had a larger population than Helsinki (in 1900 a total of 156,611 inhabitants). Like Helsinki, Halle had had a high rate of growth in the 1890s.

In 1907 a veterinary surgeon, Oskar von Hellens, and an architect, Karl Lindahl, had already been sent on the suggestion of the Municipal Health Board to study foreign abattoirs in order to gain the latest information for the new municipal slaughterhouse in Helsinki. According to von Hellens and Lindahl a large site was required for a cattle market. Another important observation was that sick animals should be isolated in their own section. Storing meat required chilled storing places while separate accommodation for veterinary surgeons, research, trading and administration were required in addition to the actual slaughterhouse. A new innovation was to place lighting in the ceiling of all workplaces. Already during their journey Lindahl and von Hellens started to plan a comprehensive abattoir for the Sörnäinen area of Helsinki, planning each building, each room and a yard with the necessary rail tracks and loading and unloading bays. They also planned separate premises not only for cows, pigs and horses but also for smaller animals, such as sheep and calves. This applied both to the actual slaughtering premises and the chilled storage rooms for meat.[46]

In the Health Care Regulations compiled in 1915 detailed instructions were also given concerning the types of food that could be offered for sale in butchers' shops. Besides meat and poultry these included, among others, eggs, honey, bread, cheese, butter and butter substitutes.[47] These regulations also prohibited the storing of meat that had not been inspected.

New innovations, such as disinfection ovens, Lysol and ambulance services were keeping the Municipal Health Inspector busy. Amid the new developments in health care the Municipal Health Board of Helsinki was particularly keen to follow the decisions made in Stockholm and Gothenburg.

Finally one can conclude that in Finland there was a strong desire in many fields to keep abreast of developments taking place in the civilized nations of Europe and that in many respects the City of Helsinki became a member of the league of European big cities. The reference groups for Finnish decision makers on many matters were drawn from Nordic and Central European cities. Hygiene and food control were no exceptions.

Notes

1. Martti Kovero, Tilastollisen päätoimiston perustamisen alkuvaiheet, Kansantaloudellinen aikakauskirja XII, 1940, p. 219.
2. The term bacteria was first used in the Finnish Medical Literature in 1873. Prof E.A. Homen was the first to use bacteriological concepts in pathological anatomy at the University of Helsinki and he became the first professor of this discipline. Leo Hirvonen, Wilhelm Joachim Sucksdorff (1851–1934), Suomen ensimmäinen hygienian professori, *Sosiaalilääketieteellinen Aikakauslehti*, 1990: 27, p. 227–35.
3. E.g. Anton Labisch, *Homo Hygienicus, Gesundheit und Medizin in der Neuzeit*, Campus, Frankfurt/New York, 1992, pp. 129–32.
4. Alfons Fischer, *Grundriss der sozialen Hygiene. Für Mediziner, Nationalökonomen, Verwaltungsbeamte und Sozialreformer*, Springer, Berlin, 1913, pp. 1–7.
5. Sven-Erik Åström, *Kaupunkiyhteiskunta murrosvaiheessa*. Helsingin Kaupungin historia IV: 2, Helsinki, 1956, p. 189.
6. Marjatta Hietala, Helsinki – edistynyt eurooppalainen kaupunki, *Innovaatioiden ja kansainvälistymisen vuosikymmenet*, Tietoa, taitoa, asiantuntemusta, Historiallinen Arkisto 99:1/ Helsingin kaupungin tietokeskuksen Tutkimuksia, 1992:5:1, Helsinki, 1992, pp. 209–44.
7. Marjatta Hietala, *Services and Urbanization at the Turn of the Century. The Diffusion of Innovations*. Finnish Historical Society, Studia Historica 23, Helsinki, 1987, pp. 301–95; Marjatta Hietala, *Berlin und andere deutsche Grosstädte als Vorbild für Beamten in Helsinki und Stockholm*, in Gerhard Brunn und Jürgen Reulecke eds., *Blicke auf die deutsche Metropole*, Hobbing, Essen 1989, pp. 201–23.
8. Bertel von Bonsdorff, *The History of Medicine in Finland 1828–1918*, Societas Scientiarum Fennica, Helsinki, 1975; Suomen Terveydenhoitolehti 1889–1915.

9. Albert Palmberg, Om den hygieniska undervisningen, *Finska Läkaresällskapets Handlingar*, Band XLVII II, 1905, pp. 435–8.

10. Hannu S. Vuorinen, Hygienian oppituolin perustaminen Keisarilliseen Suomen Akatemian Yliopistoon Helsingissä, *Sosiaalilääketieteellinen Aikakauslehti* 1990:27, pp. 221–6.

Selonteko Keisarillisen Aleksanterin yliopiston opettajain toiminnasta lukuvuonna 1904–1905, Helsinki, 1905.

11. Keisarillisen majesteetin Armollinen Asetus terveydenhoidosta Suomenmaassa, annettu Helsingissä 22. päivänä joulukuuta 1879, Suomen Aseutuskokoelma, 1879, no 31.

12. Hälsovårdsnämndens årsberättelse,n 1890.

13. Marjatta Hietala, *Services and Urbanisation at the Turn of the Century. The Diffusion of Innovations*, pp. 210–15.

14. Terveydenhoitotoimiston vuosikertomukset 1888, annex C, 1888–90.

15. Nurses Wera Stenberg and Karin Kotilainen were appointed from among 19 applicants to the vacant inspectoral posts, Hälsovårdsnämndens protokoll, 6 February 1908.

16. Terveydenhoitotoimiston vuosikertomukset 1890, annex B.

17. Terveydenhoitotoimiston vuosikertomukset 1889, annex D.

18. Complaints to the Municipal Health Board in Helsinki by Lukuisa Ostajapiiri March 1906, Hälsovårdsnämndens protokoll, 1906.

19. Sven-Erik Åström, *Kaupunkiyhteiskunta murrosvaiheessa*, Helsingin kaupungin historia IV:2, Helsinki, 1956, p. 208.

20. Hälsovårdsnämndens protokoll, 31 October 1879, Helsinki City Archives.

21. Hälsovårdsnämndens protokoll, 17 February 1883, 3 March 1883, 21 March 1883, 4 June 1883, 3 September 1883 and 3 April 1883, Helsinki City Archives.

22. Hälsovårdsnämndens protokoll, 16 December 1886, Helsinki City Archives.

23. Hälsovårdsnämndens protokoll, 25 July 1890, Helsinki City Archives.

24. Hälsovårdsnämndens protokoll, 1 October 1890 and 22 September 1910, Helsinki City Archives.

25. Hälsovårdsnämndens protokoll, 27 December 1892 and Helsingfors stadsfullmäktiges tryckta handlingar, 24 January 1893.

26. Hälsovårdsnämndens årsberättelser 1890, 1895.

27. A letter of A. Zilliacus, Hälsovårdsnämndens protokoll, 13 June 1902, Helsinki City Archives.

28. Komiteanmietintö Helsingin kaupungin terveydenhoitojärjestyksen ehdotuksen johdosta, Helsingfors stadsfullmäktiges tryckta handlingar, No 34, 1916.

29. Ibid.

30. Hälsovårdsnämndens protokoll, 22 February 1906, Helsinki City Archives.

31. A proposal for appointment of a bacteriologist to the health laboratory in Helsinki. Terveydenhoitotoimiston vuosikertomus 1906, pp. 163–5.

32. Hälsovårdsnämndens protokoll, 10 January 1907, Helsinki City Archives.

33. A report of the bacteriologist of the health laboratory in Helsinki. Hälsovårdsnämndens protokoll, 11 April 1907, Helsinki City Archives.

34. Gustaf Bergman worked in 1906 in the Chemisches Staats Laboratorium in Hamburg and worked as a voluntary assistant in Wiesbaden. Hälsovårdsnämndens protokoll, 18 April 1907.

35. Sven-Erik Åström, *Kaupunkiyhteiskunta murrosvaiheessa*, Helsingin kaupungin historia IV:2, Helsinki, 1956, s. 206–7.

36. Hälsovårdsnämndens tryckta årsberättelser, 1886, p. 26, 1888, p. 33.

37. Albert de la Chapelle, F.A. Lilius, A. Zilliacus, O.A. Hellens and Wilhelm Sucksdorff were members of the committee, Hälsovårdsnämndens protokoll, 30 April 1908 and 14 May 1908, Helsingfors City Archives.

38. Oskar von Hellens, *Om mjölken ur sanitär synpunkt*, Hygieniska spörsmål VII, 1898; Helsingfors stads statistik I: 5, 1914, pp. 26–7.

39. Jorma Kallenautio, *Kunnallistalous*, Suomen kaupunkilaitoksen historia 2, 1870-luvulta autonomian ajan loppuun, Suomen Kaupunkiliitto, Vantaa 1983, pp. 319–20.

40. Max Oker-Blom, *Yhteistoimintaan terveydenhoidon alalla I. Mietteitä lihantarkastuksesta pienemmissä kaupungeissamme*, Duodecim, 1902, pp. 466–7.

41. Förhandlingar vid Finska Läkaresällskapets femtonde allmänna möte i Helsingfors, 1895.

42. Utskottsbetänkande i fråga om införande af en obligatorisk köttkontroll, Berättelse angående Helsingfors stads kommunalförvaltning 1901/34.

43. Hälsovårdsnämndens protokoll, 2 November 1896, Helsinki City Archives.

44. Hälsovårdsnämndens protokoll, 29 September 1897, Helsinki City Archives.

45. Hälsovårdsnämndens protokoll, 1 March 1906, Helsinki City Archives.

46. Oscar von Hellens and Karl Lindahl, Till hälsovårdsnämnden i Helsingfors, 22 November 1907 (report of a study trip), annex, Hälsovårdsnämndens protokoll, 28 November 1907, Helsinki City Archives.

47. Komitean mietintö Helsingin kaupungin terveydenhoitojärjestyksen ehdotuksen johdosta, Helsingfors stadsfullmäktiges tryckta handlingar no 34, 1916.

9 Quality control and research: the role of scientists in the British food industry, 1870–1939

Sally M. Horrocks

By 1939 a considerable number of the large firms in the food manufacturing industry employed scientists and had their own laboratories. Laboratory-based science had come to be seen by many as an essential adjunct to food production, despite the fact that the food manufacturing industry had found little need to call upon science in its early stages. Once scientists were given an opportunity to demonstrate how useful their skills might be, they rapidly succeeded in extending the range of problems over which they had control. The practices of science came to be used throughout the firm, and to control operations beyond its boundaries. The changes wrought by scientists in methods of food production and in the nature of the food itself can be seen, in part at least, as a consequence of legislation which brought the skills of the analytical chemist to the attention of the food industry to a much greater extent than ever before. This legislation was aimed at combating adulteration, but the closer involvement of food manufacturers and trained scientists which it precipitated meant that other changes also occurred. Government policy in the field of public health can thus be seen to have led to changes in food supply which had little to do with the original intentions of the policy.

This chapter will discuss the growing involvement of scientists with food manufacturers in the period 1870 to 1939, focusing especially on large companies which pioneered techniques of mass production of a range of branded packaged products. It begins by looking at the early involvement of consulting chemists, and then traces the establishment and development of in-house laboratories. By looking in detail at the activities of scientists employed within the firm, it is possible to build up a picture of the many different functions which came to be performed by industrial food scientists, and to see some of the ways in which these affected the food supply.

Scientific employment in the food industry

British firms in a number of industries employed scientists before the middle of the nineteenth century, but this did not become commonplace until its final few decades, when scientific expertise began to establish for itself a secure and permanent place within the firm.[1] By the inter-war years industrial chemistry was a recognized profession and, according to Pilcher's handbook, was used 'in practically all productive industries'.[2] The *Industrial Chemist* put the number of chemists in industry in 1933 at between ten and twelve thousand,[3] suggesting that the number of scientists was even larger.

Scientists first entered the food manufacturing industry in much the same way that they had become involved with other industries, initially as consultants and only later as employees. The initial growth of large-scale food manufacturing had, however, relied little on the systematic application of scientific knowledge. Process control was carried out by skilled operators whose experience was vital to the maintenance of quality; new pieces of machinery were usually developed by independent inventors outside the firm, and novel recipes were either bought from outside or resulted from random 'experiments'.[4] This is not to say that there were no connections between scientists and food manufacture, but rather that the links were not with the emerging or existing large-scale manufacturers. Pasteur's connections with the wine trade have been well documented, while Liebig is well known for his extract of beef.[5] A British example of a chemist who turned to food manufacture is Alfred Bird, who produced custard powder and other instant desserts.[6]

Chemists were first employed by food companies to carry out routine analysis in the wake of legislation to control the quality of food supply in the mid-nineteenth century.[7] The Adulteration of Food and Drugs Act, 1872, was far more powerful than its predecessor of 1860, and led to the appointment of a considerable number of public analysts by local authorities charged with enforcing its provisions. Although enforcement was patchy and fines generally low, some companies found that a reputation for honest trading paid dividends and advertised accordingly.[8] Efforts to enforce this legislation gave a strong boost to the development of techniques of food analysis, reinforced by the formation of the Society of Public Analysts (SPA) in 1874. Its meetings and journal, *The Analyst*, provided a forum in which new techniques could be presented and results discussed. Many public analysts supplemented their incomes through consultancy work as the role of chemical analyst spread to the

Table 9.1 Employment in consulting practices involved with food in 1947.[12]

Staff employed	London Non-specialist practices	Specialist practices	Outside London	National totals
Qualified	29	16	19	64
Total	77	41	100	218

food industry.[9] Firms soon learnt that chemical expertise had uses beyond the simply defensive need to avoid prosecution.

It is impossible to ascertain the numbers of consultants involved with the food industry during this period. Many of them carried out work for other industries as well, and the total number of active consultants is unknown. It is clear that the number of consulting analysts grew steadily from the 1870s onwards, for in 1907 the SPA added 'And Other Analytical Chemists' to their title. The earliest clear evidence dates from a survey carried out in 1946–47.[10] Given the difficulties of establishing such a business during the war, we can assume that this information is close to representing the situation immediately before it. Of the 75 replies, 28 specifically mentioned that they specialized in food-related activities. The majority of those who specified their activities undertook analytical work and acted as consultants. More than half carried out research work for clients, with development work and patents also occupying staff in a few cases. Between them they employed a total of 218 people, a breakdown of which is given in Table 9.1. A directory of consultancies produced in 1947 gave very similar figures.[11]

Once scientists started to be employed within firms we have a slightly better idea of their numbers, although conclusions must remain tentative. Evidence from individual firms suggests that by 1900 there were just a handful, but that the figure grew rapidly in the years between then and World War I. Commentators in the 1930s tended to suggest that it had only been in the preceding 25 or 30 years that science had been important to the food industry. By the late 1920s, the presence of chemists in the food industry invited little comment, although it is probable that few small companies were able or willing to employ them. The food trade press portrayed the industry as modern and scientific, and indicated that the majority of large companies employed their own scientists.[13] There are a number of indirect indications but these need to be treated with caution. Comparison of the totals obtained by the Federation of British Industries for research personnel and the estimate of ten thousand chemists in 1933 suggests that a rough estimate of well in excess of one thousand chemists in the food industry in 1935 is not unreasonable.[14] In 1932 Sir George Newman, the Chief Medical Officer of Health, stated that the food industry employed more chemists than any other in Britain.

Whereas 50 years ago it was the rarest thing for a food manufacturer to employ a chemist, now every factory of any consequence is equipped with its research laboratory, and there are actually more chemists employed in the various branches of the food industry than in any other single industry in the country.[15]

Unfortunately he gives no source for this information.

It is far easier to offer an assessment of the extent of research in the industry, thanks to the efforts of the Federation of British Industries (FBI) Industrial Research Committee (IRC) which undertook a survey of industrial research and development in 1943 covering the 1930s.[16] The figures which they gathered accord well with the information available from other sources to indicate not only which firms carried out research but which were most active.[17] (see Table 9.2).

The most striking feature of the distribution of research was its concentration in a small number of companies, a trend which reflects that of British industrial research in general.[19] The largest spenders were among the top 35 companies who gave details to the IRC, out-spending companies in branches of industry more often associated with research for at least part of the period.[20] The general trend in total expenditure was upwards for the entire period, but with some significant fluctuations for some of the largest companies. The high degree of concentration meant that the decisions of one company could have a big impact on sectoral totals, as the emergence of Metal Box as a large research spender in the late 1930s demonstrates.[21] Increases in the sector totals were as much a result of increased expenditure in existing laboratories as of new companies engaging in research. Most companies only employed a small number of qualified staff to carry out research work, but they were often supported by others engaged primarily on routine testing and by qualified staff who often gained a detailed knowledge of procedures through experience. The ratio of qualified to unqualified staff varied considerably.

High levels of expenditure seem to have been more common in some branches of the industry than others, with chocolate and confectionery the dominant sector. Other areas which seem to have supported more limited but nevertheless widespread research were canning and medicinal foods. Firms involved in handling, transport and storage of fresh foodstuffs do not seem to have become involved in research.[22] A number of firms expressed an interest in research, but did not carry it out themselves. They either used the services of consultants or relied on the research associations. Several US-based firms, such as Heinz and

Table 9.2 Research spending and employment in the food industry, 1930–41.[18]

Company	Rank 1935	Expenditure (£000s)				Employment of qualified staff			
		1930	1935	1938	1941	1930	1935	1938	1941
Lever Bros/Unilever	1	35	65	85	100	30	57	79	85
Rowntrees	71	30.5	27.3	31.5	26.2	28	34	40	34
Cadbury	29	26	27	28	14	21	21	23	15
Metal Box			4	28	24		4	28	19
Lyons		28	22	25	24	71	70	84	80
United Dairies		21	21	21	21				
Glaxo		1	2	11	16	7	12	21	64
Manbre & Garton			2.5	5	4	2	3	5	3
Heinz		1.9	2.3	4.5	3.2	2	3	4	5
Horlicks		1.5	1.5	4.5	4.5	3	3	3	3
Aplin & Barrett		5	5	4	3	4	4	3	3
Virol		1.5	2.5	3.5	4	1	1	2	2
Chivers		3	3	3.4	4.8	4	4	5	5
Huntley & Palmer	54	3	3	3	3	3	3	3	3
Reckitt & Colman	44	1.2	2	2.8	3	3.	4	5	5
Geo. Bassett		2	2.5	2.7	2	2	3	3	2
Rank		2	2	2	2	5	5	5	5
Wm Crawford		1	1.3	1.7	2				
Vitamins Ltd			1.5	1.5	2.2				
Foster Clarke		0.7	1.2	1.4	1.7	1	6	6	6
Marsh & Baxter			1.1	1.4	1.3		2	2	2

There is evidence to suggest that the following companies spent more than the lowest included above:

Crosse & Blackwell
Tate & Lyle
Distillers
Co-operative Wholesale Society

The remaining companies spent the following totals during the respective years:

Rank	Expenditure (£000s)				Employment of qualified staff			
	1930	1935	1938	1941	1930	1935	1938	1941
Total	2.9	3.7	5.2	8.5	10	11	13	18
Number of companies	7	9	11	12	6	8	9	12
Overall total	167.2	203.4	276.1	274.4	197	250	334	359
Number of companies	25	30	32	33	22	26	27	30

Note: Ranking in this list is determined by expenditure in 1938
Rank 1935 refers to the place in the list of largest manufacturing firms in 1935, based on number of employees, see L. Johnman, 'The large manufacturing companies of 1935', *Business History*, 28, 1986, pp. 226–45.

Source: MRC, FBI Archives, MSS 200 F/3/T1/127 c).

Horlicks, had established active research programmes in the UK but these were not among the very largest spenders. The information obtained by the FBI IRC provides the basis for assessing the extent of research activities in the food manufacturing industry. Drawing on a range of other sources, especially company archives and trade journals, it is possible to establish a much clearer picture not only of the nature of research but also of the routine activities which accompanied it. Details of the work carried out by consultants can be added to this to give an indication of the full range of ways in which scientists came to be used by the firm.

The role of consultants

The activities of consultants have been little documented but it is clear that they continued to be important for many firms – especially smaller ones – throughout the period. The careers of Otto Hehner and William Jago give some indications of the possibilities available. Hehner established his own consulting practice in London in 1877 after a period of working with the pioneering food analyst Arthur Hill Hassall.[23] He quickly rose to prominence within the profession, playing an active role in the organization of both the SPA and the Institute of Chemistry. Besides his appointment as public analyst to a number of boroughs, he acted as an agricultural analyst and as a technical expert to numerous Parliamentary Committees. During World War I he worked on problems of glycerine manufacture. His published work, mostly dealing with foodstuffs, appeared in *The Analyst*.[24] Jago was best known for his work on cereal chemistry, and delivered several courses of related lectures at the Royal Society of Arts. He offered his services as an analyst and sold various pieces of testing apparatus designed for both bakers and millers. His contributions to the *Millers' Gazette* were collected and published as *Chemistry of wheat, flour, bread and technology of breadmaking*. Jago also wrote textbooks on organic chemistry and after being called to the bar in 1904, aged over 50, wrote a treatise on 'Forensic chemistry and chemical evidence'.[25] Both men were well respected within their profession, and maintained an extensive network of contacts.

Many companies engaged consultants prior to employing a chemist within the firm. One such was Huntley & Palmer, who during the course of 1891 called upon at least two different local experts.[26] Alfred Ashby, the local Medical Officer of Health, carried out at various times analyses of colouring agents, condensed milk and of broken biscuits.[27] Their suppliers of manufacturing equipment also made extensive use of analytical chemists.[28] At this stage, firms used consultants mainly for analytical work, but they also had some input into the development of new processes. By using outside expertise a company was able to claim that the quality of its products had been independently established, and used this fact in advertising material. The role of the chemist was restricted to what the firm demanded, leaving little space for individual initiative.

While larger companies began to employ their own chemists from the mid-1890s onwards, smaller enterprises continued to rely heavily on the services of consultants. As they themselves grew larger they were more likely to bring this service inside the company. J. Sainsbury's, primarily a retailer but also a producer of preserved meat products, relied on outside expertise until 1935 when an internal laboratory was opened.[29] Companies with their own facilities drew upon specialized consultants when necessary, using universities and technical colleges as well as commercial consultants.[30] Many more companies considered scientific expertise to be essential than felt able to employ their own scientists.[31] The cereal chemistry laboratories operated in Dover by D.W. Kent-Jones offer an interesting example of the commercial possibilities open in this area. Not only did he and his partner, A.J. Amos, supervise the routine analysis of samples and contract research projects, but they also offered lectures and courses to the milling and baking industry and published widely. The laboratories were equipped with specialist apparatus which would have been beyond the budgets of most firms in the industry.[32] Highly specialist consultancy services were offered by other firms, including Vitamins Limited, which undertook vitamin assays.[33]

A successful consultant during the inter-war period was Henry Cox. Cox held various industrial and public analyst posts before joining the practice of Otto Hehner in 1923. He specialised in patent litigation and dermatitis but most of his published work concerned foodstuffs. This included two standard textbooks on the chemical analysis of foods.[34] He held office in a number of chemical societies, including the Food Group of the Society of the Chemical Industry and the Society of Public Analysts, as well as serving on several government committees.[35] Consultants such as Cox and Thomas Crosbie-Walsh, who held a number of posts before devoting his energy to technical journalism, operated in a different climate from their predecessors, facing competition from both in-house chemists and, to some degree, the research associations. The nature of their work changed too, moving away from simple analysis towards much more specialized services. This gave them a unique position within the extended range of technical facilities to which firms now had access. They also had new opportunities, including journalism in the expanding technical press and active involvement in specialized professional societies.

Internalizing science within the firm

It is difficult to ascertain what caused the shift from using consultants to the employment of chemists by individual firms. The services of consultants had undoubtedly made valuable contributions, but the benefits of engaging permanent employees were not obvious. The earliest evidence of a food manufacturer employing its own scientists comes from Colman's, who had two chemists working in the Mustard Mill Laboratory by 1893. Their task was to check the quality and condition of incoming mustard seed.[36] Other companies followed suit in the period before the start of World War I including Cadbury, Rowntree, the CWS, Huntley & Palmers, Fry's and George Payne.[37] Although we know little about why chemists moved inside the firm, this shift had important consequences for the variety of tasks which they performed. It brought them into closer contact with the manufacturing process and enabled chemists to bring their skills to bear on a whole range of company operations which had previously been closed to them.[38]

By 1915 the chemical staff of the Silvertown confectionery works of the CWS were regarded as indispensable, since 'without science today no business, co-operative or otherwise, can permanently succeed'.[39] A number of new laboratories were founded in the latter years of the war and the succeeding decade. Lyons appointed Leslie Lampitt to the position of chief chemist in 1919 after he had met Samuel Gluckstein during the course of wartime service in Flanders. The post was largely self-created, and the firm's historian tells us that 'his employment by the firm was largely the result of chance rather than intention . . . there is clearly a case for arguing that the scientific service was also originally more the result of luck than of careful economic or technical evaluation'.[40] Similar stories emerge if we look at other firms who also started their laboratories during this period, including Chivers and Crosse & Blackwell.

Once inside the firm, what did these scientists do? This question will be explored by looking at a number of laboratories, primarily those of Lyons, but also Rowntree's, Colman's and Crosse & Blackwell. Between them they reveal some of the range of activities which came to be performed by in-house laboratories, and the ways in which these affected the output of the firms. By considering several companies simultaneously it becomes clear that, while they shared many common attributes, there were also variations in scientific activities and in their position within the overall organization. Each firm found its laboratory to be useful in distinct ways.

The largest laboratory in the industry was that of Lyons, which was established in 1919, and whose subsequent growth gives an indication of how rapidly the skills of trained scientists became part of the firm's activities. Prior to this the company had relied on traditional methods, and the decision to employ Lampitt seems to have been more an experiment than a move calculated to improve prosperity. From uncertain beginnings he had, by 1939, established an operation which was staffed by nearly 200 people, carried out 60–70 thousand analyses annually, and was regarded as the leading laboratory in the food industry[41] (see Table 9.3).

Table 9.3 Total number of staff employed in Lyons' central laboratories, 1919–39.[42]

Year	Staff
1919	4
1924	37
1927	72
1929	100
1931	140
1936	150
1939	200

The opening of a new laboratory building, which had an area of 35,000 sq ft, in 1929 received considerable attention.[43] Large sums of money were spent on equipment for the building, which included small-scale industrial plant as well as scientific instruments.[44] There was, however, no strict division between research staff and those who carried out routine work, since Lampitt felt that such separation was not only artificial, but did not get the best results.[45]

In most food companies chemists began by devoting most of their time to analytical work for the control of quality of both raw materials and products.[46] Initially raw materials received the most attention, but this gradually extended to include the development of new analytical techniques and attention to production problems. Gradually more and more functions were added, including the investigation of customer complaints, the examination and imitation of competitors' products, and the profitable use of waste materials. It was not only raw materials and products which came under scrutiny but also fuel and water supplies and many other aspects of the general running of the factory itself. Much of this work could legitimately be regarded as research but took place alongside and in close conjunction with routine work. It was only later that there were any moves to separate research and routine work, although in many companies this never took place. As standardized procedures were established for quality control they often moved from the laboratory to the factory floor.

The vast majority of research carried out in food companies was very closely related to the immediate needs of production and its control. Much of it consisted of applying standard techniques to new materials, or in developing methods of analysis and production control. Research was also used to find profitable uses for waste materials and to modify existing recipes so that they could be produced more cheaply. The lack of dramatic breakthroughs and distinctly new technologies which emerged from laboratories in the food industry should not be allowed to obscure their role in incremental change which was of considerable importance.[47] Many of the effects of this research were invisible to the consumer. Firms placed a considerable emphasis on continuity of taste in established products, but often also sought new and cheaper ways of producing them. This was true of Crosse & Blackwell's Branston pickle, which had first been sold in 1922. Despite recipe changes and the adoption of new production techniques, the intention was to sell a product which appeared unchanged.[48] As each laboratory became firmly established it began to develop a unique knowledge-base specific to the product range of the firm. The establishment of these firm-specific knowledge-bases involved lengthy research projects into the chemistry of the raw materials used by each company. These were usually based on painstaking analytical investigations. At Colman's, company scientists mixed fundamental investigations into enzyme activity, chemical composition and fermentation with projects intended to find new uses for mustard, including its possible application for mending leaky car radiators and as a treatment for athlete's foot. These projects show clearly how the establishment of a knowledge-base was linked to its commercial exploitation.[49]

The role of the laboratories in the development of new products varied considerably between firms. Laboratories were not generally the source of new product ideas but were an important part of the process which turned ideas into innovations. At Colman's, however, new products were central to the activities of the Research Department, which had been established specifically to work on a new product line.[50] In a number of cases the laboratory itself was used for the development and production of specialist chemical production used within the company. The motivation for this was primarily financial but was also related to dissatisfaction with the available alternatives. At Rowntree's the financial savings generated by the production of flavourings and colourings early in its history was a useful argument for more resources for the laboratory.[51] At Crosse & Blackwell a small manufacturing section produced hydrolysed protein, lacquer for cans and essences.[52]

The inter-war research environment

None of these laboratories worked in isolation, and all relied heavily on information from outside. All of them placed an importance on staff keeping up-to-date with publications and several had extensive technical libraries.[53] They also encouraged staff to attend the meetings of both local and national scientific societies. Although there were several organizations oriented around academic disciplines which included papers on food among those presented at meetings, there was only one organization for which it was the main focus. This was the Society of the Chemical Industry Food Group, founded in 1931.[54] The membership of this group was dominated by scientists based in industry but it also included those working in other institutional contexts. Group activities and the papers presented at meetings were very much oriented towards the needs of industrial scientists, often including factory tours. The formation and success of the SCI Food Group were largely the result of a core of enthusiasts who supported it for a number of years. Leslie Lampitt of Lyons was the most prominent, supported by Alfred Bacharach from Glaxo and Basil McLellan of Rowntree among others. As the group expanded and developed it formed two separate panels for nutrition and bacteriology.[55] Membership of the group is indicated in Table 9.4.

Table 9.4 Membership of the Food Group.[56]

Year	Total membership
1932	163
1933	294
1934	
1935	376
1936	
1937	452
1938	539
1939	721

The group met regularly, usually in joint meetings with other professional bodies or regional sections of the SCI. It worked closely with both the Society of Public Analysts (SPA), to which many of its members also belonged, and the Royal Sanitary Institute. At meetings one or more papers were usually read and discussed. Work done within industry and in university and government laboratories was presented, although industrial contributions tended to come from a small number of large firms. From the outset there was concern that the group should be more than just a London-based organization, and the annual summer meeting was usually hosted by a major regional food manufacturer such as Colman's or Chivers. These meetings included factory tours, the presentation of papers, and both formal and informal discussion. The appearance of specialist technical journals, *Food Manufacture* from 1927 and *Food Industries Weekly* from 1933, helped to promote shared standards and techniques among food scientists.

Summary

Between 1870 and 1939 the number of scientists employed by the food manufacturing industry grew considerably, and their activities broadened from the defensive to encompass a wide range of company operations. Although legislation played a role in bringing scientists into food manufacturing companies, it played only a minor role in the subsequent development of their role in the firm. Once the utility of science had been established many companies enthusiastically advocated the importance of 'scientific control' over production and turned to technical experts in the drive to achieve efficient production methods and avoid any wastage of raw materials. The work of these specialists affected both the nature of products and the way they were produced, often radically reducing labour requirements. Simultaneously the importance of routine analysis to oversee these new methods of production increased. For the consumer these changes meant that a growing range of mass-produced goods became an affordable reality.

Notes

1. D.E.H. Edgerton and S.M. Horrocks, 'British Industrial Research and Development Before 1945', *Economic History Review*, forthcoming, 1994.
2. R.B. Pilcher, *The Profession of Chemistry*, Fourth edn, London, Institute of Chemistry, 1938, pp. 66–81.
3. *Industrial Chemist*, 8, 1933, p. 37.
4. Rowntree's Archives, York, hereafter RA, papers of J.W. Rowntree, Box 1, Arch 354, 372–74.
5. M.R. Finlay, 'Quackery and Cookery: Justus von Liebig's Extract of Meat and the Theory of Nutrition in the Victorian Age', *Bulletin of the History of Medicine*, 66, 1992, pp. 404–18.
6. J.Foley, *The Food Makers: A History of General Foods*, Banbury, General Foods, 1972, pp. 1–12.
7. A.S. Wohl, *Endangered Lives: Public Health in Victorian Britain*, London, Methuen, 1984, pp. 52–5. See also, I. Paulus, *The Search for Pure Food: A Sociology of Legislation in Britain*, London, Robertson, 1974.

8. Cadbury and several other firms advertised in *The Analyst*. The CWS traded widely on their reputation as the friend of the consumer, while Quaker food manufacturers in general benefited from their honest reputation, see T.A.B. Corley, *Quaker Enterprise in Biscuits: Huntley & Palmers of Reading, 1822–1972*, London, Hutchinson, 1972.

9. The formation of the SPA is discussed in C.A. Russell, N.G. Coley and G.K. Roberts, *Chemists by Profession*, Milton Keynes, Open University Press, 1977, pp. 106–7. In his presidential address in 1880, Dr Muter encouraged members to, 'Prosecute researches at every spare moment, so that Great Britain may continue to be what she undoubtedly is at present, the nursery of the science of food analysis' *(The Analyst*, 5, 1880, p. 16).

10. Replies from consultants to the FBI questionnaire are to be found in Modern Records Centre, University of Warwick, hereafter MRC, FBI Archives, MSS 200/F/T2/7/2 c).

11. P. Dunsheath, ed., *Industrial research 1947*, London, Todd, 1947, pp. 379–91.

12. MRC, FBI Archives, MSS 200/F/T2/7/2 c).

13. It would be theoretically possible to produce an estimate of the number of scientists based on an average figure for the number employed related to the total number of a firm's employees, but in practice evidence suggests that there is such wide discrepancy between firms that such a figure would be hopelessly inaccurate.

14. If we compare the estimate of between ten and twelve thousand chemists in industry as a whole in 1933 with the FBI's admittedly low figure of 1381 research personnel in 1930 and 2566 in 1935, we can estimate that the ratio of research staff to total staff is between 1:5 and 1:6, giving us a range of between 1,250 and 1,500 for total staff in food. This must be regarded as a very rough approximation, since it is unlikely that the same ratio was to be found in all industries, or that it was in any way consistent between companies in the same industry. Lyons considered that virtually all qualified staff carried out some research, while at Cadbury there was a nominal division between research staff and others.

15. G. Newman, *On the State of the Public Health, 1932*, London, HMSO, 1933, pp. 136–7.

16. The aggregate results of the survey were published as FBI, *Industry and Research*, (London, FBI, 1943).

17. Details are found in MRC, FBI Archives, MSS 200/F/3/T1/127 c).

18. Ibid.

19. Edgerton and Horrocks, 'British R&D'.

20. Kodak spent £7,000 in 1930, £16,000 in 1935 and £32,000 in 1938. A more detailed account of spending throughout British industry is given in Edgerton and Horrocks, 'British R&D'.

21. Metal Box is included with food firms because of the nature of its research, which was oriented towards increasing the range of goods in cans. A feature of their laboratory was the support services offered to customers, *(Food Manufacture*, 14, 1939, p. xviii and *Food Industries Weekly (FIW)*, 9 July 1938, pp. 8–9.

22. MRC, FBI Archives, MSS 200/F/T2/1.

144 *Sally M. Horrocks*

23. Hassall's prominence in the development of new methods of analysis resulted from the *Lancet's* campaign against food adulteration. He was a member of the Analytical Sanitary Commission organized by its editor, Thomas Wakley. Hassall published a number of books and for a while edited a magazine called *Food, air and water*, which campaigned against adulteration.

24. Biographical details from his obituary, *Chemistry and Industry*, *(C&I)*, 43, 1924, pp. 988–9.

25. Biographical details from his obituary, *C&I*, 57, 1938, pp. 391–2.

26. Reading University Library, Huntley & Palmer Archives (hereafter, HP Archives), HP 143, letters from Alfred Shilton of 12 August 1891, 25 September 1891, and 30 September 1891, and reply from A. Palmer 1 October 1891.

27. HP Archives, HP 143, letters from Alfred Ashby, 20 May 1891 and 19 July 1894 and HP 200 references to analyses of condensed milk.

28. HP Archives, HP 129, correspondence between Alfred Palmer, Furnishing, Ironmongery and Gas Fitting Warehouse, J. Cuthbert Welch, FCS analytical chemist and Alex E. Tucker of the Birmingham Laboratory and Assay Offices.

29. J.H. Mallows, 'The science behind the seen', *JS Journal*, Feb 1951, pp. 22–6 and Sainsbury's Archives, letter from Dr Bernard Dyer, 19 March 1930, concerning the analysis of gelatine sample.

30. The Foodstuffs Department of the Manchester Municipal College of Technology gave advice to local firms (UMIST Archives, F3 and F6, Minutes of the Chemistry Sectional Committee).

31. PRO, DSIR 16/40, Memorandum of Interview of 11 June 1917.

32. 'Cereal chemistry at Dover', *FIW*, 14 October 1938, pp. 13–15.

33. MRC, FBI Archives, MSS 200/F/T2/7/2.

34. H.E. Cox, *The Chemical Analysis of Foods*, London, Churchill, 1926; and *Foods: Their Composition and Analysis*, London, Churchill, 1927.

35. Biographical details from his obituary in *C&I*, 71, 1952, p. 84.

36. A picture of the laboratory appeared in *Commerce* on 15 November 1893, and is reproduced in 'The story of Colman's mustard', one of the firm's recent publicity brochures.

37. PRO, DSIR 16/40, Memorandum of Interview of 26 July 1917.

38. W.P. Dreaper, *The Research Chemist in the Works with special reference to the Textile Industry*, London, Institute of Chemistry, 1914, makes this point for the textile industry.

39. *The Wheatsheaf*, 1915, p. 167.

40. D.J. Richardson, 'The History of the Catering Industry with special reference to J. Lyons & Co to 1939', unpublished Ph.D. thesis, University of Kent, 1970, p. 363.

41. W. Buchanan-Taylor, 'How Lyons control quality', *FIW*, 7 April 1939, pp. 7–9.

42. Ibid, and Richardson, thesis, p. 364.

43. Including a mention in the *Daily Express (Industrial Chemist*, 4, 1929, p. 135).

44. *Industrial Chemist*, 4 1929, p. 191.

45. L.H. Lampitt, *Laboratory Organisation*, London, Institute of Chemistry, 1935, pp. 4–10.

46. The major exception to this was Colman's, where the laboratory had been established specifically with research in mind.

47. Lampitt stated in 1935 that 'the application of chemistry to the study of food problems has, during the last twenty-five years, possibly been more intense than in other branches of applied science – yet it has not witnessed any great revolutionary discoveries' (*C&I*, 54, 1935, p. 426).

48. Interview with S. Back, former chief chemist, Crosse & Blackwell, May 1992.

49. Colman's Archives, typescript.

50. Ibid.

51. RA, Gum Dept. Box 5, Arch 805, Sept 1905, and Arch 808, Feb 1907.

52. Back, interview.

53. Lampitt, *Organisation*, pp. 11-13, RA, typescript.

54. The activities of the group are discussed in more detail in H.D. Kay, 'A Short History of the Food Group', *Journal of the Science of Food and Agriculture*, 23, 1972, pp. 127–60.

55. *C&I*, 57, 1938, p. 496.

56. *C&I*, 58, 1929, p. 467 and 52, 1933, p. 466.

10 Food adulteration and the beginnings of uniform food legislation in late nineteenth-century Germany

Hans J. Teuteberg

During the last 20 years there has been an increasing movement in Germany to protect the environment from dangerous substances. This has also caused a growing interest in governmental food control. Food scandals have regularly been the topic of the mass media and often led to legal actions to save the consumer from unhealthy or low quality foodstuffs. Today, the supervision of food quality is regarded as a basic governmental responsibility. A milestone in this context is the 'Gesetz zur Gesamtreform des Lebensmittelrechts' (Food Legislation Reform Law) of 1975 which repealed 16 older laws and 40 decrees, most of them dating back to the nineteenth century.[1] This important legislative reform raises the question of how food control developed as part of governmental food policy in Germany. Unfortunately, only a small amount of historical research has been done in this field.[2] This chapter intends to summarize some initial results and points out some lesser-known sources.

As in some other European countries, the guilds and their different local market regulations tried for centuries to save town-dwellers from falsification of food before the age of industrialization. Bakers especially, but also butchers, brewers, fishmongers and vintners were controlled very strictly as they often adulterated their goods.[3] From the mid-nineteenth century, official supervision of victuals became more and more urgent as the quickly growing urban population changed their food habits. They turned more and more from self-supply to food markets and became dependent on food retailers; urban food processing was expanding and modern food industries developed.[4] The growing distance between producer and consumer as well as the developments in organic chemistry, by constantly analysing new ingredients which could secretly be added to the food, increased the possibilities of food manipulation.[5]

There were growing adulterations of coffee substitutes, milk, flour, sausages, beer and wine.[6] We can assume that the high rate of child mortality in German towns until the end of the nineteenth century was partly due to these adulterations as well as to hygienic problems.

Especially dangerous to public health was the adulteration of milk,[7] which partly caused the high mortality of babies. In 1847, a well-known agrarian expert wrote:

Products which are consumed in a high degree, which are indispensable, and which are produced near the consumer, guarantee a frequent sale and a remarkable price. This fact often arouses some people's greed and a criminal want for even more money so that they increase the amount of milk by falsifying the product in various ways.[8]

As it was difficult to judge the quality of milk only by using one's senses, it was very tempting to adulterate this product. Even in 1870 one could hardly find pure milk in the urban milk trade.[9] Apparently, adulterating milk was the rule and may account for the fact that some urban administrations refused the sale of skimmed milk, which was not very popular with many Germans anyway before World War I – despite a relatively low standard of living, people mixed skimmed milk with the pigs' fodder rather than drink it themselves. As chemists proved with the help of laboratory analyses, full-cream milk was systematically mixed with skimmed milk and water; then flour and sugar were added, sometimes even brains, soap, potato starch, or bone glue in order to make up for the low viscosity. In order to slow down lactic fermentation people added sodium carbonate, boric acid and hydrogen peroxide.

There were also various possibilities of contamination of milk through carelessness. In the middle of the nineteenth century, for instance, a milk specialist still found it necessary to point out that the locations where milk was stored should be made inaccessible to rats, mice, toads and other reptiles.[10] In addition, it was natural in those times that after milking the milk came into contact with various foreign substances. Around 1900, the participants in a course for dairy specialists declared that the milk which they were given lacked something. When the course tutor added some straw from a barn, they found the taste acceptable.[11] Frequent changes of container made the transportation of milk especially unhygienic, and the milk supply of the growing cities, in general, was so unsatisfactory that Germany's leading economists saw the need for special research into this subject.

The bad conditions of the rural milk trade and the fast-growing milk retail trade in the cities called for quick legislative control. However, it was not before pharmacists, agricultural researchers and chemists of the first *Molkereifachschulen* (special dairy schools) had analysed and compared the ingredients of cow's-milk with those of mother's milk in the 1860s and had pointed out different ways for an efficient control of the quality of milk, that some bigger German cities passed bills to stop the adulteration of milk and profiteering in the months of low productivity.[12] The milk trade also became a concern of the German federal states' industrial inspection, which came into being at the same time. It seems that Switzerland served as a model: Fridolin Schuler, an industrial inspector of Basel, wrote in 1884 in one of his reports that his Board had milk frequently analysed.[13] Schuler's interest in milk was based on his assumption that he could fight the workers' increasing consumption of alcoholic drinks by fostering their consumption of milk. Government food control in the late nineteenth century was also indirectly influenced by the expanding agitation of the temperance movements, which were modelled after English and American organizations.[14] The propaganda for an increased consumption of milk went along with the intention to fight alcoholism. There were, however, many different drinking habits and problems of taste which had to be overcome.

In the last third of the nineteenth century, pasteurized milk became available from cows which had been carefully fed and had been examined by veterinarians. This milk was above all sold to private *Milchkuranstalten*. It was, however, three to four times more expensive than ordinary milk, and so it does not come as a surprise that workers stuck to their beer, home-made wine, cider, and chicory-coffee. The existence of *Milchkuranstalten* for anaemic children and ladies of 'higher degree', on the other hand, underlined the fact that the nutritive value of hygienic milk had by now been recognized. The majority of the babies and small children of the German Reich, however, had, until the end of World War I, to be satisfied with thin 'blue' milk, the content and purity of which was only slowly improved by food controls.[15]

Uniform governmental food legislation in Germany started with obligatory meat inspection in Prussia in 1868. This law, which had to do with the detection of trichinas in the 1860s, confined private slaughtering to certain locations in order to do away with the deplorable state of affairs caused by the widespread private slaughterhouses and the uncleanliness, contamination of the air and the dangers connected with leading animals through the narrow streets.[16] In addition, the authorities wished to reduce the danger of eating unhealthy meat. In the new community slaughterhouses, veterinarians examined the animals. Until 1880, however, only 14 public slaughterhouses had been built in Prussia and this first law contained a number of shortcomings. The meat which came from out of town, for instance, did not have to be examined, so there were several possibilities to evade the official meat inspection. The number of public slaughterhouses increased when the examination of all meat became obligatory.[17] Comprehensive decrees for the construction

Table 10.1 The construction of community slaughterhouses in Prussian towns, 1750–1900.

Date	Total	Date	Total
c. 1750	1	1886	10
1830	1	1887	12
1866	1	1888	18
1874	1	1889	20
1875	1	1890	27
1876	4	1891	23
1877	1	1892	24
1878	1	1893	26
1879	3	1894	27
1880	3	1895	20
1881	5	1896	18
1882	5	1897	18
1883	6	1898	12
1884	8	1899	25
1885	13	1900	14

Source: Heinrich Silbergleit, *Die Lage der preußischen Schlachthöfe und die Freizügigkeit des frischen Fleisches,* Magdeburg 1903, p. 2–17.

and working conditions of slaughterhouses were issued.[18] The other German federal states followed these improvements and enacted similar laws.[19] In 1903 the official meat inspection was expanded to the rural areas as well. This ended the urban monopoly of meat inspection. The community slaughterhouses, however, still remained important, as most of the fat stock came from urban cattle markets to the nearby slaughterhouses. The concentration of marketing and slaughtering was welcomed by the state. The official meat inspection proved a major success, for the consumption of meat infected by trichinas decreased substantially after the turn of the century.[20] The control of the quality of sausages, however, remained a problem. Tables 10.1 and 10.2 show the increase and the distribution of community slaughterhouses in Prussia.

However, the question remains how uniform food legislation developed. As we can gather from mostly incomplete research, there were various reasons. Public discussion of the best means of preventing the various food scandals had started in the eighteenth century and continued then through the nineteenth century. The German pharmacist Friedrich Accum was the first to write on the idea of a scientific and uniform food control, having examined food for certain adulterations in London in 1820. As soon as his book was translated into German, many similar books followed, describing the various ways of detecting falsified

Table 10.2 The distribution of community slaughterhouses in Prussia according to the size of towns in 1908.

Inhabitants	Number of of towns	Number of slaughterhouses	Percentage having slaughterhouses
>100,000	41	39	95.1
50,000–100,000	44	43	97.7
20,000–50,000	134	101	75.4
5,000–20,000	602	352	58.5
2,000–5,000	873	223	25.5
<2,000	615	56	9.1

Source: Wolfgang Hofmann: Die Entwicklung der kommunalen Selbstverwaltung von 1848 bis 1918. In Günter Püttner (ed.) *Handbuch der kommunalen Wissenschaft und Praxis*, 2nd edn, vol. 1, Berlin, Heidelberg, New York, 1984, p. 80.

food and other frauds. Accum, who was harshly attacked by food manufacturers in London, can be regarded as one of the forefathers of governmental food control. In 1830 Accum published a critique of deliberate adulteration of food. Most of the essays were written by chemists for other chemists, and many were translated from the French and the English languages.[21] Although all these papers were very stimulating, as was Friedrich Accum's first exposé, they did not have many practical consequences: the chemical-technical and legal foundations had as yet been insufficiently developed.

Transforming scientific knowledge into efficient consumer protection was blocked by many factors, as the efforts for control of the quality of milk and meat have already shown. As the ways of preservation were extremely limited, one could often not differentiate between a careless and a deliberate adulteration of food or natural decay.

In many cases the classification of the product decided whether the addition was an allowed surrogate or was a falsification. Today, food chemists have come to understand that the adulteration or imitation of certain foodstuffs is only a mental abstraction which does not exist in reality. According to consumers' opinions and the legal definitions, there are, apparently, only people who produce 'bad' foodstuffs either accidentally, carelessly, or deliberately with the intention to cheat; or those who combine or process certain ingredients 'inappropriately' in the view of their contemporaries. In other words, opinions about whether a foodstuff has been adulterated or falsified with intent to defraud may vary from time to time and from region to region. That also means that the inspection of foodstuffs by the state is intricately interwoven with general social changes and values and is not part of an everlasting system with standards which are valid everywhere. Consequently, it is dangerous to regard today's food and environmental laws as standards for times gone by, when people had different views on food and hygiene. The *Europäische Lebensmittelbuch*, which has obviously to consider different national viewpoints on daily food, is therefore based on the expectations of consumers who have been deceived in general. The book defines a foodstuff as adulterated only if the following criteria apply:

1. If the foodstuff lacks, either partly or totally, ingredients which determine its value and are expected by the consumer.
2. If ingredients are added which diminish the value of the foodstuff.
3. If additives or adulterations represent a better quality foodstuff or conceal inferior quality. In this context the imitation of a foodstuff can also be regarded as a falsification.[22]

Until the development of modern food chemistry in the mid-nineteenth century, people were solely dependent on their senses if they wanted to examine their daily food: the smell, taste, appearance, and the consistency of the food were the only indicators of its condition. The increase of chemical analyses of individual foodstuffs and the consequences of these foods on human metabolism have to be considered in connection with the development of food sciences, nutrition-physiology and food chemistry. Food adulteration would not have attracted the attention of so many people without Lavoisier's experiments in elementary chemical analysis and the epoch-making works of Justus Liebig, Louis Pasteur, Carl Voit, and Max Pettenkofer, to mention only a few.[23] In 1800, people had knowledge of only about 500 organic chemical substances, whereas this number had increased to 150,000 at the turn of the century. It is small wonder that – especially after the first half of the nineteenth century – reports on the composition of food and on the most frequent adulterations accelerated. Most of these reports were published in magazines and then in scientific works.[24] In 1878, the first newspaper against the adulteration of foodstuffs was published. The newspaper, which was edited by Hermann Wölfert in Leipzig, was called *Zeitschrift gegen Verfälschung der Lebensmittel und sonstiger Verbrauchsgegenstände.*

The increased activities of the food chemists and the medical profession attracted the government's attention. According to the new constitution, after 1871 the German Reich was responsible for public health affairs and founded the Imperial Health Board (Kaiserliches Gesundheitsamt) in Berlin. Inspired by the upsurge of the natural sciences and the increasing amount of research conducted by food chemists, the Reichstag passed the first 'Law on the Dealings, Food, and

Utensils' on 14 May 1879.[25] For the first time a uniform food control
was guaranteed in the German Reich as well as the examination of food
and the punishment of food adulteration. An extensive network of food
controlling authorities came into being. The new authorities relied on the
experiences of the older agricultural research stations which had been
founded after 1851. One of the most efficient agricultural research
stations was led by the chemist Joseph König in Münster. He founded
the 'Zeitschrift der Nahrungs- und Genußmittel sowie deren
Gebrauchsgegenstände' in 1898 and published the important work *Die
menschlichen Nahrungs- und Genußmittel* (Human Food and Luxury
Foodstuffs) in several volumes, which set a standard for all governmental
food chemists. It was also König who promoted the first continuous
training of food chemists in Germany.[26]

From the statistics of the Imperial Health Board we can gather that all
foodstuffs were frequently controlled from 1878 in 121 German cities.
Munich, where Justus Liebig's famous pupil Max Pettenkofer worked,
took the lead in this. In 1875, he took 40,000 food analyses, in 1879
80,000. In those regions where no agricultural research stations or
Chemistry or Hygiene Departments of Universities existed, the
communities employed private laboratories or established their own
institutions of food control.

Other towns especially in Prussia, were left far behind Munich.[27] The
Grand Duchy of Baden seems to have been a pioneer in the field of food
control.[28] In the *Intelligenz- und Wochenblatt*, published in Karlsruhe, the
editors discussed different methods of recognizing bad beer or low-
quality fruit, potatoes and milk. In addition, they also gave details of an
apparatus with which people could determine the consistency of milk,
and in 1840 a booklet on food control appeared which was written by the
physician Franz Hermann Walcher. As a consequence, the police were
ordered to identify food falsifiers. Prosecution for these offences became
part of the criminal code of the police. Watering down milk, mixing
butter with butter-milk and sugar with chalk were, next to short-weight of
bread, the most important offences. Although police commissioners,
constables and sergeants were advised, the task of controlling food
proved to be beyond their capacity. This made the government ask the
Polytechnic of Karlsruhe (today's Technische Universität) to outline
guiding principles for food inspection in urban markets. This code was
published in 1876, was several times revised and served as a model for
Swedish (1878) and Russian (1881) food legislation after it had been
translated. As the police were less and less qualified for the task of food
control, special institutions for the chemical analysis of food were
established, and government food chemists were employed. After the
food law of 1879 had come into force, institutions for the control of food
spread more rapidly in Germany, but as Table 10.3 shows, there were

Table 10.3 Number of food inspections in the German Federal States per citizen, 1903–1908.

Federal state	1903	1904	1905	1906	1907	1908
Prussia	495	462	373	324	270	231
Bavaria	77	64	52	51	48	43
Saxony	41	41	41	39	39	36
Württemburg	1,135	663	283	315	212	240
Baden	188	161	131	131	152	138
Hessia	62	73	81	75	87	77
Mecklenburg-Schwerin	728	413	495	452	395	344
Saxony-Weimar	1,181	616	528	483	453	393
Oldenburg	589	428	440	411	488	464
Altenburg	–	–	183	165	153	167
Anhalt	115	99	91	67	57	57
Schwarzenburg-Sondershausen	–	–	–	31	28	27
Reuß j.L.	33	32	33	30	32	32
Lübeck	51	49	49	159	692	630
Bremen	343	324	364	326	303	332
Hamburg	182	156	117	104	89	90
Elsaß-Lothringen	808	442	391	413	347	341
German-Reich	189	173	150	141	130	114

Source: Kaiserliches Gesundheitsamt (ed.), *Jahresberichte der öffentlichen Anstalten zur technischen Untersuchung von Nahrungs-und Genußmitteln im Deutschen Reiche,* Berlin, 1904.

many variations in the enforcement of food legislation in the different German states.

The statistics show that the number of food inspections between 1903 and 1908 in 17 federal German states increased and regional differences disappeared. According to the new food legislation, the local police were entitled to enter production plants, storage warehouses and sales offices without prior notice in order to make analyses. One severe limitation was, however, the total lack of definition of exactly what food adulterations or imitations were. Thus, it was up to the various courts to determine the nature of food manipulations. A number of handbooks, commentaries and practical guides tried to interpret food legislation at the turn of the century, but it took a long time to remedy this legal uncertainty.[29]

There was a sharp controversy about the legal norms between chemists and the Association of Food Producers and Merchants. In 1898, the food industry published *The German Food Book (Deutsches Nahrungsmittelbuch)* which established its own quality norms.[30] The views of the government food chemists and the food industry were diametrically opposed. This concerned, above all, adding artificial colours, the use of chemical preservatives and the determination of maximum and minimum weights. The industry was frequently accused of trying to evade government food control with the help of hired experts and clever attorneys.[31] The food industry and the food trade from the beginning wanted clear, official and generally obligatory norms for the quality of food. Moreover, they were of the opinion that these norms should not be valid for all times as this would hinder further technical development of the food industry.

Government food chemists, on the other hand, demanded that the official standards which they had outlined should remain part of the legislation. They wanted to carry out regulations for every single foodstuff. Regulations followed for fat, cooking oil, cheese, honey and vinegar in 1912.[32] In the view of the chemists, only strict standards would guarantee uniform law and full protection of the consumer. There were several cases where economic interests and governmental responsibility for protection clashed. In such controversies, the government tried to take into account the economic interest, but the potential risk for the consumers' health always had priority. They also paid attention to the fact that official reports were not used for advertising purposes. Between 1877 and 1914, the newspapers reported several food scandals which had been discovered with the help of the new food legislation and which led to lively law suits.[33]

We can conclude from criminal statistics and reports of the food controlling authorities that by 1914 most of the falsified and imitated foodstuffs had been withdrawn from the urban markets. The quality of basic foodstuffs like bread, meat, beer, milk and butter had been improved.[34] Coffee, chocolate and tea also gained high quality standards which were maintained. There remained some doubtful areas which official control could not shed light on. Adulteration of sausages, wine and spices, which were not produced in factories, was a real problem for a long time.

The increase of laws and edicts between 1850 and 1975 shows the slow beginning of the reform process, which speeded up in the late 1920s. Although the number of legal acts at first sight appear rather small, one can see that by the turn of the century the state control of food production was clearly a part of the solution of the 'social question' and a remarkable step towards a wider national health and food policy. Systematic education of state-certified food chemists began at the same time. The government already recognized the full importance of a standard of nutrition for its people which was not only quantitatively sufficient but was also of a high quality. The Berlin physiologist Max Rubner called for an independent Reichsernährungsamt (National Nutritional Board) to combine research, production and systems of control, and chaired the 14th International Congress for Hygiene and Demography, which discussed food adulteration and food legislation all over Europe.[35]

The extent to which food chemists' knowledge of adulteration, imitation, low quality and freshness of food reached the private household, is historically hard to reconstruct. As poison cases proved, the consumer's household remained a potential source of danger in preparing daily meals. To this day, there are no statistics on food poisoning through the consumer's own fault. By the means of popular advice literature the German government tried hard to spread the necessary knowledge on better feeding.[36]

The First World War caused a four-year break in the debate on the further development of German food legislation. From 1916 the Kriegsernährungsamt (KEA) (War Office of Nutrition) was occupied with testing the risks to health of the numerous substitutes for foodstuffs, which were developed as a result of the general shortage. Some of these new substitutes which were distributed were of low quality and hardly edible.[37] In this way, the War caused further intensification of public food control. Finally on 1 October 1927 the first food law was basically amended, whereby the old controversies between food chemists and the food industry were ended by a compromise.

From that time there were public decrees which completely regulated both ordinary and luxury foods. The government was now able to lay down definitions concerning the quality of single products as well as the principles by which these articles would be regarded as adulterated, imitated or spoiled. On the other hand, the Reichsgesundheitsamt (National Health Board), which was mainly set up by producers, traders, consumers and experts, had to be heard before decrees and laws could be passed. This requirement was considered as a step towards making the economy more democratic. This solution took into account the interests of the economy, technology and research without neglecting those of the consumer. Later extensions of food protection in Germany were based on this concept.

Notes

1. Zipfel, 1974.
2. See, for example, Hansen/Wendt 1965; Schmauderer, 1976; Teuteberg, 1986.
3. Schmauderer, 1975; Wassermann 1879.
4. Teuteberg, 1987; Burnett, 1989.
5. Accum 1822; Burnett, 1976.
6. There is, for instance, a rich contemporary literature on coffee falsification: Bibra, 1858; Chevallier, 1854; Teuteberg, 1991.
7. Schreiber, 1847.
8. Martiny, 1871, p. 401; Feser, 1866; Danckworth, 1860.
9. Martiny, 1871; Goltz, 1890, p. 535; Siedel, 1904, p. 523.
10. Schreiber, 1847, p. 151, footnote 13.
11. Neuhaus, 1954, p. 82; Teuteberg, 1981.
12. Trommer, 1859; Vogel, 1862; Herz, 1889; Sommerfeld, 1909; Morres, 1913; Exner, 1892; Gerber, 1890.
13. Schuler, 1884, p. 22.
14. Tappe, 1987.
15. Berg, 1912, p. 102; Treue, 1967.
16. Zürn, 1864; Pagenstecher, 1865; Johne, 1896; Fischoeder, 1890. See the whole contemporary literature in Ostertag, 1904.
17. Silbergleit, 1903.
18. Schwarze, 1903.
19. Heiß, 1924, Rieß, 1924.
20. Kaiserliches Gesundheitsamt, 1907; Schlampp, 1902; Edelmann, 1903.
21. Accum, 1822; Accum, 1833; Sobernheim, 1833; Walchner, 1840; Duflos and Hirsch, 1842; Brumm, 1842; Chevallier, 1856–57; Klencke, 1856; Günther, 1858.
22. Lindner, 1963.
23. Mani, 1976.
24. See, for example, Vogel, 1872; Löbner, 1877; Geißler, 1877; Klencke, 1879; Hilger, 1879.
25. Würzburg, 1894. An exhaustive description of the origin of the legislation, comments on the content and comparisons between the Reich and the Federal States.
26. König, 1883; König, 1907.
27. *Stenographische Berichte*, 1897, pp. 148–87.
28. Reusch, 1986.

29. Hilger, 1882, pp. 241–308; Dammer, 1885–87; Neufeld, 1910.
30. Bund Deutscher Nahrungsmittel-Fabrikanten, 1905.
31. Neufeld, 1910, p. 308.
32. Kaiserliches Gesundheitsamt, 1912.
33. Ellerbrock, 1987, pp. 170–71.
34. Juckenack, 1911.
35. Rubner, 1908; Beythien, 1911.
36. Kaiserliches Gesundheitsamt, 1904.
37. Roerkohl, 1991.

Bibliography

Accum, Friedrich, *Von der Verfälschung der Nahrungsmittel und von den Küchengiften* . . ., Leipzig, 1822.

Accum, Friedrich, *Der Chemiker für das Haus. Oder praktische Unterweisung zur Auffindung der Verfälschung bei vielen sowohl im gewöhnlichen Leben als in der Medizin und den Künsten angewendeten Stoffen sowie die Vergiftungen in Speisen* . . . *Aus dem Englischen übersetzt,* Leipzig, 1833.

Berg, Georg, Die Milchversorgung der Stadt Karlsruhe, *Schriften des Vereins für Socialpolitik,* vol. 140, part 1, München, Leipzig, 1912.

Beythien, A., 'Die Nahrungsmittelchemie in ihrer Bedeutung für die Volkswohlfahrt', *Zeitschrift zur Untersuchung der Nahrungs-und Genußmittel sowie deren Gebrauchsgegenstände,* vol. 22, 1911, pp. 8–24.

Bibra, Baron von, '*Der Kaffee und seine Surrogate*', Abhandlungen der naturwissenschaftlich-technischen Commission bei der Königlich Bayerischen Akademie der Wissenschaften vol. 2, Tübingen, 1858, pp. 219–328.

Brumm, Franz, *Hilfsbuch der Untersuchungen der Nahrungsmittel und Getränke, wie deren Ächtheit erkannt und ihre Verfälschungen entdeckt werden können* . . . Wien, 1842.

Bund Deutcher Nahrungsmittel Fabrikanten und -Händler e.V. (ed.), *Deutsches Nahrungsmittelbuch,* Heidelberg, 1905.

Burnett, John, 'Food Adulteration in Great Britain in the 19th Century and the Origins of Food Legislation', Edith Heischkel-Artelt (ed.), Ernährung und Ernährungslehre im 19. Jahrhundert, Göttingen, 1976, pp. 117–36.

Burnett, John, *Plenty and Want. A Social History of Food in England from 1815 to the Present Day,* 3rd edn, London, New York, 1989.

Chevallier, Jean-Baptiste Alphonse, 'Du café, son histoire, ses fabrications, ses falsifications et des moyens de les reconnaitre', *Journal de chimie médicale, de pharmacie et de toxilogie,* IIIe série, vol. 5, Paris, 1854, pp. 276–86.

Chevallier, Jean-Baptiste Alphonse, *Wörterbuch der Verunreinigungen und Verfälschungen der Nahrungsmittel, Arzneimittel und Handelswaaren nebst Angaben der Erkenntnis-und Prüfungsmittel* . . . *Frei nach dem Französischen in alphabetischer Ordnung bearbeitet und mit Zusätzen versehen von A.H.I. Westrumb,* 2 vols Göttingen, 1856–57.

Dammer, O. (ed.), *Illustrirtes Lexikon der Verfälschungen und Verunreinigungen der Nahrungs-und Genußmittel* . . . *Mit Berücksichtigung des Gesetzes vom 14. Mai*

1879 betr. den Verkehr mit Nahrungsmitteln, Genußmitteln und deren Gebrauchsgegenständen sowie aller Verordnungen und Vereinbarungen, 2 vols, Leipzig, 1885–87.

Danckworth, W., '*Uber polizeiliche Milchprüfungen*', Monatsblätter für exakte Forschung auf dem Gebiete der Sanitäts-Polizei, vol. 1, Berlin, 1860, pp. 193–201.

Duflos, Adolf and Adolf G. Hirsch, *Die wichtigsten Lebensbedürfnisse, ihre Ächtheit und Güte, ihre zufälligen Verunreinigungen und ihre absichtlichen Verfälschungen mit gleichzeitiger Berücksichtigung der in den Haushalten, den Künsten und Gewerben benutzten chemischen Gifte* Breslau, 1842.

Edelmann, Richard Heinrich, *Die Fleischbeschaugesetzgebung des Deutschen Reiches und des Königreiches Sachsen* Leipzig, 1903.

Ellerbrock, Karl-Peter, Lebensmittelqualität vor dem Ersten Weltkrieg: Industrielle Production und staatliche Gesundheitspolitik, Hans J. Teuteberg (ed.), *Durchbruch zum Massenkonsum* Münster, 1987, pp. 127–88.

Exner, Franz, *Die Milch, ihre Verfälschung und deren Nachweis* Neustadt/ Oberschlesien, 1892.

Feser, Johann, *Der Wert der bestehenden Milchproben für die milchpolizei* München, 1866.

Fischoeder, Franz, *Leitfaden der praktischen Fleischbeschau* . . . 3rd rev. edn Stuttgart, 1890.

Geißler, E., *Ein Beitrag zur Frage der Verfälschung der Lebensmittel in der Stadt Dresden* Dresden, 1878.

Gerber, Nicolaus, *Die praktische Milchprüfung*, 5th rev. edn Bremen, Wien, 1890.

Goltz, Theodor von der, *Handbuch der Landwirtschaft*, vol. 3, Tübingen, 1890.

Günther, Johannes, *Das Surrogatbuch oder die vorzüglichsten Ersatzmittel für Kapern, Oliven, Citronensaft, Kartoffeln, Eier, Sago, Kaffee, Arac, Rum, Ratafia, Mandelmilch, Zucker, Schokolade, Thee, Tabak und viele andere Gegenstände*, 3rd edn, Eisenberg, 1858.

Hansen, E./W. Wendt, 'Überblick über die Geschichte der Lebensmittelkontrolle und-verfälschungen', Johannes Schormüller (ed.), *Handbuch der Lebensmittelchemie* vol. 1 Berlin, Heidelberg, New York, 1965, pp. 1–75.

Heiß, Art., 'Schlachthöfe (Technisches)', Josef Brix *et al.* (eds), *Handwörterbuch der Kommunalwissenschaften*, vol. 3, Jena, 1924, pp. 599–606.

Herz, Franz-Josef, *Die gerichtliche Untersuchung der Kuhmilch sowie deren Beurteilung* Berlin/Neuwied, 1889.

Hilger, Albert, *Die wichtigsten Nahrungsmittel und Benußmittel, deren wesentliche Bestandteile, Verfälschungen nebst Prüfung* Erlangen, 1879.

Hilger, Albert, 'Verfälschung der Nahrungs-und Genußmittel', *Handbuch der speciellen Pathologie und Therapie, vol. 1: Handbuch der Hygiene und Gewerbekrankheiten*, part 1, Leipzig, 1882, pp. 241–308.

Johne, A., *Der Trichinenbeschauer*, 5th edn Berlin, 1896.

Juckenack, Adolf, *Die Verdrängung verfälschter, nachgemachter und minderwertiger Erzeugnisse vom Nahrungsmittelmarkt als Folge intensiver Lebensmittelüberwachung, gemessen an den Erfolgen statistischer Erhebungen*, Zeitschrift für Untersuchung der Nahrungs-und Genußmittel sowie deren Gebrauchsgegenstände, vol. 21, 1911, pp. 83–91.

Kaiserliches Gesundheitsamt (ed.), *Gesundheitsbüchlein*, 10th edn Berlin, 1904.

Kaiserliches Gesundheitsamt und Kaiserliches Statistisches Amt (eds), *Das deutsche Reich in gesundheitlicher und demographischer Beziehung* Berlin, 1907.

Kaiserliches Gesundheitsamt (ed.), *Entwürfe zur Festsetzung über Honig, Essig, Speisefette und Speiseöle, Käse* Berlin, 1912.

Klencke, Hermann Philipp Freidrich, *Die Verfälschung der Nahrungsmittel und Getränke der Kolonialwaaren, Droguen und Manufacte der gewerblichen und landwirthschaftlichen Producte* Leipzig, 1856.

Klencke, Hermann, *Illustrirtes Lexikon der Verfälschungen der Nahrungsmittel und Detränke*, 2nd edn Leipzig, 1879.

König, Josef, '*Über die Bedürfnisse der deutschen Nahrungsmittelgesetzgebung*', Zeitschrift zur Untersuchung der Nahrungs- und Genußmittel sowie deren Gebrauchsgegenstände, vol, 14, 1907, pp. 621–36.

König, Josef, *Die menschlichen Nahrungs- und Genußmittel, ihre Herstellung, Zusammensetzung und Beschaffenheit, ihre Verfälschung und deren Nachweisung, mit einer Einleitung über die Ernährungslehre*, 2nd edn, 3 vols, Berlin, 1883, 4th edn 1903–19.

Löbner, Arthur, *Maßregeln gegen die Verfälschungen der Nahrungsmittel* Chemnitz, 1877.

Mani, Nikolaus, 'Die wissenschaftliche Ernährungslehre des 19. Jahrhunderts', Edith Heischkel-Artelt (ed.), *Ernährung und Ernährungslehre im 19. Jahrhundert*, Göttingen, 1976, pp. 22–75.

Martiny, Benno, *Die Milch, ihr Wesen und ihre Verwertung*, vol. 1, Danzig, 1871.

Morres, Wilhelm, *Praktische Milchuntersuchung*, 2nd rev. edn Berlin, 1913.

Neufeld, C.A., 'Zur Neuregelung der Lebensmittelgesetzgebung im Deutschen Reiche', Zeitschrift zur Untersuchung der Lebensund Genußmittel sowie deren Gebrauchsgegenstände, vol. 20, 1910, p. 308.

Neuhaus, Ulrich, *Das Lebens Weiße Quellen. Das Buch von der Milch*, Berlin, 1954.

Ostertag, Robert von, *Bibliographie der Fleischbeschau*, Stuttgart, 1904.

Pagenstecher, H. Alexander, *Die Trichinen*, Leipzig, 1865.

Reusch, Helmut, *Zur Geschichte der Lebensmittelüberwachung im Großherzogtum Baden mit seinen Nachfolgeterritorien (1806–1954)*, Karlsruhe, 1986.

Rieß, Art., '*Schlachthöfe (Rechtliches)*', Josef Brix et al. (eds), Handwörterbuch der Kommunalwissenschaften, vol. 3, Jena, 1924, p. 607.

Roerkohl, Anne, *Hungerblockade und Heimatfront. Die Kommunale Lebensmittelversorgung in Westfalen während des Ersten Weltkrieges*, Stuttgart, 1991.

Rubner, Max, *Volksernährungsfragen*, Leipzig, 1908.

Schlampp, Karl Wilhelm, *Die Fleischgesetzgebung in sämtlichen deutschen Bundesstaaten des Deutschen Reiches zum Gebrauche für Staats- und städtische Behörden, Polizei und thierärztliche Beamte und Thierärzte*, Stuttgart, 1902.

Schmauderer, Eberhard, *Studien zur Geschichte der Lebensmittelwissenschaft*, 2 vols, Stuttgart, 1975.

Schmauderer, Eberhard, 'Die Beziehungen zwischen Lebensmittelwissenschaft, Lebensmittelrecht und Lebensmittelversorgung', Edith Heischkel-Artelt (ed.), *Ernährung und Ernährungslehre im 19. Jahrhundert*, Göttingen, 1976, pp. 131–98.

Schreiber, J. von, *Die Milchwirthschaft im Innern großer Städte und deren nächster Umgebung*, Prague, 1847.

Schuler, Fridolin, *Zur Alkoholfrage. Die Ernährungsweisen der arbeitenden Klassen in der Schweiz und ihr Einfluß auf die Ausbreitung des Alkoholismus*, Bern, 1884.

Siedel, Johannes, *Die Milchwirtschaft*, Leipzig, 1904.

Silbergleit, Heinrich, *Die Lage der preußischen Schlachthöfe und die Freizügigkeit des frischen Fleisches*, Magdeburg, 1903.

Schwarze, Oscar, 'Bau, Einrichtung und Betrieb öffentlicher Schlachthöfe und Viehhöfe', *Ein Handbuch für Sanitäts- und Verwaltungsbeamte*, 3rd edn, Berlin, 1903.

Sobernheim, Johann Friedrich and J. Franz Simon, *Handbuch der praktischen Toxikologie*, Leipzig, 1833.

Sommerfeld, Paul, *Handbuch der Milchkunde*, Wiesbaden, 1909.

Stenographische Berichte über die Verhandlungen des Deutschen Reichstages, 4. Legislatur-Periode, II. Session, vol. 7, Berlin, 1897, pp. 148–87.

Tappe, Heinrich, Der Kampf gegen den Alkoholmißbrauch als Aufgabe bürgerlicher Mäßigkeitsbewegung und staatlich-kommunaler Verwaltung, Hans J. Teuteberg (ed.), *Durchbruch zum Massenkonsum*, Münster, 1987, pp. 189–206.

Teuteberg, Hans J., 'The Beginnings of Modern Milk Age in Germany', Alexander Fenton and Trevor T. Owen (eds), *Food in Perspective*. Proceedings of the Third International Conference of Ethnological Food Research, Edinburgh, 1981, pp. 282–311.

Teuteberg, Hans J./Günter Wiegelemann, *Unsere tägliche Kost. Geschichte und regionale Prägung*, 2nd edn, Münster, 1986.

Teuteberg, Hans J. (ed.), *Durchbruch zum Massenkonsum. Lebensmittelmärkte und Lebensmittelqualität im Städtewachstum des Industriezeitalters*, Münster, 1987.

Teuteberg, Hans J., 'Zur Kulturgeschichte der Kaffee-Surrogate', Daniela Ball (ed.), *Kaffee im Spiegel europäischer Trinksitten*, Zürich, 1991.

Treue, Wilhelm, *Zur Geschichte der Ernährung in Berlin. Proceedings of the 7th International Congress of Nutrition, Hamburg 1966*, vol. 4, Braunschweig, 1967, pp. 66–73.

Trommer, C., *Die Prüfung der Kuhmilch in Bezug auf ihre Verdünnung und Verfälschung mit Wasser und anderen Substanzen*, Berlin, 1859.

Vogel, Alfred, *Die neue Milchprobe*, Erlangen, 1862.

Vogel, Heinrich, *Die Verfälschung oder Verschlechterung der Lebensmittel*, 2nd edn, Schwelm, 1872.

Walchner, Franz Hermann, *Darstellung der wichtigsten im bürgerlichen Leben vorkommenden Verfälschungen der Nahrungsmittel und Getränke nebst den Angaben wie dieselben schnell und sicher erkannt werden können*, Carlsruhe, 1840.

Wassermann, Ludwig, *Der Kampf gegen die Lebensmittelverfälschung vom Ausgang des Mittelalters bis zum Ende des 19. Jahrhunderts*, Mainz, 1879.

Würzburg, Arthur, *Die Nahrungsmittelgesetzgebung im Deutschen Reiche und in den einzelnen deutschen Bundesstaaten*, Leipzig, 1894.

Zipfel, W., *Lebensmittelrecht*, 8th edn, München, 1974.

Zürn, Friedrich August, *Anleitung zur rationellen Fleischbeschau*, Leipzig, 1864.

PART 4: DIETARY TRENDS

11 Food policies in Sweden during the World Wars

Mats Essemyr

Introduction

In this chapter I shall discuss the characteristics of Swedish food policy during the First and the Second World Wars. The main objective is to establish whether the policy changed from the first crisis to the latter, and whether the outcome of the policy affected the standard of nutrition in the country. Three factors will be considered. First, the state of Swedish agriculture and food supply at the outbreak of the wars will be discussed. In relation to this, I will point out some important differences in the structure of Swedish food supply between 1914 and 1939. In this respect, the role of domestic food production versus the role of imports is of particular interest. This relationship can be assumed to have had particular influence on the food policy that was employed during periods of restrictions in the international trade.

Second, the food policy as such – in terms of aims and means – will be examined in order to reveal changes over time. Emphasis will be placed on the ideology behind the decisions taken and on the systems of rationing. Here, the aim is limited to pointing out some important factors behind the change in food policy. An explanatory model, of course, must be based on a broader concept of socio-economic and political changes that took place during the inter-war period. In many respects, Sweden moved from a traditional agricultural society (in its wider meaning) to a modern industrial nation between 1918 and 1939. The introduction of political democracy, the first steps towards a social welfare system and the rise of important export industries are examples of this.

Thirdly, it seems reasonable to pay some attention to the outcomes of the food policy. Did people starve? Did food intake decline or was it possible to maintain energy and nutritive intake on a pre-war level? To what extent did the situation affect health standards and the death rate? These questions are to be examined in the following sections.

Agriculture and food supply before the Wars

Concerning the structure of ownership in Swedish agriculture, the system of family-based farming was to a great extent already established prior to the First World War. In 1914, about 75 per cent of the land under cultivation was owned by the cultivators themselves, whilst only about 25 per cent was tenanted. Hence, the average size of a farm was quite modest, around 20 acres. Therefore, the system of capitalist farmers employing agricultural labour on a large-scale basis is a concept which is not valid for twentieth century Sweden.[1]

In 1914, the use of land was quite evenly distributed between grain and fodder crops. We can see in Table 11.1 that rye, oats and hay took the bulk of the land under cultivation. To this should be added large areas of pasture. As cultivation was dominated by oats and fodder crops, it is clear that livestock was the dominant sector of Swedish agriculture at the outbreak of the First World War. Not only did the producers keep a great number of draught animals but also the number of cattle, sheep and swine had increased significantly since the beginning of the century. Although the population was quite small in absolute terms, it was rising rapidly.

This circumstance of an unbalanced agricultural production caused Sweden to seek foreign markets, for imports as well as for exports. In 1914, the domestic supply of grain, especially wheat, was too small to meet the demand and it was necessary to import great quantities from Germany, Russia and Denmark. In 1911–13 the annual net imports of grain were nearly 300,000 tonnes, about one-third of the total consumption.[2] Other vegetable food items that were available through foreign trade alone were coffee, tea, rice, spices, etc. Another problem was the growing use of artificial fertilisers and refined fodder. These certainly increased productivity, but on the other hand, they made the agricultural sector more vulnerable to interruptions in foreign trade.

As has been suggested above, Sweden had a surplus of animal products during the first decade of the twentieth century. Consequently, around 37,000 tonnes of butter, beef and pork, and 31,000 cattle could be exported annually. A survey by the National Commission on Wartime Supply estimated that the total annual energy need amounted to 6,225 billions of calories, of which 5,123 billions – or 82 per cent – could be

Table 11.1 Land usage in Sweden 1914.

Crop	Land under cultivation (%)
Wheat	3.2
Rye	10.6
Barley	4.6
Oats and mixed grain	26.2
Podded plants	1.0
Potatoes	4.1
Root crops	2.8
Fodder crops	38.2
Other plants	0.1
Fallow	9.2

Source: Heckscher (1926) p. 45.

produced within the country. However, concerning vegetable food items the domestic deficit was 23 per cent, while for animal products only 9 per cent of the energy came from other countries.[3] In general, at the outbreak of the First World War the food situation did not seem too bad. The government, which in 1914 had taken but few steps towards a systematic food emergency policy also accepted this view: it was borne out when, in 1940, the Research Institute of Industry (IUI) published a volume of essays concerning the supply situation during the war. One of the essays, dealing with the development in Swedish agriculture since the late nineteenth century, describes the 'magnificent' rise in production capacity. The average yield-to-land ratio went up by 79 per cent between 1881–90 and 1928–37, whilst population increased by only 33 per cent.[4]

Through investment rather than rationalization, the many small-holdings became effective production units. Mechanization was rapid in the latter part of the 1930s, and the number of tractors is likely to have increased from 9,000 to 22,600 between 1937 and 1940. Also, electricity had been introduced, not only on the large estates but also on many smallholdings, making it possible to introduce new machines and tools. Improvements in seeds, fertilisers, and stock-breeding contributed as well.[5]

As can be concluded from Table 11.1 and Table 11.2, two major changes occurred between 1914 and 1939 concerning the usage of land. First, concerning bread-grain, wheat increased its share threefold, at the expense mainly of rye. Earlier, the growing taste for wheaten bread had been met mainly by imports, due to the unfavourable natural conditions for domestic production. During the inter-war period, however, the scientific development of plants made it possible to increase home

Table 11.2 Land usage in Sweden 1939.

Crop	Land under cultivation (%)
Wheat	9.0
Rye	4.7
Barley	2.8
Oats and mixed grain	24.4
Podded plants	0.5
Potatoes	3.5
Root crops	3.2
Fodder crops	45.9
Other plants	0.2
Fallow	5.8

Source: Ekholm (1976) pp. 18, 23.

production. Secondly, the share of fodder went up steadily during the inter-war period, indicating an even stronger concentration on cattle and animal food production than was the case prior to the First World War.

In general, the food supply situation was better in 1939 compared to 1914. One scholar argues that 90 per cent of the calories needed were produced domestically, compared to 82 per cent in 1914.[6] For certain products, however, the situation was problematic. Most worrying was the rapid increase in imports of artificial fertilisers – 366,000 tonnes in 1939. A cut-off from foreign suppliers could affect the food situation negatively.[7]

Food policy during the Wars

There are two major similarities in the Swedish situation during the periods of war. First, in both cases Sweden's neutrality kept the country out of the wars and, consequently, free from destruction and occupation. The military forces, however, were used to maintain neutrality and a great number of people were mobilized. Secondly, in both cases foreign trade was severely hit by blockades. During the First World War the allied objective to stop German trade had a massive impact on Swedish imports. In the Second World War, naval warfare put great obstacles in the way of Swedish merchant fleet operations. However, there is one important political difference to mention. During the First World War party politics persisted for the whole period, while a government with members from all great parties was established at a very early stage in the Second World War.

Food policy during the First World War

At the outbreak of the First World War, Swedish dependence on external supplies of grain and other vegetable food items was the basic problem. As many of the nearby suppliers were unable to provide the products, Sweden was forced to open up trade with sellers in overseas countries. Between 1914 and 1916, the problem was not of access to sufficient quantity, but rather that relative shortages and increasing transportation and insurance costs made the prices of imported grain rise. As the Swedish farmers demanded the same price, the general price level of grain increased significantly. At the same time, Swedish exports of animal food items were not only allowed, but also maintained. Rising foreign demand caused prices to increase, and, hence, prices in Sweden went up as well, as demonstrated in Figure 11.1. It was, however, still possible to buy enough on the world market.

The price increase caused a change towards animal production, thus worsening the food situation. In general, during the First World War prices went up much more than did wages, so that it became known as a 'time of dearth'. Consequently, during the first two years the main efforts made by the government focused on the stabilization of food prices. To a great extent this objective was the result of political pressure from workers and consumers, who suffered from rapidly diminishing real wages. The producers, on the other hand, who expected large profits from the rising prices, were opposed to government intervention in the market system. Indeed, it was the basic opinion of the liberal government as well that prices and consumption should be left to the free market system. Theory and practice, however, were far removed from each other.

Up to the winter of 1916 only one product – wheat – was subject to restriction in price. Instead, the government's policy was to reduce import tariffs, make price agreements with the producers and – for animal food items – to establish a system of compensation for the exporters.[8] In the latter system, introduced in 1915, the producers agreed to export no more than 400 tonnes per week, and to distribute an amount equal to one-quarter of the exported quantity within the country, at a much lower price. Later, the ratio was raised to 50 per cent, and even later to 75 per cent.[9]

In the long run, however, it became impossible not to use price restrictions. In November 1915 maximum prices on rye, barley and oats were introduced. As the domestic supply of potatoes was quite good, their price did not rise during the first two years. It was not until April 1917 that restrictions on the price of potatoes were put into force.[10]

The overall opinion amongst historians is that the food price policy during the War was, in general, a failure. Three factors are emphasized.

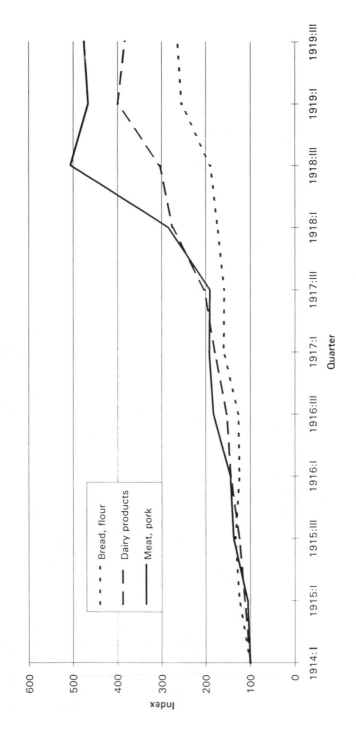

Figure 11.1 Food prices in Sweden 1914–19. Quarterly, index July 1914 = 100.

Table 11.3 Swedish food imports 1911/15–1919.

Year	Grain (tonnes)	Vegetable oils (tonnes)	Artificial fertilisers (tonnes)	Coffee (tonnes)
1911/15	498 859	29 533	224 576	33 277
1916	354 483	19 479	230 424	38 200
1917	151 105	802	61 951	8 552
1918	111 705	817	164 260	11 199
1919	258 460	40 935	224 019	39 007

Source: Heckscher, 1926, p. 63.

First, the policy failed to keep the cost of living in parity with wages, thus lowering real wages and creating a situation of relative poverty. Generally, from 1916 the gap between food prices and wages was growing.[11] Secondly, the price policy up to 1918 favoured a transition of agriculture towards livestock and cultivation of fodder crops. The farmers were able to get more profit from pork compared to wheat or rye. This came into conflict with the main objective of the food policy, to feed the people at a pre-war level. It was not until the last years of the War that a return to cultivation of grain occurred.[12]

Thirdly, the regulations were so full of loopholes that the results often became the opposite of what had been intended. 'The maximum price of butter, e.g., was set too low and without regard to the quality. Consequently, the farmers kept the milk, produced their own butter and gave the skimmed milk to the livestock, thus causing a shortage of milk together with a permanent shortage of butter. At the same time the price of butter went up on the black market.'[13] Also, as the price of pork was increasing faster than the grain price, producers were able to raise their profits by using grain as fodder instead of selling it.

From the latter part of 1916, the problem of shortage became acute. Four reasons are pointed out. For nearly three years, restrictions, export prohibitions and naval warfare made it almost impossible to find sellers of grain, vegetables and artificial fertilisers. The lack of fertilisers affected domestic production adversely, and resulted in comparatively low yields. Also, the turnover of farms went up as a result of the general speculative boom. In many cases, this interrupted the natural cycle of cultivation. Lastly, the wartime boom in industry and forestry caused a relative shortage of agricultural labour.[14]

Apart from the price control another aim has to be added to the food policy, namely self-sufficiency and distribution of food equally to the population. The first thing to do was to reduce exports of food through prohibition. Gradually, from 1916, Swedish exports dropped to reach an

Table 11.4 Swedish food exports 1911/1915–1919.

Year	Livestock (number)	Pork (tonnes)	Meat (tonnes)	Butter (tonnes)	Fish (tonnes)
1911/15	48 047	11 936	8 491	20 186	54 466
1916	13 598	14 114	4 981	13 020	46 107
1917	2 675	4 766	5 761	1	9 731
1918	5	4	57	1	635
1919	27	1 620	3 348	35	6 800

Source: Heckscher, 1926, p. 63.

absolute minimum in 1918 (see Table 11.4). Secondly, a number of reclamation projects were started all over the country in order to increase domestic cultivation of grain and potatoes. The projects stretched from the draining of vast areas of fenland, to propaganda for potato cultivation on small plots in cities.

It was, however, the system of rationing that became the main issue in food policy during the second part of the War. Sugar was the first item to be rationed, in the summer of 1916, at the level of one kilogram/month. It turned out to be successful. All available sugar was brought into the system, and a maximum price was established.

A more radical rationing, of bread-stuffs, was planned during the autumn of 1916 and put into force early in 1917. It stipulated an allowance of 250 grammes/day. Hard-working labourers were allowed an extra 50 grammes. The whole thing was based on the idea of putting all available grain into the system of rationing, with the exception of seed-grain and the grain that the farmers needed for their own consumption. An inventory, however, showed that the quantities available for consumption among non-farmers were too small to maintain the stipulated allowances. Consequently, in April 1917 the allowances were cut down to 200 grammes/day. Also, all kinds of flour, oatmeal and peas were subject to rationing. While the rationing of bread and bread-stuffs lasted up to the end of August 1919, the consumption of flour, oatmeal and peas was freed in February 1919.

Another wave of rationing occurred in late 1917 and early 1918. From October to February coffee, milk, butter and pork were rationed. Milk was given primarily to children at a rate of a half to one litre a day depending on age. Butter was allowed in quantities of 25 to 100 grammes/week. Rationing was abolished for these items during the first six months of 1919.

During the winter of 1916 there were several indications of potato shortages, such as a sudden increase in the price level. A number of actions were taken in order to secure the supply, like the prohibition of using potatoes as fodder. Concerning this basic item, however, rationing was looked upon as a last resort and consequently, no legal restrictions in consumption were introduced at the start. However, the authorities were forced to establish a maximum price for potatoes, thus causing a permanently high demand which almost emptied the stores.[15] During the first months of 1917 the situation became explosive. Starting in Västervik – a small city in the south of the country – hunger-riots spread all over the country, and continued until the stores were refilled by the new harvest. In Stockholm, police forces suppressed the riots, but the government felt threatened and prepared a system of potato rationing in order to secure distribution. Amongst historians, the 1917 riots are generally considered to be as close as Sweden ever came to a revolution.[16] Through social democratic influence, rationing and increasing supplies during the autumn, further violence was avoided.

As hostilities on the continent ceased in 1919, rationing was gradually abolished between May and August 1919, as can be seen in Figure 11.2

Food policy during the Second World War

The planning of the food sector started immediately after the outbreak of the Second World War. The Food Supply Commission, which was given its terms of reference by the government during the autumn of 1939, had to work out guidelines in order to reach four main objectives. First, the government wanted the population to be fed on an acceptable nutritional level. Second, it was desirable for agriculture to keep its level of profitability, and for real wages to remain stable. It is clear that this objective was perhaps the most important lesson that was learned from the First World War. Third, it was thought desirable to concentrate on feeding the population by the most important vegetable food items, namely grain, potatoes and sugar. Unlike in the First World War, sugar was regarded as an item of high priority. It put some 'luxury' into a diet that consisted of nothing but 'necessities'. A precondition for the priority of sugar was the growth of domestic cultivation of sugar-beet that had occurred during the inter-war period. Fourthly, concerning animal food items, priority was given to milk. Production should, if possible, be kept at the pre-war level. Therefore, the limited supply of fodder must be reserved for milk production.[17]

In many ways, Swedish agriculture became part of a system of economic planning during the Second World War. For priority products, specific goals were settled. It was the main task of the Food Supply Commission continually to ensure that production results did not diverge from these goals. Altogether, for grain the goal was very well achieved. The production of potatoes and sugar-beet, however, showed alarming

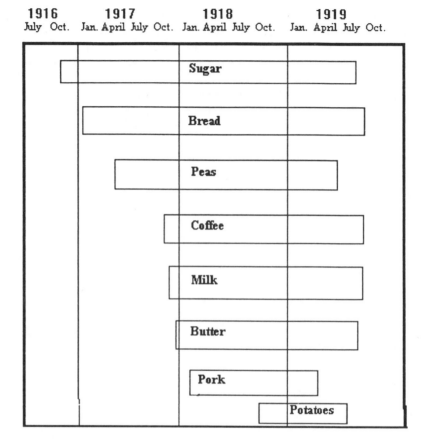

Figure 11.2 The duration of rationing of foodstuffs in Sweden, 1916–19

deficits. In the case of potatoes, it was decided to limit the amount used for fodder in order to maintain the level of human consumption. The figures for annual production are given in Table 11.5.

Although the means to carry out the food policy – price policy and consumption restrictions – were the traditional ones, they were used differently during the two World Wars. As concerns price policy, maximum prices – which caused so much trouble during the First World War – were rarely used. The principal idea that governed the Board of Price Supervision was to accept an increase in food price only if it was caused by a real – that means it had already occurred – rise in costs, like a sudden change in the transportation costs. Speculation on possible rising costs in the future was not allowed.[18] This meant, however, that consumer prices were allowed to increase. In order to compensate the

Table 11.5 Average annual agricultural production in Sweden 1939–45.

	Production goals (tonnes)	Production results (tonnes)	Difference (%)
Grain	775 000	774 900	0.0
Potatoes	2 100 000	1 897 100	−9.7
Raw sugar	319 000	291 739	−8.5

Source: Ekholm, 1976, p. 63.

consumers and, at the same time, alter consumption in the desired direction, a system of subsidies and price reductions was worked out.

The subsidies were directed towards certain food items, and simply meant that these items were sold at a lower price. The system focused on bread-stuffs, milk, dairy products and to some extent on meat. An investigation in April 1942 showed that average household food expenditure was reduced by 8 per cent due to the subsidies.[19] At least for bread-stuffs and milk, the subsidies are likely to have had a very positive impact on the consumption of the majority of the population, as was the intention.[20]

Price reductions focused both on certain groups of the population, and on specific food items, especially butter and milk. The background is to be found in the growing surplus of butter, which was the result of the decrease in exports during the blockade. The food policy programme, however, presupposed a rise in the price of butter, and in order to increase consumption amongst the most needy stratum of the population, price reduction coupons were distributed. The system was intended primarily for children under the age of 16 and adults over the age of 67. Together with pregnant women and disabled persons they formed the largest group.

However, a second group of ordinary people could also have the price reductions, depending on their income and wealth. As a result of the mobilization of the armed forces, the number of individuals in this group increased significantly. In 1942 about 50 per cent of the whole population was entitled to receive price reductions. As incomes rose, the number of individuals entitled to price reductions went down.

On average, the reductions cut the expenditure on milk by 33 crowns/year and on butter by 78 crowns. Their impact upon consumption is likely to have been significant, as the low-income groups were able to maintain high consumption of items with high nutritional value. The subsidies and price reductions together amounted to around 14 per cent of the total food expenditure.[21] Consumption restrictions were carried out through rationing. A system of rationing is generally based upon coupons with either fixed values and variable duration of the periods of validity or the reverse, coupons with variable values and fixed duration. Sweden chose the first system, which was easy to adjust to changes in the supply situation. The coupons for sugar, for example, had periods of validity from 28 to 42 days, depending on the domestic supply. The allowance was always two coupons per period, each for one kilogram of sugar. Also, coupons were often valid for different items, for example, one kilogram of sugar could be substituted for 1.4 kilogram of treacle.

In 1939/40 only one item, sugar, was subject to rationing. In general, it was after April 1940 that the important items like bread-stuffs, oatmeal, butter and meat were rationed. In 1941/42 peas and beans were rationed. However, these vegetables, as well as root crops, like potatoes, were subject to extensive household cultivation. Milk and potatoes were never rationed.

On the basis of the duration of coupons, the allowances of the different food items can be calculated (see Table 11.6). Although some important fluctuations occurred, the main impression is one of considerable stability. Regarding bread-stuffs, for example, the difference between the highest and the lowest allowance was only 25 per cent. The allowance of sugar was cut by 30 per cent between 1939/40 and 1940/41, but was maintained approximately at this level for the rest of the war.

Standard of Nutrition

On the basis of household budgets food consumption was regularly studied during the First World War. In terms of nutrition two important points are worth emphasizing. Firstly, during the first part of the war calorific intake was stable. However, the vegetable share of the energy consumed increased at the expense of animal energy. From mid-1917 onwards, total energy consumption declined, mainly caused by the declining supply of vegetable food items. (see Table 11.7).

Secondly, an important change in diet occurred from 1916 onwards. The shortage of potatoes and bread caused an increasing consumption of fish. As has been pointed out above, total energy intake went down, but on the other hand the intake of protein went up. As a consequence, the percentage of energy that came from protein rose, from 12 per cent to 15 per cent. If we assume that the total energy and protein intake was satisfactory in relation to needs, this change can be regarded as an improvement in the nutritional quality of the diet. Table 11.8 – describing conditions in the Swedish cities – indicates that the absolute intake of energy was between 2,400 and 3,000 calories a day and protein intake between 88 and 92 grammes a day. As the survey does not include

Table 11.6 Daily ration allowances in Sweden 1939/40–1948/49.

Year	Bread-stuffs (g.)	Oat-meal (g.)	Barley-grain (g.)	Peas (g.)	Beans (g.)	Sugar (g.)	Cheese (g.)	Butter (g.)	Eggs (g.)	Meat (pork) (g.)
1939/40	–	–	–	–	–	103.2	–	–	–	–
1940/41	198.9	12.0	–	–	–	72.4	8.2	38.2	–	46.0
1941/42	172.2	0.0	0.0	9.7	9.7	75.4	6.0	35.9	12.1	47.1
1942/43	167.6	20.7	11.0	7.3	2.1	77.2	4.6	36.6	8.4	43.2
1943/44	175.1	17.1	11.0	16.8	4.1	71.6	8.6	42.6	13.0	72.4
1944/45	174.8	13.8	10.8	–	3.4	68.0	10.5	39.9	14.0	47.0
1945/46	159.2	12.8	0.0	–	–	66.5	14.0	35.7	7.6	55.7
1946/47	153.7	16.5	0.0	–	–	67.0	–	37.2	–	49.5
1947/48	147.9	15.9	0.0	–	–	69.1	–	37.2	–	55.6
1948/49	151.5	–	0.0	–	–	67.4	–	37.1	–	59.7

Source: Ekholm, 1976, p. 81.

Table 11.7 Average daily intake of energy in Sweden 1914–18 per consumption unit. (May 1914 = 100)

	May 1914	May 1916	July 1917	July 1918
All foods	100	101	89	87
Vegetables	100	109	84	86
Animal	100	92	96	87

Source: Heckscher, 1926, p. 136.

Table 11.8 Daily food consumption in Sweden 1907–18 per consumption unit.

	Meat (pork) (g.)	Fish (g.)	Milk (l.)	Butter (g.)	Bread-stuffs (g.)	Sugar (g.)
1907/08	126	16	1.10	46	431	104
1916	64	54	0.81	29	167	40
1917	26	127	0.61	33	162	11
1918	60	200	0.10	3	190	22

Source: Hirdman, 1983, p. 261.

Table 11.9 Daily nutrient intake in Swedish cities 1913–18 per consumption unit.

	Protein (g.)	Fat (g.)	Carbo-hydrate (g.)	Energy value (kcal.)	Composition of nutrients protein (%)	fat (%)	carbohydrate (%)
1913	88	94	420	2957	12	30	58
1916	92	96	431	3037	12	30	58
1917	88	97	346	2681	13	34	53
1918	91	74	331	2408	15	29	56

Source: Hirdman, 1983, p. 261.

potato consumption, the values are somewhat underestimated. For the average man, doing normal work, the total levels are likely to have been sufficient.

Also, as we can assume that food supplies were greater amongst the rural population, it gives further support to the opinion that the nutritional standard in general did not deteriorate during the First World War (see Table 11.9). Although certain food items of high social esteem temporarily disappeared from the table, from a nutritional point of view people did not starve. Another circumstance that might indicate a

Table 11.10 Daily energy intakes in Sweden 1939–45 per consumption unit.

| | Energy value (kcal.) | Index (%) | Sources of energy | |
			Vegetable foods (%)	Animal foods (%)
1939	3921	100	59.1	40.9
1940	3768	96	58.7	41.3
1941	3555	91	60.1	39.9
1942	3478	89	61.1	38.9
1943	3637	93	60.0	40.0
1944	3709	95	57.4	42.6
1945	3715	95	58.2	41.8

Source: Ekholm, 1976, pp. 67, 101.

constant nutritional standard is the continuously declining mortality from common diseases. Only diphtheria showed a constant mortality rate – 1.5 deaths per 10,000, between 1904 and 1918.[22] The mortality rate in general in the country was stable between 1914 and 1919.[23]

In 1939 average energy intake was much higher than in 1914, at about 3,900 calories per day. Between 1939 and 1942 it went down by about 10 per cent. In 1945 intake again was relatively high at 3,700 calories per day. The relationship between vegetable and animal energy showed only minor changes. The share of vegetable energy went up by 2 per cent during the first half of the war. By 1945, though, the share of animal energy was 1 per cent higher than it had been in 1939 as shown in Table 11.10.

1942 was obviously the critical year during the Second World War and both total energy intake and the share of animal energy reached their lowest points. Concerning the total levels, however, both energy and protein intakes are likely to have been sufficient for nutritional needs, as was predicted by Professor Ernst Abrahamsson, the expert on nutrition in the Food Supply Commission during the Second World War.[24] During the War, mortality in Sweden went down from 11.5 to 10.8 per thousand.[25]

Conclusion

As I have suggested above, in terms of nutritional standards, the food situation did not deteriorate during the war periods, at least for the average person. However, it is obvious that the food policies in both World Wars to some extent were carried out differently. The most important difference is the late introduction of rationing during WWI. It is evident that the opportunities of maintaining foreign trade were different during the two wars. Consequently, this must be regarded as one of the explanations.

It has been pointed out, however, that price policy did influence food consumption more in the First World War than in the Second. In terms of food policy, the main difference between the two periods is that the government's reluctance to interfere in the free market system was much stronger during the First World War than it was during the Second World War. When in 1914 it became necessary to introduce some form of food policy, the strategy was clear – price control. In 1939, though, food policy was an important part of the planned economy. The aim was not only to maintain food consumption in general, but also to secure nutritional standards among the most needy groups of the population. Therefore planning, in terms of rationing, became the self-evident strategy.

Notes

1. Mannerfelt, 1926, p. 44.
2. Heckscher, 1926, p. 46.
3. Heckscher, 1926, p. 49.
4. Åkerman, 1941, p. 5.
5. Ekholm, 1976, p. 12.
6. Juréen, 1953, p. 252.
7. Ekholm, 1976, p. 57.
8. Heckscher, 1926, pp. 58–61.
9. Hirdman, 1983, p. 216.
10. Östlind, 1945, pp. 133–4.
11. Heckscher, 1926, p. 131.
12. Heckscher, 1926, p. 131.
13. Hirdman, 1983, p. 212.
14. Heckscher, 1926, pp. 52–5.
15. Heckscher, 1926, pp. 102–10.
16. Hirdman, 1983, pp. 231–4.
17. Ekholm, 1976, pp. 58–60.
18. Lundberg, 1941, pp. 77–82.
19. For the average household, the subsidies amounted to SEK 156 of a total of SEK 1921 spent on food. The SEK 156 were distributed on the specific items as follows: bread-stuffs 70, milk 48, butter 32 and cheese 6. Ekholm, 1976, p. 71.
20. Ekholm, 1976, pp. 70–71.
21. Ekholm, 1976, pp. 72–4, 81.
22. The diseases covered were measles, scarlet fever, diphtheria, whooping-cough, tuberculosis, pneumonia, stomach catarrh. Hirdman, 1983, p. 265.

23. The temporarily high mortality in 1918, 18 per thousand, was due to the influenza epidemic.
24. Abrahamsson, 1941, p. 71.
25. National Central Bureau of Statistics, 1969, table 28.

Bibliography

Abrahamsson, E., 'Folkkost i kristid'. In *Vår folkförsörjning i avspärrningstider*, part II, Stockholm 1941.

Åkerman, Å., 'Nya produktioninriktningar inom jordbruket'. In *Vår folkförsörjning i avspärrningstider*, Industriens Utredningsinstitut (IUI), Stockholm 1941.

Ekholm, G., *Det svenska jordbruket och folkförsörjningen under andra världskriget*, Lund 1976.

Heckscher, E.F. (ed.), *Bidrag till Sveriges ekonomiska historia under och efter världskriget*, Stockholm 1926.

Hirdman, Y., *Magfrågan – Mat som mål och medel*, Stockholm 1870–1920, Kristianstad 1983.

Juréen, L., *Jordbruksproduktionen och Sveriges försörjning med livsmedel*, Utredningar verkställda på uppdrag av 1942 års jordbrukskommitté. Unpublished 1953.

Lundberg, E., 'Prisövervakningen', In *Vår folkförsörjning i avspärrningstider*, part II. Stockholm 1941.

Mannerfelt, C., 'Livsmedelspolitik och livsmedelsförsörjning 1914–1922'. In Heckscher, E.F. (ed.), *Bidrag till Sveriges ekonomiska historia under och efter världskriget*, Stockholm 1926.

National Central Bureau of Statistics. *Historisk statistik för Sverige*, part I, Stockholm 1969.

Östlind, A., *Svensk samhällsekonomi 1914–1922*, Stockholm 1945.

12 The beginnings of potato cultivation in Transylvania and Hungary: government policy and spontaneous process

Eszter Kisbán

The potato was not accepted wholeheartedly in its early days. In central Europe it first became established as a field crop around 1680–1700 in German centres of innovation. It had to overcome much disinterest, ignorance and several misconceptions but in the end it won the day throughout the whole area. The innovation process has been well investigated but, while the German and Austrian picture is readily accessible in publications, the Polish and Hungarian one is not because of the language barriers. Among these regions it is in Hungary that production and consumption of potatoes was always lowest. This does not affect the point I would like to discuss here, however.

The introduction of potato cultivation was done through individual, spontaneous efforts, but besides these, a recurring phenomenon in the eighteenth century was the attempt by the government to promote the spread of the new crop and foodstuff by central direction. Potato cultivation on the crown estates of the Polish King August III of Saxony (1733–63), carried out by German estate managers and stewards who came from the King's homeland, set an example which not only made potatoes widely known but also had a knock-on effect on their cultivation among the local people.[1] Centrally directed campaigns for potato-growing started in Sweden after 1739,[2] and in Prussia and Prussian Silesia under Frederick the Great in 1743 as part of his ambitious programme for the improvement of agriculture generally,[3] and in parts of the Austrian Habsburg Empire from 1767 onwards.[4]

Government policy, however, does not seem to have been especially successful in so far as it did not significantly shorten the time-span for the whole innovation process for larger areas. This is the time during which potatoes came to be accepted and actually grown by all possible producers, as well as eaten regularly by all.

In the view of Gösta Berg, there were only a few ineffectual attempts at cultivation before the start of the Government campaign for the introduction of the potato in Sweden in 1740. The centrally directed campaign went on, using all possible means, for six decades. All the same, the breakthrough of the crop into general cultivation came only in the 1820s, and the general, regular consumption of potatoes in the 1830s. The adoption of the potato, therefore, covered a 90-year span for the area as a unit.[5]

In Germany, then divided into several smaller and larger individual states, the cultivation of the potato started in 1680–1700 in two middle-German innovation centres in the Palatinate (Unterpfalz, the Electorate and a smaller princedom) and Vogtland in Saxony where it became a field crop. The spontaneous spread from there, with Dutch and English influence in some regions, was helped in several cases by the intervention of regional authorities, but progress was often interspersed with great delays. Only by 1770 were potatoes widely known and their cultivation underway nearly everywhere in Germany. The shortage of grain during the great famine of 1771–72 emphasized the significance of the potato crop and quickly led to an increase in its sown acreage in the areas which had long been hesitant. Including the scattered smaller areas which lagged behind, it was only by 1800 that potatoes reached all the possible producers and consumers. The process really started in the mid-seventeenth century with the first attempt at potato-growing in the areas which were to become the innovation centres. Considering the dimensions and diverse orientation of the German territory, it might not be fair to take it as a unit but, if we do, the complete innovation process took 150 years, i.e. five generations for the region as a whole. The wide-ranging increase in the acreage of potato cultivation after 1817–24, which, according to Teuteberg, did not follow a shortage but rather an overproduction of grain and a fall in grain prices, was no longer part of the innovation process.[6]

In Austria, the first attempts at small-scale planting took place in Vorarlberg in the 1730s. During the next two decades individual experiments followed in other districts as well, but by no means in every one. Both contemporary writers and production data point to the great famine in 1770–72 as a turning-point in attitudes towards the new crop. From the 1770s the potato began to gain ground as an arable crop, yet in the last decades of the century several areas in the country were still without potatoes. Central government promotional policy started in 1768–69 and was carried out in a selective way, recommending potatoes for regions permanently short of grain but not for those where it was abundant. The completion of the innovation process came after the next great famine in 1816–17. In the immediately ensuing years (1818–22) it was still necessary for the local authorities, for example in Steiermark, where the beginnings of potato cultivation go back to the 1740s, to start a five-year campaign to teach people how to grow potatoes by running a demonstration farm and distributing seed tubers to the peasants. Consolidation of the cultivation pattern is documented by the 1830 statistics, which report potatoes as a regular field crop in every region of Austria.[7] From the 1730s to the 1820s the time-span of the innovation process is again about 90 years.

From the beginning of cultivation in Poland in the 1740s, the potato here too took about 90 years to become a regular field crop and a necessity so that 'folk would have felt it difficult to live without them' in the 1830s. Even a decade earlier this was not universally the case. It seems that the rate of introduction accelerated again after 1770. For the period 1774–1830, 36 calendars were found which urged propagation of the potato. Under Austrian supremacy in Galicia there was a government campaign for the crop in the late eighteenth century, as reports of 1783 about its results demonstrate.[8]

Private initiatives and central direction often intertwined during the introduction of the potato. In Hungary, in one case, the two different approaches diverged in two larger neighbouring regions. It is worth looking more closely, to see if the speed of the process was significantly different according to the different circumstances.

The Transylvanian campaign

The first real food-policy campaign of any government in Hungary started in 1767; its aim was to stimulate the cultivation of the potato. During the Turkish occupation of central Hungary in the sixteenth and seventeenth centuries, the non-occupied territories were divided into two parts: the Hungarian kingdom in the north and west with Habsburg kings, and the independent principality of Transylvania in the east. After the liberation of the Turkish province, central Hungary was again incorporated into the kingdom, while Transylvania was not integrated administratively but governed separately from Vienna. This meant that Hungarian and Transylvanian matters were treated separately at the imperial aulic councils and each territory had its independent regional administration, i.e. government. The Hungarian kingdom bordered on Austria, while Transylvania, surrounded by the Carpathians, was the most south-eastern part of central Europe.

The Viennese aulic councils chose this farthest corner, Transylvania, for one of their earliest experiments in encouraging cropping with the potato. The choice was not specifically explained, but implied a recognition that the region's subsistence economy was not soundly based on grain.

When government intervention in the spread of potato cultivation started in Transylvania in 1767, the plant was not totally unknown there. Intellectuals who had travelled in Germany and western Europe had met it there and had already spoken of it in Hungarian publications (for example, the medical doctor István Mátyus in his first small book, *Dietetics*, in 1762) but potatoes were also grown locally in small quantities, for example on the estates of Lord Gabor Bethlen, Chancellor and holder of one of the largest landed properties in Transylvania in the 1760s.[9]

Preceding the hesitant start of its potato campaign in the Austrian homelands, Maria Theresa's government issued a decree for Transylvania on 21 October 1767, ordering the local authorities to encourage the whole population, but especially those living in infertile mountain areas, to grow potatoes.[10] Although aware that there were hardly any potatoes as yet in Transylvania, Vienna ordered the development of the distillation of brandy from potatoes instead of grain in 1769, at the same time repeating the prohibition of grain distillation that in any case had been in force for 50 years. In 1770, Vienna at last provided arguments in favour of the potato and made suggestions as to how to make its use known. The arguments were that all kinds of grain fields were suitable for the potato, that the plant was very productive, weather-resistant, and a food as good as maize. This meant that people would have potatoes to consume and could release their grain for sale. The Transylvanian government sought to persuade not only the peasant population but also magnates, noblemen and high officials to plant potatoes. Bread and brandy could be made with and from them and the regional government should bring in people familiar with such kinds of processing to teach the methods. Such folk were to be found in the independently governed military border zones which formed the frontiers on the south of Hungary against the Turkish Empire. This last suggestion, however, was never put into practice.

The Transylvanian regional government took the matter seriously and immediately forwarded the first Viennese order to all cities and territorial units. The latter had different legal statuses but let us call them 'counties' here. The Transylvanian government then dealt with the matter continuously until 1815–17, that is for 50 years altogether. This included further ordinances of its own and the requirement that all the counties and cities should send yearly reports about potato cultivation to the regional government. The reports were commented on by the government in its replies. A random sample of the correspondence between the central and local authorities has survived. There was certainly direct communication between gentlemen and peasant farmers also on this matter, but almost no sources allow an insight into them. In a region with recurrent years of poor harvest, the regional government always had a real reason to propose the promotion of the potato as a remedial measure.

Working in close co-operation with the regional government, the first Agricultural Society (1769–72) in Transylvania regarded the promotion of the potato as one of its main tasks. The first meeting of the Society showed how unfamiliar the use of potatoes was in the region. The President, a lord, reported at that meeting that he and a county minister had succeeded in their experiments in producing potato-bread and spirits, samples of which they offered the members to taste. The spirit was approved but the bread was found too moist. Later, the Society gave support to the government regulations, and advertised a competition on questions of cultivation, storage and use of the potato. In 1771 the scientist and academic teacher, János Fridvalszky, presented a treatise on their use, especially emphasizing their value in fattening pigs. He proposed two types of bread made of a mixture of potatoes and cereal flour. The Society's work does not seem to have had much external influence. Even its suggestions that the local authorities should provide experts to teach the people how to make bread with potatoes could not be put into practice.[11]

Government officials themselves also tried to make the crop better known and esteemed. By sheer chance, at that time the regional civil government was headed, for a short time, by the military commander-in-chief who was, to judge by his name – O'Donel – an Irishman. His kitchen at least was able to demonstrate how to eat potatoes. An upper-class preparation of the tubers, served at one of his parties late in 1768, had been carefully noted.[12] The same kind of preparation in the summer of the same year at a party of a Hungarian general, where government officials were present, initiated a discussion of potatoes after the dinner, in which they were not set against grain, but the two plants, maize and potatoes, were compared. The usefulness of the potato was not questioned, but it was stated that peasants did not grow the potato very much and noblemen preferred maize.[13] Among the Hungarian lands, it was in Transylvania that the cultivation of maize had become firmly established already in the seventeenth century, and this crop was heavily used as a foodstuff by the lower classes in the eighteenth century.[14]

The regional government's argument in favour of the new plant was that potatoes would almost never fail when other food plants did. It repeatedly pointed out (from as early as 1769) that poor soil and less fertile areas were good enough for the potato, and that the plant would not take up field space because potatoes could be set among the maize. It encouraged noblemen to set a good example for the peasants, and also the local authorities, on their own estates. There is no record of such action, nor of any kind of a formal demonstration farm. Local officials were also asked to teach the people and get tubers for them to plant, from areas where some had been harvested previously. A formal description of how to grow and use the new plant was completed by the government only in 1795 for the local authorities. This was also published in the Transylvanian Calendar, the most widespread reading material after the Bible, in the following year.[15] The next piece of descriptive information, published in 1815, was still so much in demand that though 4,000 copies were distributed, several local authorities asked for more.

Over the decades, the local authorities' methods of development were by persuasion, announcements by the village drummer, and also in 1815 the repeated reading of the above-mentioned instruction to the people by parish notaries, schoolmasters and choir-masters. In the 1790s, some county authorities had already obtained seed-tubers for their villages and the county physician was commissioned to distribute them. The whole amount allowed was, for example, to enable the planting of 47 seed-holes, on average, in every village. But seed-tubers were generally provided first during the worst famine year of 1814, to be planted the following spring. At that time the regional government and the counties co-operated in food aid, of which a major aim was to ensure the potato harvest for the subsequent year. The government gave and lent money to the local authorities for the purchase of seed-tubers. The quantity aimed at was 50 seed-holes per family. Several local authorities now took more practical measures such as: assigning a field from the parish on which potato plantation could be concentrated; providing patches for potatoes for those without land; urging share-farming again in favour of the landless; sending officials to supervise the planting; and winning over noble farmers to supervise the entire operation. In the early nineteenth century, when authorities were already impatient with people opposing potatoes but complaining about famine, force was also used, i.e. peasants were formally beaten for their opposition. This was no longer necessary by 1815.

The excuses for opposition to or neglect of the central ordinances that the counties forwarded were: not enough agricultural land; poor quality land; cold climate; bad experiences of low yields, showing that potatoes were not a good crop; more profit from grain and maize than from potatoes; the peasants simply did not want it; and traditional old-style agriculture could not accommodate the potato. In some areas peasants stuck to the mistaken belief that potatoes spread the 'French disease' (syphilis). By 1814 there were no objections and everybody was eager to plant them.

There were only two potato varieties used in Transylvania in the eighteenth century – white and red. The welcome given to two new varieties (tender ones, good for soup, yellow in colour) shows that although the innovation had not as yet broken through, yet the prestige of the potato was rising. A gentleman farmer reported its arrival in a curious way. Samuel Gyarmathi, pioneer of Finno-Ugric linguistics, brought them back from his stay in Germany in 1795–97. In doing so, Gyarmathi did much more good for the nation than with his long 387-page book in which he proved the linguistic affinity of the Hungarian language with the Finno-Ugric languages (a new concept at that time, not unanimously welcomed at the beginning).[16]

Of six records of potato cultivation by the counties in 1769, only two were positive, but they reported the plant from the far away southern and northern areas. One showed a successful record for the following five decades but the other produced some negative years again later. Such fluctuation was often recorded from other counties as well. Already in the next year new counties joined the range of potato-growers. There was correspondence with 34 counties and 29 cities altogether during these decades, the highest survival rate of the sources being from 1774, 1782 and 1815. Of potato-growers in 18 counties in 1774, six reported none, six a few and six a relatively well-established level of cultivation. The proportions were similar in 1782–83 when, of 32 counties, 10 reported none and 22 some cultivation. Of the latter, 13 reported a few, two some, six several growers and one intensive cultivation in its mountain area only. At the same period, out of 20 cities, ten had no potatoes of their own, six had some and four a considerable harvest for the period. Behind the positive answers, there lay in most cases very small quantities (a few basketfuls) on a few farms or in solitary villages only. By the 1800s there was already a continuous regular cultivation in some areas. Peasants who had protested against the potato 20 years earlier now had potato harvests outdoing their grain harvests in the Carpathian areas. Successive poor harvests of grain and maize throughout the region from 1805 onwards, culminating in the disaster of 1814–17, definitely changed attitudes in favour of potatoes. Amongst the 25 surviving county reports from 1815, there are no more negatives. The reports state only 'good' (12), 'medium' (12) and 'poor for weather' (1) potato harvests. Of 15 cities, 12 had good, one a medium and two poor harvests.

Potatoes first appeared in vegetable gardens next to the dwelling houses, then spread to the fields, but at first only amongst the maize (1774). Later special fields, often specially cleared, were allocated for them outside the standard two- or three-field system (1814) and potatoes also appeared among the spring crops within the field system (1815). The first descriptive mention of potatoes as an independent field crop in connection with Transylvania was from 1788, but there is no way of knowing if it was an aspiration or an observation.[17]

The county where potatoes first became generally grown by peasant farmers reported their use in 1774 as eaten with meat, eaten with butter, and baked in ashes. Bread-making and distilling were not mentioned, but pigs were fattened on boiled potatoes. In this county potatoes were already on sale in weekly markets. Potatoes were then recorded, in 1815, as being mixed into wheaten bread and for small-scale distilling on peasant farms. In the earlier period of the innovation process it often happened that gentlemen were more interested in growing a few potatoes than peasant farmers, and also that people of the latter rank only considered the crop as a delicacy. The fact that several counties were in need of seed-tubers in 1815 indicates that on many farms and even in many villages potato cultivation had not started previously. After 1815–17, cultivation was not interrupted any more. We know also, however, that on one of the leading 'improving' estates in Transylvania potato cultivation was introduced only with modernization in the 1820s.[18] Potatoes certainly reached an established stage in the 1820s in the region so that everybody could have his own harvest for food at least. If that process was completed by 1830, the time-span of innovation from 1760 is 70 years. The fact that potatoes never became too important in Transylvania raises a different question. This was because maize had taken the place that potatoes might have occupied had there been no traditional use of maize in the region.

Before turning to Hungary, we should go back to the independently administered frontiers under military government in the south of the kingdom. They had a peasant population, holding privileges for performing military service in case of need. They were mostly living in villages made up of new settlers who came after the end of the Turkish occupation and were less bound by traditional agriculture in these places. They were not only held up to neighbouring regions from 1770 onwards as examples of people experienced in the use of the potato, but it was here that potatoes first appeared in agricultural production statistics. In 1800–01 they were included together with millet, buckwheat and leguminous plants. In 1818 potatoes alone took up 3.13 per cent of the arable land which still included 40.45 per cent fallow.[19] In Transylvania, there was also a local frontier military organization, but joined by some scattered peasant families only. The fact that these were also mentioned early (1795) as experts in the growing and use of the potato indicates that there must have been successful efforts by the Vienna administration to promote the crop in these special military zones, though direct evidence for this has not yet turned up.

Diverse spontaneous initiatives in Hungary

In Hungary itself, cultivation of the potato occurred first in 1745. This was a regular practice in one special village only. It is only in the 1760s that further reports of the potato crop began, but then in several parts of the country and in different settings.[20] The 1765, 1768, 1769 data include six crown estates in four widely separated regions. All but one were in the east, on the edge of the lowland area where it bordered the mountains, in one case running into the north-east Carpathians. Only one estate was clearly situated in a lowland area. This was in the west of the country, near to Lower Austria.

In a different setting, potatoes turned up in the 1760s amongst the inhabitants of the highest mountain areas of the north Carpathians, in an area with very small-scale tillage. Rural ministers, county officials and urban intelligentsia supported the potato positively, and peasants, though hesitant at first, adopted them very quickly. In 1787 potatoes were already reported there as the main food of the region.[21] The early spread covered a larger area here, including the northern, Polish side of the Carpathians.[22] On the Hungarian side, the region was described in the 1800s as one where, in all the fields which would have lain fallow earlier, potatoes were now grown; they were also grown in every garden and on every patch where nothing else would grow.[23] Cultivation went ahead without interruption and this became the main production area in historical Hungary up to 1918. This was also the region where human consumption of potatoes was always highest.

In the interior of the country, a village with regular potato fields was still a curiosity in the 1760s. This could only happen where there were a few German settlers. After its liberation, the previous Turkish province in central Hungary was a devastated land. Colonization started in the late seventeenth and continued during the eighteenth centuries. The settlers came from the north and west of Hungary and also from abroad, mainly from southern German provinces. German settlers from different areas intermingled in their new villages in Hungary. In most of their areas of origin potatoes had not yet become a necessity by the time they left. Hundreds of such villages came into being. Two of them are known as early potato-growers, one of them already in 1745 (settled in 1739), where potatoes were grown on fields used continuously for them, next to the grain fields of the village.[24] Production there never stopped. The other village, alongside a city, figured in a play in that city in 1768, because of its surprising potato fields.[25] Both villages were situated in the mountain area of Transdanubia. Some of the settlers in these places probably originated from the innovation centre area of the Palatinate, and from the area of Alsace.[26]

In the 1770s–80s and up to the mid-1790s, potato cultivation appeared in other counties but always only in a few villages. Some potatoes appeared, but rather exceptionally, in city markets. The newly developing academic agricultural writing both in Latin and Hungarian, and the translated popular agricultural literature, all discussed the new crop; medical doctors supported it of their own initiative in their counties and travellers planned to bring back tubers from Germany. But Debrecen, the largest and most important agricultural centre on the Great Plain, was still not making use of potatoes by the mid-1790s. The late-1790s, however, brought the beginning of agricultural improvement in the country. A few estates gave up fallowing and the whole three-field-system, introducing sown grass fodder, regular manuring and the more frequent use of wage labour instead of serfs. The reorganized estates all took up the potato as well and encouraged peasants in their area by distributing seed-tubers. This was still necessary even around the capital Pest-Buda in this decade. From 1797 there was an agricultural college in the country, attached to the large estate of the magnate, who was the pioneer in improvements. Potatoes were grown on its demonstration farm where estate stewards and prospective managers had their training.

The growing literature on agriculture, including special periodicals from 1796, was also aimed at estate managers and did not fail to encourage the new crop. But popular calendars, with more chance of reaching the villages, also agitated for the potato from 1796 onwards. However in 1814, when a qualified agricultural expert started a new agricultural journal, it was still found necessary to encourage the potato as a crop. The editor set this task as one of the main aims of the journal. The journal received and printed correspondence, mainly for gentlemen farmers on small estates. They still discussed questions such as whether potatoes should be set in soil prepared by the spade only or also in plough-land; whether it was bad for the three-field system when potatoes were grown there instead of fallowing, and the like. The general improvements in agriculture advanced very slowly. Another important topic was how to use the crop as food, especially as bread. This was also stimulated by a series of poor grain harvests in the country in 1815–17. On the tables of well-to-do burghers and noblemen in the capital city, bread with potato flour in it was still a novelty, but potatoes now began to appear in the city markets. In 1816–18 a housewife, daughter of a county physician, published three booklets of potato recipes for educational purposes. She put together a full 100 recipes, partly evidently from practice, partly newly invented. She used potatoes in all possible upper-class and peasant dishes and distributed the work to all the villages of her county.[27] Landowners at that time let ground for share-farming to their peasants on the condition that they grew some potatoes there. Contemporaries felt the 1815–17 famine years had been the breakthrough period for the potato. Neither nobles nor peasants avoided them any longer thereafter. Arguments such as that foreign potatoes were no good for Hungarians ceased, but it was not until 1830 that, outside gardens, potatoes became a regular field crop everywhere except for some areas of the Great Plain. On the large estates, based on potatoes and modernized distilling equipment, a distilling industry developed in the 1830s. When statistics begin for both regions in 1858, potatoes took up 2.38 per cent of the arable area in Hungary and 0.07 per cent only in Transylvania.[28]

The time-span of the innovation

The examples of the introduction of potatoes into larger regions as whole units, touched on and discussed above, have shown that the innovation process took longer where it started earlier, as in Germany in the mid-seventeenth century, but was shorter where it started in the eighteenth century. The tendency towards such differences is well known for the development of other phenomena as well. I am fully aware that to work out the starting points and the periods of completion of innovation in any reconstruction is not easy, and that any choice made about such points in time can be questioned. But I also think that the rough estimates for different regions can be compared. In the case of the potato in Sweden, Poland and Austria in the eighteenth century, the innovation process took about 90 years, which means it was completed in the third generation's lifetime. It was the same in Hungary, between 1745 and 1830. Here the innovation was mainly based on private initiatives and although helped by the ideas of the agricultural improvers, it remained, overall, very much a spontaneous process. Transylvania was the most traditional, or we can say backward, region of all those discussed here in its agriculture in the eighteenth century. It is enough to say that even the general introduction of the fallowing three-field-system was no more than an aspiration at that time, as the two-field variation (one sown and the other in fallow) still predominated in several areas. There was also the problem that maize had already taken up the fields where potatoes could be grown. In this region, there was a 50-year long intensive government campaign in support of the potato. We have seen how few means the government and the local authorities had to help their intention, especially in a region with illiterate lower classes. The campaign cannot be said to have been very efficient; but neither was it unsuccessful, for it resulted in a 70-year long time-span of innovation. This was also completed in the third generation's lifetime but was still two decades quicker than in other places where the processes had begun in the eighteenth century. It is very likely that without such a campaign the process would have taken a significantly longer time in this particular case.

Notes

1. Kowalska-Lewicka, 1986, p. 90.
2. Berg, 1971, pp. 159–60.
3. Teuteberg and Wiegelmann, 1986, p. 104.
4. Sandgruber, 1982, p. 179.
5. Berg, 1971.
6. For details of the whole process see Teuteberg and Wiegelmann, 1986.
7. For details see Sandgruber, 1982.
8. Kowalska-Lewicka, 1986; Jostowa, 1954. On the calendars, see Baranowski, 1960, p. 21, 34–5.
9. Trócsányi, 1986, p. 1043.
10. If not stated otherwise, the picture of the development in Transylvania is based on the following primary source, where further data are also given: Karlovszky, 1896; Kósa, 1980 includes Transylvania as well.
11. On the society's activities see Kárffy, 1898.
12. Trócsányi, 1986, p. 1043.
13. Halmágyi, 1906, p. 402.
14. Balassa, 1960.
15. *Erdélyi . . .*, 1796.
16. An anonymous correspondent from the Transylvanian city of Kolozsvár in the journal *Nemzeti Gazda*, 1814, vol. II, pp. 109–12.
17. Benkő, 1778, p. 110, quoted by Kósa, 1980, p. 59.
18. Csetri, 1957, pp. 166, 173–4.
19. Benda, 1973, pp. 360–62, 329.
20. For details from the 1760s onwards see the monograph by Kósa, 1980, pp. 17–75.
21. Marczali, 1887, p. 359.
22. Kowalska-Lewicka, 1986, p. 90.; Jostowa, 1954, p. 709.
23. Melczer, 1918, p. 13.
24. Fülöp, 1985, on the village (Vértes) kozma.
25. The village Márkó next to Veszprém city (Kósa, 1980, p. 19).
26. In the group of villages to which Vérteskozma belongs, there were people from Alsace amongst the settlers, see Fülöp, 1985. In the case of Márkó, the majority of the inhabitants came from the area of Mainz. Not here, but in the surrounding villages, the Rhein-Franconian dialect prevailed during the linguistic levelling. Bakonyi, 1940; Hutterer, 1975, p. 23.
27. Rátz, 1816–18.
28. Benda, 1973, p. 232.

Bibliography

Bakonyi, János, *Márkó telepítése és nyelvjárása* [The settlement and dialect of the village of Márkó], Budapest, 1940.

Balassa, Iván, *A magyar kukorica* [Maize in Hungary], Budapest, 1960.

Baranowski, Bohdan, *Poczatki i rozpowszechnienie uprawy ziemniaków za ziemiach

Środkowej Polski [The beginnings and spread of potato cultivation in Central Poland], Łódz, 1960.

Benda, Gyula, Statisztikai adatok a magyar mezőgazdaság történetéhez 1767–1867. [Statistical data on the history of Hungarian agriculture 1767–1867], Budapest, 1973.

Benkő, József, Transilvania sive Magnus Transilvaniae Principatus olim Dacia Mediterrana dictus, Vindobona, 1778.

Berg, Gösta, 'Die Kartoffel und die Rübe', Ethnologia Scandinavica, 1, 1971, pp. 158–65.

Csetri, Elek, 'Kelemen Benjámin, a haladó gazda' [Benjámin Kelemen, an improvement agriculturist], in Emlékkönyv Kelemen Lajos születésének nyolcvanadik évfordulójára, Kolozsvár, Bukarest, 1957, pp. 157–78.

Denecke, Dietrich, 'Innovation and Diffusion of the Potato in Central Europe in the Seventeenth and Eighteenth Centuries', in R.H. Buchanan, R.A. Butlin, D. McCourt (eds) Fields, Farms and Settlement in Europe, Belfast, 1976, pp. 60–79.

Erdélyi Házi és Uti, Uj és Ó Kalendáriom [Transylvanian Calendar], Kolozsvár, 1796.

Fülöp, Éva, 'Burgonyatermesztés egy dunántuli német telepes faluban 1745-ben' [Potato production in a new German settlement in Transdanubia Hungary], Ethnographia 96, 1985, pp. 336–40.

Halmágyi, István, Naplói és iratai 1752–1785 [Memoirs and other writings 1752–1785], ed. by Lajos Szádeczky, Monumenta Hungariae Historica IV, Budapest, 1906.

Hutterer, Claus Jürgen, 'Die deutsche Volksgruppe in Ungarn', Beiträge zur Volkskunde der Ungarndeutschen, 1, 1975, pp. 11–36.

Jostowa, Wanda, 'Tradycyjne pożywienie ludności Podhala' [Traditional food and foodways in Poland], Lud 41, 1954, pp. 703–29.

Karlovszky, Endre, K., 'A burgonya meghonosodása Erdélyben' [The introduction of the potato in Transylvania], Magyar Gazdaságtörténeti Szemle, 3, 1896, pp. 293–321.

Kárrfy, Ödön, 'Az első erdélyi Földművelő Egyesület működése 1769–1772' [The first Agricultural Society in Transylvania 1769–1772], Magyar Gazdaságtörténeti Szemle, 5, 1898, pp. 287–319.

Kósa, László, A burgonya Magyarországon [The potato in Hungary], Budapest, 1980.

Kowalska-Lewicka, Anna, 'The Potato and the Polish Kitchen', in Alexander Fenton and Eszter Kisbán (eds), Food in Change, Edinburgh, 1986, pp. 90–94.

Marczali, Henrik, 'Inség 1785–1790' [Famine 1785–1790], Budapesti Szemle, 52, 1887, pp. 344–71.

Melczer, Jakab, 'Geographiai, Historiai és Statisticai Tudósítások Szepes Vármegyéből' [Geographical, historical and statistical reports from County Szepes], Tudományos Gyűjtemény, 2, 1818, XII, pp. 3–26.

Ottenjan, Helmut and Ziessow, Karl-Heinz, Die Kartoffel. Geschichte und Zukunft einer Kulturpflanze, Cloppenburg, 1992.

Rátz, Zsuzsanna, Buza szükségben felsegéllő Jegyzések [Advice when wheat is scarce], vol. 1–3, Miskolc, 1816–18.

Sandgruber, Roman, 'Die Einführung der Kartoffel in Österreich. Sozialgeschichtliche und volkskundliche Interpretation', in Ernst Hinrichs and

Günter Wiegelmann (eds), *Sozialer und kultureller Wandel in der ländlichen Welt des 18. Jahrhunderts*, Wolfenbüttel, 1982, pp. 163–94.

Teuteberg, Hans Jürgen and Wiegelmann, Günter, 'Einführung und Nutzung der Kartoffel in Deutschland', in Hans Jürgen Teuteberg and Günter Wiegelmann, *Unsere tägliche Kost. Geschichte und regionale Prägung*, Münster, 1986, pp. 93–134.

Trócsányi, Zsolt, 'Gazdaság és társadalom 1771–1830' [Economy and society 1771–1830], in Béla Köpeczi (ed.), *Erdély története* [History of Transylvania], Budapest, 1986, vol. II. pp. 1039–67.

13 Sugar versus saccharin: sweetener policy before World War I[1]

Christoph Maria Merki

Since the time of its introduction in Europe, sugar has always been a highly political commodity. The same can be said of its rival saccharin, the oldest synthetic sweetener. Accidentally discovered in 1878, saccharin was first introduced commercially nine years later in Germany. Though scientists and, as a result, public health officers more or less unanimously declared it to be non-toxic, its free trade was soon forbidden in most European countries, and the consumption of saccharin became limited to those who had to avoid sugar for reasons of health. Because saccharin remained available on grey and black markets, several countries on the continent decided to co-ordinate the suppression of saccharin internationally. Eight of them signed a corresponding convention just before the war, in April 1914.

This chapter will examine the anti-saccharin policy before World War I, and especially the influence of the European sugar-beet industry on this policy. In order to be able to understand the sweetener legislation at all, it is necessary to look first at the changes in the consumption of both sugar and saccharin over the long term.

The story of sugar (i.e. sucrose) has always been adventurous, and it is now passing through a very exciting phase. Known in Europe since the turn of the millenium, sugar served first as a medicine, before it came into vogue as a spice in the gentleman's cuisine, where it began to displace the usual honey. As sweetener for the new colonial beverages (tea, coffee and chocolate), as well as a chief ingredient in sweet things like lemonade and ice-cream, sugar was appreciated as a scarce luxury.

At that time sugar developed into a major status symbol, which played an important role in the process of cultural distinction during the fifteenth, sixteenth, seventeenth and eighteenth centuries.[2] By indulging themselves in this luxurious pleasure, courtly circles made themselves stand out from the common people. The courtiers prepared the way for larger consumption, encouraging the other social classes to try the same sweet delight. With the crisis of the absolutist society, courtly show began to lose its importance. The more the prestige of sugar faded, the more important it turned out to be for nutrition.[3] It kept its exclusivity until the second half of the nineteenth century, when domestic beet sugar began to compete with colonial cane sugar and, as a consequence, the price of sugar fell. Owing to its great functional flexibility, sugar was destined to become a pacemaker of modern nutrition. In this context, 'modern' refers essentially to two developments: first, the increasing tendency of people to eat outside the home,[4] and secondly, their increasing consumption of industrially produced foods like jam or chocolate. Around the year 1500, per capita consumption of sugar in Europe averaged two ounces per annum;[5] today twice as much is used – not per annum, but per day.

In the developed countries[6] sugar reached saturation point in the 1960s and 1970s. Since then consumption has stagnated at this high level but in some countries has even declined. Today we witness the dramatic end of this long socio-cultural *Absinkprozess*[7]: the highly regarded medicine has turned into a common, sometimes even despised food, which is permanently attacked by the media, consumer organizations and dentists.[8] Sugar does not heal any longer, it is – in a complete reversal of the original views – accused of causing illness. The list of diseases it is supposed to cause becomes longer every day. The French sociologist Fischler recently diagnosed a general 'saccharophobia'.[9] Nothing better illustrates sugar's loss of image than the positive connotations of the expression 'sugar free', which has been used for promoting sweets without sucrose for a decade now.

On the other hand, synthetic sweeteners[10] have undergone the opposite development. At the beginning of our century the coal-tar product saccharin achieved great success in the areas in which sugar had retained its luxury image – thus rather in the countryside than in the towns, and rather in the eastern parts of the continent than in the western ones. Having risen in social status, today saccharin and its numerous successors are no longer consumed *in spite of* having no caloric value, but *because* they have none, which means by affluent people who want to reduce their energy intake without being forced to renounce sweet foods in general. The diet-foods industry is getting increasingly fat on consumers' never-ending quest to slim down.

The sweetness of saccharin, which can be detected at a dilution of one part in 100,000, was discovered accidentally in 1878 by Constantin Fahlberg, a German expert on sugar chemistry who worked temporarily at Johns Hopkins University in Baltimore (USA). There, under the tutelage of Professor Ira Remsen, he searched for a new dye-stuff based on the oxidation of toluenesulfonamide.[11] While German literature attributes the discovery of saccharin to Fahlberg alone or to Fahlberg and Remsen, the American literature credits the discovery to Remsen alone or to Remsen and Fahlberg. Perhaps the discovery of saccharin was due to both of them, but the recognition of the economic possibilities of the discovery and their technical development and industrial exploitation was due to Fahlberg alone.

Nine years later, having improved the method of production, which starts from toluene, Fahlberg introduced saccharin commercially in Germany. Decorated with several awards it had won at international exhibitions, the pioneer of non-nutritive sweeteners achieved great success as a sugar substitute for diabetics. After an abortive attempt to introduce it as an additive in the dextrose industry, saccharin came into use as a sweetening agent in other food-processing industries, for example in the production of lemonade and of special beers, which had the peculiarity of fermenting when sweetened with sugar. Initially saccharin was quite expensive but improved processes, greater volume of use and competition combined to bring the price steadily down. Until 1892, the worldwide pioneer, Fahlberg-List & Co., had no competitor. The firms which later entered this small, specialized market – for example, Bayer (Germany), Sandoz (Switzerland), Monsanto (USA) – manufactured saccharin normally as one of several products of their quickly expanding new pharmaceutical divisions.

Around the turn of the century, saccharin became a substitute for those people who could not afford sugar: its price had fallen below 10 per cent of its original level, and there was an upward trend in sugar prices at the same time. Housewives provided themselves by the penny-worth with the cheap pills, which helped them to sweeten their bitter lives. Saccharin was particularly successful in those areas in which sugar had retained its luxury image. Indeed, sugar had not yet lost its luxury touch completely at that time. In Germany, its income elasticity of demand was still greater than one.

Shortly before saccharin was banned in 1902, its consumption reached a first peak. As Table 13.1 demonstrates, nearly 200 tons were consumed in Germany, which was no less than 10 per cent of the total German sugar consumption (on an equivalent sweetness basis).[12] However, sugar consumption itself was increasing too, and the manufacturers of saccharin did not tire of pretending that their product did not replace sugar, but only complemented it: nobody who was able to afford sugar would prefer saccharin, they said.[13]

From a social history point of view, saccharin can be considered a late example of the substitutes or surrogates that spread in the nineteenth century, after the barriers between classes had fallen and the imitation of the representative forms of cultural behaviour was restricted only by financial considerations.[14] Instead of pure coffee one had chicory, instead

Table 13.1 Saccharin consumption in Germany 1888–1900.

Year	Saccharin consumption in metric tons (sweetening power 550) (tonnes)	Saccharin consumption in metric tons of sugar equivalent (tonnes)	Saccharin consumption as percentage of sugar consumption (%)
1888	0.15	83	0.02
1890	0.8	440	
1892	1.6	880	0.17
1894	2.3	1,265	
1896	5.7	3,135	0.52
1898/99	32.2	17,710	2.54
1900/01	118.9	65,392	9.17

Source: Merki, 1991, p. 71.

of butter the so-called 'economical butter', margarine, instead of sugar, saccharin. Before the time of saccharin, the same purpose was served by cheap beet syrup, which was an undesirable by-product of sugar production. It goes without saying that the substitute was rather abhorred than adored by those who were not dependent on it. Those who had become acquainted with the original and were then forced to be content with the surrogate judged this restriction as an insult to their good taste. That is why some servants formed a union whose members were required never to take a job in a house where they got only saccharin.[15] Well-refined sugar was the prestigious taste that all other sweeteners had to try to imitate.

The modifications in the social assessment of both sweeteners, sugar and saccharin, are complicated processes, which not only complement and influence each other, but also overlap and intersect, both spatially and in time as well as with respect to social class. Thus, in the world depression at the end of the 1920s, saccharin made a comeback as the 'sugar of the poor'.[16] At the same time, however, when there were the first, timid beginnings of an affluent society, saccharin was discovered as an alternative for the foodstuff sugar, an alternative with which it should be possible to avoid *unerwünschte Körpergewichtszunahmen* (unwanted increases in body weight).[17] While sugar was a good indicator of wealth in the industrialized countries until the end of the nineteenth century, during World War II (and in the countries of eastern Europe, for example, even later), saccharin and the people who had to eat it were branded with the stigma of poverty. Since then the relationship between the two sweetening agents has reversed.

The politics of sugar

The mutual relation between sugar and saccharin is not only interesting to social history; the two substances are also intimately connected with each other in an economic and political way, and the interaction that results from this association is much more important than the restricted conflict between a product of the chemical industry and one of agriculture might appear to be. There is, in my opinion, no better object than saccharin with which to analyse and illustrate the politico-economic power held by the European beet sugar industry before its breakdown in World War I. However, the sweetener legislation could be realized only because the state took a very active role.[18] In particular, the Ministry of Finance cared about the well-being of the sugar industry and of the proceeds of the sugar tax, which grew in importance after several reforms and constituted 5 per cent to 10 per cent of all revenues of the Kaiserreich at the beginning of the twentieth century.[19] The most important fact motivating the state to act in compliance with the beet sugar industry's wishes was that saccharin did not yield tax revenue but threatened the very elaborate system of sugar taxation. In Imperial Germany the links between the fiscal system and the industry were so close that they gave rise to the malicious saying '*Preussisch-deutscher Zuckerrübenstaat*' (Prussian-German Sugar Beet State).

Both in Germany and in Austria-Hungary there was not only a sweet affinity between the bureaucracy and the industry. The political influence of the industry was also due to the great economic weight it had – something that has not been acknowledged by economic history so far. By the close of the century sugar was the most valuable export, earning more than iron, steel or chemicals, both in Germany and Austria-Hungary. Sugar production was a progressive rural industry with a heavy reliance upon the integration of advanced agricultural methods and rationalized, highly capitalized processing.[20] Werner Sombart – perhaps not totally unprejudiced, being the son of a sugar entrepreneur – equated the role of the sugar industry in the capitalistic development of Germany with that of the textile industry in Great Britain.[21] In any case, the connection between field and factory, which took effect in the 'Saccharin Question', was not a fragile political construction, but the result of a deep-rooted relationship.

Sweetener policy in the era of the Emperor William II led to a first law in 1898 and to a second in 1902, which was valid till 1916. While the law of 1898 limited the use of saccharin in the food industry, the law of 1902 prohibited the consumption of saccharin totally. Only persons who had to avoid sugar for reasons of health and who could prove this by documentary evidence were allowed to buy saccharin at the pharmacy and even then only in small quantities. Fahlberg, List & Co., the firm which had founded the sweetener industry, was allowed to take charge of the supply to the pharmacies; the five other manufacturers, who had to stop their production, recovered damages for the loss of earnings.

The law of 1902 signified a massive intervention in the freedom of trade, which was possibly unique in its rigour for the Kaiserreich, even if it is easy to rank it among other related interventions. Under the spell of the *Gründerkrise* of 1873 and of the recession afterwards, the state had recovered many of its old functions and acquired many new ones. After a short era of liberalism, protectionism achieved great triumphs, for example, the establishment of tariffs on imported grain (1879), or the preferential treatment of the schnaps industry (*Branntweinindustrie*) by way of the method of taxation.[22]

There is no doubt that the laws of 1898 and 1902 were due to a certain extent to considerations of public health as well, to an attempt, for example, to protect consumers from adulteration of food. But in the foreground of the discussion were always motives related to economic or fiscal policy, something that Graf Posadowsky, the Prussian Minister of the Interior, admitted frankly. In an internal memorandum of March 1898, he said that to justify the Saccharin Amendment, the interests of the Nahrungsmittelpolizei (public food quality control) were of secondary importance in comparison with the interests of the Treasury and of the sugar industry.[23]

In 1902, when the second saccharin law was enacted in Germany, sugar policy even figured directly in sweetener policy. The German sugar industry demanded a package deal: it linked its consent to the Brussels Convention with the *Rezeptpflicht* of saccharin (availability only by prescription). The Brussels Convention, which dismantled export subsidies, forced the German sugar industry to orient itself more to its domestic market.[24] After the treaty was signed, a conservative member of the Reichstag said that the saccharin law was the only thing he could take home to his constituents.[25] When formulating and putting through its proposals, the sugar industry could rely not only on its own association, founded already in 1841,[26] but also on other industrial and agrarian organizations, such as the mighty Central League of German Industry; it could also count on numerous supporters in parliament, especially among the National Liberal Party.[27]

A situation comparable to the German one existed in the Danubian Monarchy, where an innovative but regionally unevenly distributed sugar industry advanced the modernization of agriculture, and where the fiscal system also intervened in the sugar market with a tax on consumption and a well-contrived system of subsidies. Because there was no autonomous sweetener industry, the prohibition of import and consumption of saccharin – desired by the sugar industry – was not really opposed. At most, resistance to a radical prohibition was offered by the departmental bureaucracy itself, especially by the liberal-minded Ministry of the Interior.

After saccharin had established itself as a popular sugar substitute in northern Bohemia within a few months, the government of Cisleithania[28] reacted quickly. On 20 April 1898, it published four decrees which submitted the artificial sweetener to the *Rezeptpflicht*. Unlike in Germany, sugar had kept the character of a luxury food in many regions of Austria. Thus, the Saccharin Question remained of topical interest. Not only were there many consumers who did not accept the four decrees, but also several courts refused to do so.[29]

When combined with some other food products, saccharin could threaten sugar only as a luxury food (*Genussmittel*), but not as a food of nutritive value (*Nahrungsmittel*). Realizing this, the German sugar industry tried to convince its customers in a huge promotion campaign[30] that its product was an indispensable food and not worthless stuff – like the *Gaumenkitzel* (palate-tickler) saccharin. But the sugar industry did not realize that with this campaign it contradicted the marketing strategy of its own cartel. Instead of reducing prices and changing the image of sugar to a real *Volksnahrungsmittel* (food of the people), the industry dumped its sugar on the international market at lower-than-prevailing prices but kept the domestic price high. The taxation policy of the German government – and other governments – was contradictory too, because as soon as sugar became a common food, the sugar tax lost its legitimacy as *Luxusabgabe* (luxury tax). But the revenue would not give up earnings that were more lucrative than ever on the eve of the war.

Primarily because these contradictions became manifest thanks to the success of saccharin, saccharin became a 'dangerous substance' and the 'most important enemy'[31] of the sugar industry, although in reality the industry was never seriously threatened by it. This was – in my opinion – the basic motive of the sweetener legislation: to safeguard a price policy that discriminated against the domestic consumer, a policy that was established by the sugar industry and supported by the revenue. At the risk of overstatement, one could say that the prohibition of saccharin was due to protectionism on the one hand and to the need for money for armaments (particularly for the Kaiser's pet naval project) on the other hand.

However, it is doubtful whether the state was among the winners from the sweetener legislation. It cannot be proved that the profits from the sugar tax rose as a result of the prohibition. Moreover, in addition to the compensation the state had to pay to the chemical industry, there was resistance by consumers in the form of illegal consumption.

The illicit trade in saccharin

In the areas in which sugar had retained its aura of luxury, even a Draconian law could not manage to change saccharin back into a mere dietary food. In spite of smuggling and secret manufacturing, the artificial sweetener continued to be a desired surrogate, available on grey and black markets. The smugglers settled in Switzerland, where the consumption of saccharin was allowed, and sold the 'hot stuff' underground to the east, following the European welfare gradient. As the stronghold of the smugglers, Zurich gave shelter – according to the police – to at least 1,000 professional black-market dealers in 1912. Their originality knew no frontiers. Saccharin was smuggled as a liquid in bottles of champagne, as a powder in tyres, and *en bloc* in suitcases with a false bottom or in special waistcoats. The method of a chiefly Austrian gang was simply Kafkaesque: they dissolved the saccharin with wax in ether, and then formed it into candles which they sent to Einsiedeln, a famous centre of pilgrimage in Switzerland; there the candles were consecrated and sent to Vienna, to a shop for devotional articles that had been set up especially for that purpose; there the candles were immersed in a solution of caustic soda, from which the saccharin could be separated with hydrochloric acid.

At the suggestion of the sugar industry, the police formed special squads like the Zentralevidenzstelle für den illegalen Saccharinverkehr in Vienna which, however, did not manage to get the smuggling under control. On the contrary, the severe repression contributed a great deal to the fact that professional organizations took shape on the illegal market. In 1913, 950 persons were convicted of having offended against the German saccharin law. Most of them were Austrians, caught on the way from Switzerland across Germany to Austria-Hungary.[32] Some of them were popular heroes at home, because there saccharin smuggling was often supported by public opinion. In Bischofsreut, at the German-Czech border, I found a chapel which had been built in honour of 'The Saccharin Saint of Bischofsreut'. The Saint was a wooden statue, in which the residents of this little village hid their saccharin when customs officers made their raids. In fact, resistance to the interventions of the state in the area of luxuries has a long tradition; such interventions have always been a cause of riots, protest, and smuggling.[33]

In Switzerland saccharin was not only easy to obtain, but the international sweetener industry also had its seat there. As early as the 1890s the chemical factories of Basle had included saccharin among their products and, with the repressive laws in the surrounding countries, Switzerland grew in importance as a centre of the sweetener industry. In 1904 Swiss producers, whose foreign trade suffered from the prohibitions in the main marketing areas, formed a cartel, from which the International Sweetener Syndicate (Internationales Süßstoff-Syndikat) resulted five years later. It divided up the markets that were left after the restrictions.[34]

Efforts to control the sweetener market internationally in order to bring smuggling to an end started some time around 1907, first at a transnational level, then at an inter-governmental one. After a highly informal meeting in Brussels, which was dominated by the deputies of the sugar-beet industries, the French government organized an official conference in Paris in 1909. The driving force behind this project was not France, but Tsarist Russia, a country with a high sugar tax and a low consumption level, which was the worst affected by the smuggling of saccharin. Fearing coercive measures by its beet-sugar producing neighbours, even Switzerland was compelled to join the conference. After a second conference in 1913, on 16 April 1914, eight continental countries[35] signed the International Convention for the Regulation of Saccharin, an agreement which would have forced them to prohibit saccharin in food-processing industries and to control the trade of artificial sweeteners with special care.

Even though the eight countries mentioned above were not able to ratify it before the war, this convention represents a supranational intervention in the freedom of trade that is perhaps unique for this time and that can be best compared with the Opium Convention of 1912, which recommended similar controls. But while the international crusade against opium was understandable from a socio-medical point of view, artificial sweeteners were persecuted – as we have seen – almost exclusively for politico-economic reasons.

The breakdown of regulation

In the course of the last hundred years saccharin has been most widely used – at least on the European continent – neither during its pioneer time (as 'the sugar of the poor') nor in the last few decades (as a 'sweet alternative for the preservation of health'), but during and shortly after World Wars I and II, when it was consumed in large quantities because of sugar shortages. In most European countries, the repressive laws against saccharin were lifted in the middle of the war – in Germany at the end of 1916. During the first part of the war, sugar was available in plenty, because continental countries had the possibility of falling back on the sugar they had exported in pre-war times. The authorities tried to allow saccharin only for special uses, which meant only for uses in which sugar had no nourishing function. Thus, saccharin was allowed in place of sugar in a café, but not in a public soup kitchen.

The raw material for the production of saccharin is toluene, a hydrocarbon which is also used for the production of TNT, a military explosive. During the second half of the war, therefore, not only was sugar scarce but also its substitute, saccharin. In June 1917 when the state-run Sweetener Monopoly of Austria demanded five tons of toluene, the War Office did not want to deliver it, because – as they said – 'these five tons would be enough for the production of 26,000 shells'. To defuse this situation, the German Food Department switched from saccharin to dulcin, another sweetener. But this sweetener was not totally harmless, and two children who took too much of it died a sweet, but certainly not honourable, death for their fatherland.

During the 1920s neither Germany nor Austria returned to the prohibitive laws of the pre-war time, due to a basic change in socio-economic circumstances. The sugar industry was occupied with itself, digesting the setback caused by the war; the tax system was no longer annoyed by an excessive consumption of non-nutritive sweeteners because it received its share of the profits of the sweetener industry (e.g. in Germany), or was interested in keeping sugar imports low for monetary reasons (e.g. in the Republic of Austria). Lastly, in the 1920s saccharin did not really compete with sugar, because sugar had become firmly established as a common food.[36]

Conclusion

When Constantin Fahlberg presented saccharin to the public, its sweetening power astounded doctors, chemists, and physiologists. Within a few years, nearly all experts agreed that saccharin in the normally used quantities was 'really remarkably harmless'.[37] Medical-toxicological reservations about saccharin therefore played only a small role in the formation of sweetener policy until the second half of our century, and that is why they are ignored in this article.[38] That saccharin came under the suspicion of being carcinogenic in 1977 has much less to do with new toxicological findings than with an increasing feeling of general insecurity in view of changing nutrition. The perception of such risks caused by civilization is primarily culturally conditioned, and that saccharin has probably been better studied epidemiologically than any other substance (except tobacco) is – considering its possible harmfulness – paradoxical. Apart from such toxicological considerations, the dietetic desirability of the substitution of aspartame, cyclamate, saccharin or acesulfame-K for sugar will remain controversial. While the use of such non-nutritive sweeteners is accepted by members of the affluent society keen to look slim, adherents of raw or 'natural' food refuse such a technical solution of their sweet problem: they swear by honey (*retour à la nature*), prefer brown and hardly refined raw sugar (which from a nutritional point of view has just the same value as the white variety), or preach bitter abstinence.

Notes

1. This chapter is based on a dissertation, accepted by the University of Berne in February 1991 (C. Merki, *Ein Jahrhundert Zucker gegen Saccharin. Die künstlichen Süßstoffe im Spannungsfeld von Wirtschaft, Staat und Gesellschaft*, (448 pp.)) A shortened version of this dissertation will be published soon (*Zucker gegen Saccharin. Zur Geschichte der künstlichen Süßstoffe*, Frankfurt/ New York, Campus). Although the role of synthetic sweeteners is becoming more and more important to the food industry, there has been little or no recognition of the long history of these sweeteners. Recommended for a first survey are some older handbook-articles, for example A. Hempel, 'Benzoesäuresulfinid', in F. Ullmann (ed.), *Enzyklopädie der technischen Chemie*, Berlin/Vienna, Urban & Schwarzenberg, 1915, vol. 2, pp. 346–59; and W. Lange, 'Süßstoffe', in K. von Buchka (ed.), *Das Lebensmittelgewerbe*, Leipzig, Akademische Verlagsgesellschaft m.b.H., 1919, vol. 4, pp. 138–228.
2. This is demonstrated by G. Wiegelmann ('Zucker and Süßwaren im Zivilisationsprozess der Neuzeit', in H.J. Teuteberg and G. Wiegelmann (eds), *Unsere tägliche Kost*, Münster, F. Coppenrath, 1986, pp. 135–52), following Norbert Elias' theory of the process of civilization.
3. See S.W. Mintz, *Sweetness and Power: The Place of Sugar in Modern History*, New York, Viking Penguin Inc., 1985. *Sweetness and Power* is an important work, which, unfortunately, completely neglects the development of the sugar-beet industry; besides this, Mintz underestimates, in my opinion, the impact of fiscal policy upon consumption. Mintz's study is discussed in *Food & Foodways* Harwood Academic Publishers, 1987, vol. 2, no. 2, pp. 107–97.
4. Mintz (*ibid.*) points out that sugar helped to destroy the old agrarian pattern of meals, which had centred around food prepared and eaten in the family. Like a kind of early fast food, both the tea-snack between meals and the sweet sandwich spread with jam favoured an economy of time whose rhythm was dictated by the factories.
5. See H.H. Mauruschat, *Preise und Verbrauch des Kolonialzuckers im vorindustriellen Europa*, Berlin, Technische Universität Berlin, 1985, p. 27.
6. While the few very rich societies are beginning to reduce their consumption of sugar the correlation between increasing wealth and increasing sugar consumption, so noticeable in Europe during the eighteenth and nineteenth centuries, is still holding true today in the developing world.
7. See H.J. Teuteberg, 'Zuckerwirtschaft und Zuckerkonsum im historischen Rückblick', in *Zucker*, M. Hannover and H. Schaper (eds), 1974, vol. 27, no. 9, pp. 484–8.
8. One of the most striking books about the ills and evils attributed to sugar is W. Dufty's *Sugar Blues* (New York, Warner Books, 1975).

9. C. Fischler, 'Attitudes towards Sugar and Sweetness in Historical and Social Perspective', in J. Dobbing (ed.), *Sweetness*, Berlin, Springer, 1987, pp. 83–98.

10. Synthetic or artificial sweeteners such as saccharin, cyclamate, or aspartame differ substantially from caloric sweeteners (sucrose, corn syrup etc.); they are highly concentrated and provide no or almost no nutritional value. The 'natural' synthetic sweeteners, like thaumatin, are not synthesized chemically, but extracted from plants. Saccharin, a white crystalline powder, is 200 to 700 times sweeter than sugar.

11. See G.B. Kauffman and P.M. Priebe, 'The Discovery of Saccharin', in *Ambix*, Cambridge, Heffers, 1978, vol. 25, pp. 191–207.

12. A detailed analysis of the development of early German sweetener consumption is very difficult for several reasons; thus, we only know figures of production, but not of export, for the time before 1899. My estimates are grounded on the information of the German treasury (*Zentralarchiv Potsdam*, Bestand 21.01, vol. 3965–70) and of the sugar industry (periodical publications); the most important producers (Fahlberg-List in Magdeburg and Heyden in Radebeul) left no files on the 1890s.

13. It is impossible to measure the impact of non-nutritive sweeteners on the nutritive sweetener markets with complete accuracy because some uses of non-nutritive sweeteners are complementary and not substitutional. A cross price elasticity between sugar and saccharin existed at least in as much as the sugar cartel of those years could not raise prices as much as desired without being at risk of losing regular customers to the competing industry.

14. G. Wiegelmann, 'Tendenzen kulturellen Wandels in der Volksnahrung des 19. Jahrhunderts', in E. Heischkel-Artelt (ed.), *Ernährung und Ernährungslehre im neunzehnten Jahrhundert*, Göttingen, Vandenhoeck & Ruprecht, 1976, pp. 11–20.

15. The union is mentioned in a debate at the *Reichstag* (see *Stenographische Berichte*, vol. 6, 1900/03, p. 5574).

16. Also 'The Unemployed of Marienthal' were forced to fall back on saccharin. 'Some families have had no single piece of sugar in their home for two years', the authors of the famous study recorded in 1933 (cf. M. Jahoda, P. Lazarsfeld, H. Zeisel, *Die Arbeitslosen von Marienthal*, Allensbach/Bonn, Verlag für Demoskopie, 1960, 2nd edn, p. 27).

17. When a sweetener tax was to be introduced in Germany in 1926, the sugar industry insisted on a 'restriction of advertising for sweeteners'. It feared that this advertising could contain 'attacks on sugar, which will be based on the statement that sugar would cause undesirable increases in weight' (cf. *Bundesarchiv Koblenz*, Reichsfinanzministerium, Bestand R 2, vol. 1834).

18. Cf. the documents of the Reichsschatzamt (fn. 12).

19. See P.-C. Witt, *Die Finanzpolitik des Deutschen Reiches von 1903 bis 1913*, Lübeck/Hamburg, Matthiesen, 1970; and W.A. Boelcke, 'Industriesubventionierung am Beispiel der deutschen Zuckerindustrie. Wachstumsanalyse für eine Industriebranche 1830–1914', in *Scripta Mercaturae*, München, 1976, vol. 10/1, pp. 53–101. This tax had a similar significance in other countries with an important sugar industry (France, Russia, Belgium, etc.).

20. See Boelcke (*Industriesubventionierung*), G.B. Hagelberg, 'Anhaltspunkte zur

vergleichenden Wirtschaftsgeschichte von Rohr- und Rübenzucker bis zur Mitte des 20. Jahrhunderts', in *Jahrbuch für Wirtschaftsgeschichte*, Berlin, Akademie-Verlag, 1971, part III, pp. 141–80, and J.A. Perkins, 'Volkswirtschaftliche Aspekte des Zuckerrübenanbaus im kaiserlichen Deutschland', in *Jahrbuch für Wirtschaftsgeschichte*, Berlin, Akademie-Verlag, 1984, no. 4, pp. 75–102.

21. Cf. W. Sombart, *Der moderne Kapitalismus*, Leipzig, 1902, vol. 2 (Die Theorie der kapitalistischen Entwicklung), p. 14.
22. See the classical study of H. Rosenberg (*Grosse Depression und Bismarckzeit*, Berlin, Walter de Gruyter & Co., 1967). Still of central interest to historians are the protective duties that secured economic advantages for the grain-producing landowners in eastern Germany, the so-called *Junkers*. That the consumption taxes were also quietly turned into profitable sources of subsidies is often overlooked.
23. Cf. *Zentralarchiv Potsdam*, Bestand 21.01, vol. 3959, pp. 257–61.
24. Prior to 1902/03 the sugar industry on the continent benefited from a system of *de facto* market protection supplemented by export subsidies from the treasury. The abolition of subsidies for continental beet-sugar exports was forced on European governments by the Conservative government of Britain, as a means of providing support for the ailing West Indian sugar industry. See, for example, Ph.G. Chalmin, 'The Important Trends in Sugar Diplomacy before 1914', in W. Albert and A. Graves (eds), *Crisis and Change in the International Sugar Economy 1860–1914*, Norwich/Edinburgh, ISC Press, 1984, pp. 9–19.
25. *Stenographische Berichte*, vol. 6, 1900/03, p. 5572 (Graf Carmer).
26. See H. König, *Entstehung und Wirkungsweise von Fachverbänden der Nahrungs- und Genußmittelindustrie*, Berlin, Duncker & Humblot, 1965, pp. 19–62. Concerning 'The Question of Saccharin', see *Protokolle des Ausschusses des Vereins der Deutschen Zucker-Industrie* (1886ff.).
27. See G.S. Vascik, *Sweet Affinity: The National Liberal Party and the German Sugar Industry, 1867–1914*, University of Toledo, n.d.
28. The Austrian part of the Danubian monarchy.
29. See Merki, 1991, *op. cit.*, pp. 206–93. The chapter about the sweetener policy of Austria is based on the files of the *Oesterreichisches Staatsarchiv* (Allgemeines Verwaltungsarchiv, Finanz- und Hofkammerarchiv) in Vienna.
30. See *Ausschuß-Protokolle des Vereins der Deutschen Zuckerindustrie* (1898–1902).
31. Graf Sylva-Tarouca in front of the East-Bohemian millowners on 25 March 1898 (*Zeitschrift für Zuckerindustrie in Böhmen*, Prag, Verein der Zucker-industrie in Böhmen, 1897/98, p. 662).
32. See J. Bender, 'Der Saccharinschmuggel und seine Bekämpfung', in *Archiv für Kriminal-Anthropologie und Kriminalistik*, Leipzig, F.C.W. Vogel, 1911, vol. 41, pp. 245–67; Merki, 1991, *op cit.*, pp. 307–39.
33. See R. Sandgruber, *Bittersüße Genüsse. Kulturgeschichte der Genußmittel*, Wien, Böhlau, 1986, p. 10.
34. The files of these Syndicates are kept in the archives of the *Sandoz AG* (Basle).
35. France, Russia, Portugal, Italy, the Netherlands, Greece, Belgium, Germany (cf. the records (*Bundesarchiv Bern*)). While Hungary was ready to sign, the

Austrian parliament obstructed the repressive policy of its government. Switzerland would have had to accede sooner or later. The UK did not join the convention. It was not only the UK's liberal sugar policy that made a prohibitive dealing with saccharin impossible, but also the fact that there – in contrast to the continent – sugar had completely lost its luxury image.

36. Cf. Merki, 1991, *op. cit.*, pp. 386–425 (saccharin during and shortly after World War I).

37. Professor Lehmann (Würzburg). His opinion is quoted in: A. List, *Saccharin – Benzoesäuresulfinid*, Magdeburg, A. Wohlfeld, 1980 (1893), p. 59. 'Remarkably harmless' in comparison with other 'nervenanregenden Genußmitteln' like tea or coffee.

38. For further information: Merki, 1991, *op. cit.*, pp. 95–115.

PART 5: DIET IN AN INSTITUTIONAL CONTEXT

14 The workhouse diet in Ireland before and during the Great Famine

E. Margaret Crawford

In 1838 an 'Act for the more Effectual Relief of the Poor in Ireland' – an Irish Poor Law – was passed. The scheme, in effect, resembled the 1834 English Poor Law, whereby relief was offered only on the basis of indoor provision, within workhouses. Originally a network of 130 unions was planned for the country with a workhouse in each. In 1840 the first workhouse was opened and by 1846 all were accepting paupers. The crisis of the Great Famine revealed the inadequacy of the provision and so an additional 33 unions were formed in particularly distressed areas to make a total of 163 by 1850, though later the number was reduced to 161.

The scheme was governed by the 'less eligibility' principle. Thus every aspect of workhouse life had to be made so unattractive as to ensure that only the really destitute would apply for admission. This premise tested the ingenuity of the newly appointed Irish administrators to the full since Ireland's greatest social problem was extreme poverty. As reports of many commissions and committees testified, millions existed clothed in rags, housed in hovels and fed solely on potatoes and buttermilk. Despite the difficulty of their task the Poor Law commissioners approached their work with remarkable zeal. In particular, great care and attention was put into devising a dietary regime which would conform to the principle of 'less eligibility' yet keep the inmates in health and strength, while at the same time reflect the dietary pattern of the labouring classes. George Nicholls, the architect of the scheme, pondered on this problem as early as 1836 when the Irish Poor Law was still under consideration:

It would perhaps be in vain . . ., even if it were desirable to seek to make . . . the diet of the inmates of an Irish workhouse, inferior to those of the Irish peasantry. The standard of their mode of living is so low, that the establishment of one still lower is difficult, and under any circumstances [would] be inexpedient.[1]

Despite his doubts, the instruction sent to Assistant Commissioners in 1839 from the Commission office in preparation of prescribing a suitable diet emphasized that:

. . . the principle on which the Diet in the Irish workhouses must be regulated, will be the same as that on which the Dietaries were framed in England – namely – that the 'Dietary of the workhouse must on no account be superior to, or even equal to the ordinary mode of subsistence of the labouring classes in the neighbourhood'.[2]

Furthermore, every Assistant Commissioner was requested to enquire of the dietary served in the hospitals, jails and asylums as well as that eaten by the peasantry under his jurisdiction, and forward the findings to the Commission. On the basis of these enquiries a suitable diet for serving in the workhouses of that district was to be submitted.

The mainstay of the diet throughout the country was found to be potatoes. Additions to their menu varied according to region. In the south-west, in the counties of Limerick, Tipperary and Clare, buttermilk or skimmed milk were common adjuncts, and sometimes whole milk.[3] In the west, by contrast, Burke reported that the labouring poor, 'who seldom can afford to keep a cow, find it almost impossible to procure milk'; here herrings or more frequently salt were the only additional items to the fare.[4] In the north-east, oatmeal was often on the table of the labouring poor.[5] It was also common for thin gruel or water seasoned with an onion and salt to suffice during the lean months before the potato harvest. The absence of meat was particularly noted; that 'it is [a] matter of notoriety that meat is rarely, if ever tasted by the Irish peasant'.[6] The number of meals eaten daily by the labouring classes was also recorded; two were found to be the general rule in most of the country, a third being taken only at plentiful seasons of the year and in parts of Ulster.

Not surprisingly, each of the Assistant Commissioners pointed out the difficulty, if not impossibility, of framing a scale of diet for the workhouse which did not violate the principles laid down. The solution suggested by Mr W.H.T. Hawley, the Assistant Poor Law Commissioner for counties Limerick, Tipperary and Clare, was 'a reduction in the quantity and not in the quality of the food'.

In 1840 the first workhouses opened. These were in the unions of North and South Dublin and Cork. The diet initially suggested for use,

Table 14.1 Workhouse menus, 1840.

	5 days	2 days
Adult paupers		
Breakfast	7 oz (200 g) oatmeal (stirabout) ½ pt (285 ml) milk	7 oz (200 g) oatmeal (stirabout) ½ pt (285 ml) milk
Dinner	4 lb (1.8 kg) potatoes (raw wt.) 1 pt (570 ml) buttermilk	2 lb (0.9 kg) potatoes (raw wt.) in broth
Children 9–15 years		
Breakfast	3 oz (100 g) oatmeal (stirabout ½ pt (285 ml) milk	
Dinner	2 lb (0.9 kg) potatoes (raw wt.) ½ pt (285 ml) buttermilk	
Supper	6 oz (170 g) bread ½ pt (285 ml) milk	

Notes: Children under nine years old were to be dieted at discretion; the sick and infirm as directed by the medical officer.

Conversion from Imperial to metric values has been carried out on the basis that 1 oz is equivalent to 28.5 g/ml.

Source: Sixth Annual Report of the Poor Law Commissioners, BPP 1840(245)XVII, Appendix D, No. 21, 'Workhouse Dietaries', p. 242; *Seventh Annual Report of the Poor Law Commissioners*, BPP 1841[327]XI 1st Session, Appendix C, p. 455.

and indeed implemented in the North and South Dublin Unions, is set out in Table 14.1. Being urban unions, the suitability of the regime for city paupers was questioned because it was based primarily on information received from rural districts. The issue was resolved by making:

. . . no difference, or only a very trifling difference . . . between the dietaries of the rural Union workhouses and those for the city Unions; and that it would be especially inexpedient to make any great difference where a city or town Union, as is the case in Dublin, comprises also a considerable rural population.[7]

In effect, broth was incorporated into the diet on two days each week to prevent, 'in some degree, against mischief which might arise to the city paupers from having recourse suddenly to a diet from which all animal food but milk is excluded'.[8] Because 'the establish[ed] dietaries in the different unions . . . should accord with the general habits of the people,'[9] slight variations appeared from region to region. In the north-east, where three meals a day were common, workhouse dietary regimes reflected this pattern. In the Lurgan workhouse rations were divided thus:

Breakfast:	6 oz (170 g)	Oatmeal (stirabout)	1/3 qt (380 ml) Buttermilk
Dinner:	3 lb (1.4 kg)	Potatoes	1/3 qt (380 ml) Buttermilk
Supper:	4 oz (115 g)	Oatmeal (stirabout)	1/3 qt (380 ml) Buttermilk

Source: Minute Book of the Lurgan Poor Law Union, 1841, PRONI BG22/A/1, p. 192.

But a few miles east, in the Newry workhouse, rations were somewhat less:

Breakfast:	5 oz (140 g)	Oatmeal (stirabout)	1/3 qt (380 ml) Buttermilk
Dinner:	3 lb (1.4 kg)	Potatoes	1/3 qt (380 ml) Buttermilk
Supper:	4 oz (115 g)	Oatmeal (stirabout)	1/3 qt (380 ml) Buttermilk

Source: Minute Book of the Newry Poor Law Union, 1841, PRONI BG24/A/1, p. 168.

By 1842 almost one-third of the planned workhouses were open. The Poor Law Commissioners now considered they were 'in possession of sufficient information for enabling them to decide upon the best scale of workhouse diet for general adoption'.[10] The aim was to operate greater central control in dietary scales, thus preventing regional variation. Three menus were devised from which workhouse administrators had to choose and register their choice. Diet No. 1 consisted of the same formula as the 1840 menu. Diet No. 2 was also a two-meal regime similar to Diet No. 1, with the addition of a meat meal on two days of the week. Meat was given in soup, as ox-head, shin or other coarse pieces of beef. Diet No. 3 was included to accommodate those unions where three meals daily was the norm for the peasantry of that region.

Detailed dietary information was provided for the sick, for children, for those employed on hard-labouring duties, and for use when the market prices of foodstuffs rose to high levels. The basic diet could be varied upon the advice of the medical officer. Nevertheless four menus were set out for sick paupers as guidance. Sick Diet No. 1 was the house diet of the workhouse. The other three were of bland bread-and-milk regimes, the main differences between them being in the quantities served.

For dietary purposes children were divided into three groups according to age: nine to 14 years, five to nine years, and under five years. The eldest were to receive two-thirds of the three-meal regime

Table 14.2 Diet for children 9 to 14 years.

Breakfast	Dinner	Supper
3½ oz (100 g) Oatmeal ½ pt (285 ml) Milk	2 lb (0.9 kg) Potatoes ½ pt (285 ml) Milk	6 oz (170 g) Bread

Source: Eighth Annual Report of the PLC, p. 152.

Table 14.3 Diet for women and children under 13 years and for men not at work.

Breakfast	Dinner	Supper

6 oz (170 g) Oatmeal
½ pt (285 ml)
  Buttermilk
	3 lb (1.4 kg) Potatoes
	½ pt (285 ml)
	  Buttermilk
		4 oz (115 g) Oatmeal
		½ pt (285 ml)
		  Buttermilk

Source: Minute Book of Cookstown Poor Law Union, 1842, PRONI, BG11/A/1, p. 54.

(see Table 14.2), while for other groups no stipulated menu was laid down. Their diets were left to the discretion of the Board of Guardians, the general rule being that the same items of food were to be given, though in reduced quantities. For the youngest group, rice or bread could be substituted for oatmeal or potatoes.

An awareness of the need for additional food when men and women had to undertake heavy labour was demonstrated in the document by grading menus according to type of employment:

It is usual to give the able-bodied women in the workhouse, who are employed in washing, or in hard household, or out-of-door work, the same quantity and description of food as the able-bodied men; ... and the able-bodied women employed in needle-work and other sedentary occupations, are allowed somewhat less.[11]

Table 14.3 shows the diet served to women on sedentary duties at the Cookstown workhouse in May 1842; as a guide for diets suitable for those paupers not engaged in manual work the Commissioners suggested reducing the able-bodied diet by one ounce of oatmeal and half a pound of potatoes daily.[12]

Reference to the Poor Law Commissioners' revised dietary scheme of 1842 was noted in many union minute books. The Board of Guardians of the Banbridge Union recorded the receipt of the dietary circular on 1 January 1842, and decided that the 'No. 3 dietary being recommended by the Commissioners shall be adopted in this Union'.[13] Many Ulster

unions chose the three-meal regime, whereas at Enniscorthy, in the
south-east of the country, the Board of Guardians selected Dietary No.
1, the two-meal regime.[14] Such variations reflected the differences in
meal patterns outside the workhouse in these regions. Not only were the
selected menus recorded in the Union Minute Books, but the decisions
were sent to the Commissioners in Dublin. The insistence of the
Commissioners that Boards of Guardians notify them of all dietary
alterations, no matter how small, even though within the regulations,
illustrates their vigilance and control, no doubt to ensure that the 'less
eligibility' principle was not violated.

During 1843 and 1844 there were few comments about the workhouse
diet. In the autumn of 1845, however, references appeared in union
minute books with increasing frequency concerning the poor state of the
potato crop. The bad quality of potatoes thus forced the authorities to
replace them with oatmeal. In the Antrim Poor Law Union minute book
the following entry occurred on 16 October 1845:

> . . . in consequence of the contractor being unable, from the prevailing disease of
> the potato crop, to procure the full supply of a sound description, the following
> changes be made in the dinner menu for one week viz. On Sunday adult paupers
> to be allowed 7 oz [200 g] oatmeal . . . with the usual quantity of milk; on
> Monday, Wednesday and Friday adults to be allowed 4 lb [1.8 kg] of potatoes
> each . . . with the usual quantity of milk; on Tuesday, Thursday and Saturday
> adults to be served with ½lb [225 g] bread . . . with the usual allowance of
> soup.[15]

One Poor Law Union after another reported that the diseased state of the
potato crop rendered them unfit for consumption.

The crop failure in 1845 did not immediately precipitate alarm, since
millions of Irishmen regularly endured annual semi-starvation during the
hiatus between one season's crop of potatoes and the next. Time soon
revealed the enormity of the catastrophe, however. The dependence of
the vast majority of the labouring population upon the potato left them
totally destitute when the crop failed. They had little choice ultimately
but to seek admission to the workhouse or, alternatively, starve to death.
The workhouses, therefore, became inextricably involved in the famine
crisis.

Initially the authorities were reluctant to plan for the crucial role they
were compelled to play in the crisis. As Helen Burke noted, the *Annual
Report* of 1846, prepared at the peak of the famine, contained 98
paragraphs but it was not until the 94th that passing reference was made
to the failure of the potato crop with comment on an alternative dietary
strategy.[16] Burke has suggested three reasons for complacency. First, the
headquarters of the Irish Poor Law was still in London;[17] second, the

crop failure was viewed as an extreme episode of the normal annual food shortage experienced during the hiatus between the old and the new crop; and thirdly, in times of extreme distress, the poor law scheme was not regarded as an agency for support.

Meanwhile, in the autumn of 1845, alarm was being expressed at local level by the Guardians as the crisis accelerated and guidance was requested from the Dublin administrators on modifying the dietary regime. On 27 October 1845 a General Order was issued by the Poor Law Commissioners authorizing the Guardians to 'depart from the established dietaries by substituting the use of oatmeal, rice, bread or other foods in lieu of potatoes, whenever the Guardians may deem it advisable to do so'.[18] Changes, nevertheless, were supposed to be submitted to the Commissioners for approval before implementation took place. Following this directive, the Belfast Board of Guardians asked Messrs Sheil & Co. of Liverpool for quotations of various grades of rice,[19] though potatoes were still being ordered despite their diseased state. On 3 February 1846 a letter was sent to Mr Boyd, the potato contractor, complaining that he delivered 182 lb (82.7 kg) of diseased potatoes unfit for consumption and requesting that these be replaced by a supply of sound potatoes.[20] Later that month a special meeting of the Belfast Board was called 'to take into consideration the propriety of making an alteration in the diet by substituting bread in place of potatoes on the days that soup is given'.[21] As famine conditions intensified, one Board of Guardians after another reluctantly ceased to use potatoes, substituting cereal foods on the menu.

The government nurtured the hope that diseased potatoes could be salvaged. To this end the scientists Lindley and Playfair were retained with instructions to advise on ways and means of preserving the potato crop. Among the suggestions proffered was a complex method of converting diseased potatoes into edible starch for making bread. The Commissioners considered:

. . . that the proposed conversion of potatoes into potato-flour, or into starch and pulp, may afford a suitable employment to certain classes of inmates of the workhouse; and the Guardians will have the goodness to consider the means by which [these] wishes . . . can be carried out.[22]

The necessary implements and machinery were to be supplied along with exact details on the method of processing. A *Minute Book of the South Dublin Union* records the setting up of the apparatus in the workhouse yard.[23] The scheme failed because of difficulties with the drying apparatus, and the great expense of overcoming the problems.

By 1846 and 1847 the influx of paupers into the workhouses increased to a point of massive overcrowding. T.P. O'Neill, quoting from correspondence regarding the state of the workhouses at this time, states that, 'ninety-three of the one hundred and thirty workhouses contained more inmates than they were built to contain'.[24] For example, in the Enniscorthy workhouse, 'there were about 700 "paupers" . . . although the number of beds was only 378'.[25] All over the country this situation was repeated.

One of the farinaceous products introduced into the workhouse at this time was Indian meal. This grain is a derivative of maize and had to be imported from America. The attraction of Indian meal as a substitute for the potato was its low cost. It was much cheaper than oatmeal. In March 1846 when Indian meal was released onto the market by the government – who at that time controlled supplies – it was priced at one penny per pound, rising to 2d per pound in 1847. Initially the food was very unpopular; indeed so strong was the feeling against Indian meal that even workhouse paupers refused to eat it. Writing from Wexford, the Deputy Commissary-General Dobree remarked on 'the prejudices which still exist against Indian corn [even] when it is doled out as charity', and, 'in [the] poorhouse, . . . it was sturdily refused as an article of diet'.[26] The opposition to the food stemmed from paupers believing that they would die of poisoning if they ate Indian meal.[27]

The use of Indian meal initially had a major drawback. It could not be processed like other grains as it was particularly hard and so it had to be chopped in steel mills instead of being ground. In addition, it was susceptible to sweating and overheating; consequently unloading and processing had to be done quickly on arrival in Ireland. Early consignments were of old, dry and inferior corn, which exacerbated the technical difficulties of milling it into a digestible form. Furthermore, the population was ignorant of the methods of preparing and cooking Indian meal. Some even tried to eat the meal raw, because they lacked fuel for cooking. Many discovered that consumption of the flint-hard grain caused severe intestinal disorders; and hence strongly opposed the food in the early stages of the famine. As the season progressed, however, and dearth intensified, Indian meal became more acceptable. Workhouses increasingly used it extensively, incorporating it into the diet as stirabout, frequently mixing it with oatmeal. Some Irish workhouses served quite enormous quantities of Indian meal. In the Castlereagh workhouse the daily ration of Indian meal was 15 oz (428 g raw weight); in Cashel workhouse 16 oz (456 g raw weight); and at Lisnaskea the workhouse menu contained 20 oz (570 g raw weight) daily.[28]

The financial difficulties of the unions had a direct bearing on the quality of the workhouse diets. The entire system was financed by rates levied locally according to value of property. As the grip of famine intensified, more and more rate-payers defaulted: consequently the flow of income declined to a trickle, resulting in many unions becoming bankrupt. In general, therefore, finances were in a perilous state from 1846 to 1849. Contractors frequently refused to supply food, and the diet deteriorated because Guardians' cheques were dishonoured. Evidence to this effect abounds in correspondence between the Boards of Guardians and Inspectors to the Poor Law Commissioners. A resolution of the Cavan Board of Guardians indicates that because of:

. . . the extraordinary increase of paupers admitted into the poor-house during the existence of the calamity which has afflicted the country, has completely exhausted the funds, and the establishment is consequently indebted to the contractors in a very considerable sum, about 800, while the arrear likely to be collected does not exceed 250. . . . Under these circumstances the contractors have refused further supplies, and unless funds be raised for the immediate expenditure, it will be necessary, however painful . . . not only to close the house, but actually to put out the unfortunate paupers'.[29]

Similar pleas were prevalent in the west. The Guardians of the Swineford Union, County Mayo, lamented in January 1847:

. . . we therefore are forced to the reluctant conviction that if money be not advanced by the State on the security of the rates, no means at our disposal can prevent the inmates of the house this day, 644 souls in number from perishing by starvation, we therefore put this fearful state of things before the Government, as we have no alternative left, and we deeply feel the responsibility resting on us.[30]

At Ballyshannon Union the food contractor stopped supplies as there were unpaid bills to the tune of £220. To prevent eviction of the inmates three members of the Board of Guardians were persuaded to lend £100 for paying the contract provisioner as an inducement for him to supply bread, meal and milk to the workhouse for three or four weeks longer.[31] Because of non-payment of bills many contractors to the union workhouses tore up their contracts: thus paupers received irregular meals of reduced rations.

The effects of severely curtailed rations soon became evident in the physical appearance of the paupers. In January 1847, the Rev. Richard Gibbons, shocked after visiting the Castlebar workhouse, wrote to Mr T.N. Redington, Under Secretary for Ireland: 'I am pained to have to state that almost every individual [is] showing striking signs of haggard and famished looks; the provisions, oaten or Indian meal, are supplied very irregularly'.[32] Mr Gibbons continued that he 'had thought the Poor Law Commissioners might have secured the good treatment of the few confined in the house . . .; the contrary is almost the case'.[33]

Further evidence of the defective quality of diet during the famine years is the increasing incidence of scurvy among the paupers. Dr J.O. Curran, investigating the prevalence of scurvy in Dublin hospitals, noted

that 60 per cent of all cases were in the North and South Unions'
hospitals in Dublin, and:

> . . . all the patients (with but four or five exceptions) . . . had been in the Poor
> House for periods varying from six months to five years, and for at least six
> months had been using the following dietary: South Union – 7 oz [200 g]
> oatmeal in porridge, with ½ pt [285 ml] milk for breakfast; 8 oz [228 g] bread,
> with ½ pt [285 ml] milk for dinner . . . . In the North Union, the patients when
> attacked were using for breakfast 1 qt [1.1 l] of porridge (containing 7 oz [200 g]
> oatmeal) with ½ pt [285 ml] milk; the bread used at dinner being replaced on
> Tuesdays and Fridays by 1 qt [1.1 l] of boiled rice.[34]

Scurvy was not confined to Dublin. Reports of its appearance in
various towns and rural districts confirmed its presence throughout the
country. Unquestionably the cause of scurvy was the absence of potatoes
from the diet and failure to replace with another antiscorbutic vegetable.
In the majority of cases bread, cereals, milk and tea had become the
main items of diet. The widespread appearance of the disease in the
workhouses eventually prompted the Commission to issue a circular on
the subject in July 1849.[35] The circular attributed scurvy to insufficient
vegetables and milk in the diet. The Commissioners were correct in
blaming the lack of vegetables in the daily fare, but unfortunately their
directive to the Boards of Guardians was not totally sound. They
recommended the inclusion of *well cooked* vegetables, so ruining the
vitamin C content of the meals before the paupers ate them.[36]

Scurvy was not the only vitamin deficiency disease present in Ireland's
workhouses. A prolonged lack of vitamin A damaged the sight of many
workhouse children. Although not identified at the time, the dietary
evidence and medical reports confirm the eye disease to be
xerophthalmia.[37] Reference to Wilde's historical survey of diseases in
Ireland reveals that an eye affliction which contemporaries called
ophthalmia (an infectious eye disease) had long been endemic in
Ireland.[38] Insufficient quantitative dietary material precludes analysis of
earlier episodes, but it is certain that in 1849–50 many people diagnosed
as having ophthalmia in fact were suffering from xerophthalmia. The
Poor Law medical records provide the clearest evidence.[39] In 1849 the
Poor Law Commissioners were greatly alarmed by an epidemic which
they described as ophthalmia in the workhouses. It was particularly rife in
the overcrowded and insanitary establishments of the south and west and
was especially common among children under 15 years of age.

Professor Arthur Jacob and Sir William Wilde, two specialists in the
field, investigated the disease. Comparison of the clinical aspects of
xerophthalmia with the symptoms described in Wilde's report is
revealing. First, he noted the highest incidence was among children.[40] In

the Tipperary workhouse 96 per cent of cases were children; their ages ranged from four to 14 years. Only 14 patients were adults.[41] Secondly, Wilde reported that in the eyes of some patients 'several . . . [ulcers] were nearly transparent, as if a piece had been clipped out of the cornea'.[42] He continued by describing corneal changes which produced 'either staphyloma or extensive Leucoma with adhesion of the [iris] to the cornea'.[43] All are clinical symptoms of xerophthalmia.

Left untreated, xerophthalmia ultimately results in blindness. Often blindness occurs in one eye only. The pattern once again reflects that found by Wilde. Of the 340 cases examined, 16 had irrecoverably lost the sight of both eyes and in 32 vision was ruined in one eye. A further 33 had one eye blemished, impairing vision though not totally destroying sight.[44] The statistics on blindness for all workhouses in Ireland during the closing years of the famine mirror the conditions in the Tipperary institution.

The cause of xerophthalmia in the workhouses is not hard to find. Menus consisted of Indian meal, oatmeal, bread, gruel, with whole milk, skimmed milk or buttermilk. The best source of vitamin A in the diet was whole milk, and when it was drunk in sufficient quantities enough vitamin A to meet body requirements was acquired.[45] However, buttermilk or skimmed milk was often used instead of whole milk, and the children then became very vulnerable to the effects of vitamin A deficiency, as buttermilk and skimmed milk are poor sources.[46] Such was the case in 1848–49. Nutritional analysis of Tipperary workhouse diets for children aged five to nine years shows that the vitamin A content was only around 130 μg retinol equivalent (RE) even when whole milk was served, and barely a trace when buttermilk or skimmed milk was substituted. Both menus were below a child's requirement (4–14 years) of 300 μg to 725 μg RE.[47]

The treatment recommended by Sir William Wilde for the eye disease, cod-liver oil, provides final proof that xerophthalmia was the disease he witnessed. In his report Wilde advised:

where the patient is much broken down in health, and . . . the disease is in a chronic stage, I beg to suggest the plentiful use of cod-liver oil, of which medicine a large supply should at once be procured, and a tablespoonful given to each child, two or three times a day. I saw I am sure fifty cases among those under your care which would be greatly benefited by the use of this remedy.[48]

Wilde's prescription predated by 60 years the general recognition that cod-liver oil was effective treatment for vitamin A deficiency.

By the end of 1847 chaos reigned in many workhouses. One extreme case, the Ballinrobe workhouse, was the subject of much correspondence. No food was in its kitchen nor eaten in the dining hall. Instead, paupers got their food rations raw in the morning and cooked them in numerous locations throughout the building, in the infirmary, the dormitories, the day room or nursery on fires often lit in rooms without chimneys. The correspondent painfully described conditions as 'a picture of demi-savage life'.[49]

Indeed, so bad were workhouse diets in the late 1840s that inmates committed crimes in order to get transferred to the relatively better conditions of the gaols. The Inspector-General of Prisons reported that 'insubordination in workhouses [was] committed solely for the purpose of obtaining gaol dietary'.[50] Perhaps it was partly in response to this ludicrous situation, though probably because of a major alteration in the administration of the Poor Relief Act in 1847, that in March 1848 the House of Commons ordered a dietary survey to be conducted in the county gaols and union workhouses for the category of the able-bodied man.[51] It was requested that the information be arranged by counties so as to show comparison between the diets of the two types of institutions.

The survey revealed a number of features worthy of note. Firstly, the variations in menu were almost as numerous as the number of workhouses, indicating that the Commissioners had lost control over prescribing the diet. Local conditions rather than edicts from headquarters dictated the menu within the workhouse, with the more destitute areas providing the most frugal fare. Thus the relatively more prosperous north-east still retained the three-meal fare, though heavily grain-based, while regions in the west and south-west recorded monotonous menus of one and two meals consisting of large though varying quantities of grain accompanied by a small ration of a milk beverage. Secondly, throughout the country Indian meal had been adopted in place of potatoes, with no other vegetable supplied as an alternative. Some 38 per cent of workhouses, however, served soup, in some cases described as vegetable soup, in others as broth or meat soup.

Although the 1848 dietary survey meticulously recorded all items and quantities of food in workhouse diets, we should not accept the amounts without question. We know that paupers on the outdoor relief programme[52] did not always receive the stipulated rations of food. Dr Dempster reported to the Commissioners that in the Union of Ballinrobe the County Inspectors of Weights and Measures seized a set of scales and weights, and placed them in the custody of the police as they were 'irregular'.[53] In Tipperary, cooked food for the outdoor scheme was discontinued 'in consequence of the numerous frauds committed by the people employed in the [workhouse] kitchens',[54] and there are comments to be found in correspondence to the effect that because of lack of discipline in certain workhouses, food was often taken out of the establishments.[55] Such incidents indicate that in the crisis era lack of finance was not the only factor reducing rations.

Table 14.4 Average daily nutrient intake of Irish workhouse diets, 1841 and 1849.[57]

	Protein (g.)	Fat (g.)	Carbo-hydrate (g.)	Energy value (kcal.)
Mean of pre-famine diets (1841–4)	93	30	535	2670
Regulation diet 1849 (minimum rations)	62	23	425	2075

Almost a year after the dietary survey and despite the rigours of the famine, new rules for framing workhouse diet were issued in February 1849.[56] Once again the Boards of Guardians were provided with two- and three-meal regimes. The basic menu for able-bodied male paupers was to be 'not less than' 8 oz (228g) Indian meal, ½ pt (285 ml) milk, 14 oz (400 g) brown bread, and 2 pt (1.1 l) of soup. Comprehensive advice was provided on the substitution of various foods, as the famine crisis had highlighted the need for greater flexibility in food exchanges. The use of the phrase 'not less than' indicates an intention to establish a minimum standard. The basic menu could be varied, and even exceeded, on the advice of the Medical Officer and with the approval of the Commissioners. Certainly the wide variation in the individual inter-pretations of the ruling substantiates this.

During the famine years the workhouse diet deteriorated not only in monotony of menu but also in nutritional quality. By comparing the nutritional analysis of the pre-famine diet with the 1849 regulation diet the poor quality of the latter is evident as shown in Table 14.4.

By focusing on the protein content and the energy value the contrast in nutritional quality is evident. Protein can be evaluated in two ways – by quantity and by quality. The pre-famine regime was ample in quantity and adequate in quality, whereas the 1849 menu was poor in both. Quantitatively, the 1849 diet was one-third below the pre-famine menu, while in qualitative terms the 1849 diet scored an abysmal 53 compared with 75 for the pre-famine diet. To place these figures in context, a good nutritious diet scores about 80, while poor diets would rate at 70 or less.[58] The better quality of the pre-famine diet is attributable to the potato, which provides higher biological value protein than the cereal foods used during and after the famine.

The energy value of both dietary regimens was poor, particularly for able-bodied paupers expected to do arduous tasks. Given that the recommended intake is 2750–3000 kilocalories per day for the moderate to very active adult male[59] the deficiency is thus even more pronounced.

In conclusion, in the minds of administrators two rules determined the diets for paupers in Irish workhouses. The first, and most important, was the 'less eligibility principle'. Meals had to be inferior to those outside the workhouse, though the menus were supposed to be sufficient to maintain the paupers in health. Up to the famine years the administrators achieved this objective. Even during the famine despite the appalling conditions in the workhouses, paupers were fed, albeit spasmodically and on low rations of monotonous fare – chiefly Indian meal. This was in stark contrast to their fellows outside who faced starvation. The second premise governing the thinking of Poor Law administrators was that health should be maintained. The aim in this respect was extremely modest, being nothing more than the prevention of a serious outbreak of disease.

The financing of the system on a local self-supporting basis controlled the amount of relief in each union. Diet was but one aspect. Hence we find the regional differences between the diets served in the wealthier north-eastern unions and the poorer west, a contrast which was maintained throughout the famine era. The crisis proved a strain for which the Poor Law administration was ill-equipped. Intervention occurred only when extreme conditions forced action.

Notes

1. G. Nicholls, *A History of the Irish Poor Law*, 1856, Reprint New York, Kelly, 1967, p. 171.
2. J. Burke, Poor Law Commission Letters PROI 1A/50/20, vol. 1. Reprinted in *Sixth Annual Report of the Poor Law Commissioners*.
3. *Sixth Annual Report of the Poor Law Commissioners*, Appendix (D), Reports to Boards Ireland, No. 21 'Report on Workhouse Dietaries' British Parliamentary Papers (henceforth BPP) 1840[245]XVII, p. 244.
4. J. Burke, Poor Law Commission Letters PROI 1A/50/20, vol. 1. 1838–9.
5. *Report of Commissioners for Inquiring into the Conditions of the Poorer Classes in Ireland (Poor Inquiry (Ireland))* BPP 1836(36)XXXI Appendix D.
6. *Sixth Annual Report of the Poor Law Commissioners*, p. 239.
7. Ibid, p. 240.
8. Ibid, p. 241.
9. George Nicholls, *A History of the Irish Poor Law*, p. 253.
10. *Eighth Annual Report of the Poor Law Commissioners*, Appendix (C), 'Documents relating to Ireland', BPP 1842[339]XIX, p. 152.
11. *Eighth Annual Report of the Poor Law Commissioners*, p. 152.
12. *Eighth Annual Report of the Poor Law Commissioners*, p. 152.
13. *Minute Book of the Banbridge Poor Law Union*, 1842, Public Record Office of Northern Ireland (henceforth PRONI) BG6/A/1, p. 280.
14. 'Dietary of Enniscorthy Workhouse 1842–47', *The Past*, vol. 9, 1972, p. 57.

15. Minute Book of the Antrim Poor Law Union, 1845, PRONI, BG1/A/1, reproduced in *The Great Famine in Antrim, Randalstown and Districts*, Belfast, PRONI, 1972, p. 16.
16. Helen Burke, *The People and the Poor Law in 19th Century Ireland*, Littlehampton, WEB, 1987, p. 125.
17. Initially the Irish Poor Law was administered from London, with an office in Dublin. In August 1847 the link was severed and a new commission was established in Dublin.
18. Minute Book of the Antrim Poor Law Union, 1845, PRONI, BG1/A/1.
19. Minute Book of the Belfast Board of Guardians, BG7/A/4, p. 37.
20. Ibid, p. 116.
21. Ibid, p. 123.
22. *Twelfth Annual Report of the Poor Law Commissioners*, BPP 1846[745]XIX, Appendix A, No. 17, p. 91.
23. Minute Book of the South Dublin Union, 1845.
24. T.P. O'Neill, 'The Administration of Relief' in *The Great Famine*, R.D. Edwards and T.D. Williams (eds) Dublin, Browne & Nolan, 1956, p. 245.
25. 'Dietary of Enniscorthy Workhouse 1842–1847', p. 58.
26. Correspondence relating to the Measures adopted by Her Majesty's Government for the relief of Distress arising from the Failure of the Potato Crop in Ireland, BPP 1846[735]XXXVII, p. 89.
27. Ibid.
28. To place these quantities in perspective, 1 oz raw weight Indian meal makes 8 oz of cooked weight.
29. *Correspondence relating to the State of Union Workhouses in Ireland*, First Series, BPP 1847(766)LV, IUP Edition, p. 26.
30. Ibid, p. 41.
31. *Correspondence relating to the State of Union Workhouses in Ireland*, (Second Series), BPP 1847(790)LV, IUP Edition, p. 71.
32. *Correspondence relating to the state of the Union Workhouses in Ireland*, First Series, BPP 1847(766)LV, p. 51.
33. Ibid. Reference to 'the few confined in the house' is a consequence of the Guardians refusing to admit applicants for relief because the Union had no funds and was deeply in debt. In addition they would not set a new rate.
34. J.O. Curran, 'On Scurvy', *Dublin Quarterly Journal of Medical Science*, vol. 4, 1847, p. 100.
35. *Third Annual Report of the Commissioners for Administering of the Laws for Relief of the Poor in Ireland*, BPP 1850[1243]XXVII.
36. For a more detailed analysis of the disease see E. Margaret Crawford, 'Scurvy in Ireland during the Great Famine', *The Journal of the Society for the Social History of Medicine*, vol. 1, no. 3, 1988, pp. 281–300.
37. E. Margaret Crawford, 'Dearth, Diet and Disease in Ireland 1850: A Case Study of Nutritional Deficiency', *Medical History*, vol. 28, no. 2, 1984, pp. 151–61.
38. *The Census of Ireland for the Year 1851*, Table of Deaths, vol I, BPP 1856[2087–I]XXIX, p. 439.
39. *Fourth Annual Report of the Commissioners for Administering the Laws for Relief of the Poor in Ireland*, 1851, pp. 130–51 (hereafter *Fourth Annual Report PLC*);

Fifth Annual Report of the Commissioners for Administering the Laws for Relief of the Poor in Ireland, 1852, p. 14; W.R. Wilde, *Observations on the Epidemic Opthalmia which had prevailed in the Workhouses and Schools of the Tipperary and Athlone Unions*, Dublin, 1851.

40. *Fourth Annual Report PLC*, p. 137.
41. Ibid.
42. Ibid. p. 146.
43. Ibid. p. 145.
44. Ibid. p. 140.
45. See. E. Margaret Crawford, 'Dearth, Diet, and Disease in Ireland 1850: A Case Study of Nutritional Deficiency', *Medical History*, 28, 1984, p. 159.
46. Ibid.
47. *Recommended Daily Amounts of Food Energy and Nutrients for Groups of People in the United Kingdom*, Report on Health and Social Subjects no. 15, DHSS, London, 1979.
48. *Fourth Annual Report PLC*, p. 145.
49. *Correspondence relating to the state of Union Workhouses in Ireland*, Third Series, BPP 1847(863)LV, IUP edition p. 211.
50. *Report of the Committee appointed to inquire into the Dietaries of County and Borough Gaols in Ireland*, BPP 1867–8[3981]XXXV, p. 13.
51. *Return from the Several County Gaols and Workhouses in Ireland, of the Daily Diet allowed to an Able-bodied Man*, BPP 1847–8(486)LIII.
52. Outdoor relief was introduced as a temporary measure in a desperate attempt to deal with the escalating crisis.
53. *Papers relating to Proceedings for the Relief of the Distress and State of Unions and Workhouses in Ireland*, Sixth Series, BPP 1847–8[955]LVI, p. 59.
54. *Papers relating to Proceedings for the Relief of the Distress and State of Unions and Workhouses in Ireland*, Sixth Series, BPP 1847–8[955]LVI, p. 609.
55. *Correspondence relating to the State of Union Workhouses in Ireland*, Third Series, BPP 1847(863)LV, IUP edition p. 211.
56. *Second Annual Report Of The Commissioners for Administering the Law for Relief of the Poor in Ireland*, BPP 1849(118)XXV, pp. 165–7.
57. Nutrient content of diets calculated from R.A. McCance and E.M. Widdowson, *The Composition of Foods*, Medical Research Council, Special Report Series No. 297, London, HMSO, 1960 and 1978; United States Department of Agriculture, *Composition of Foods*, Agricultural Handbook no. 8, Washington DC, 1950.
58. Joint FAO/WHO Committee Report Series No. 522 *Energy and Protein Requirements*, Rome, 1973.
59. *Recommended Daily Amounts of Food Energy and Nutrients for Groups of People in the United Kingdom*, Report on Health and Social Subjects no. 15. DHSS London, 1979.

15 The care of the poor by the charity institutions of the Protestant Augsburgian Community in Warsaw from the eighteenth to the twentieth century

Hanna Krajewska

From its earliest days, the history of the Protestant Augsburgian Community in Warsaw was closely related to the history of Protestantism in Poland. Despite the fact that Luther's teachings flourished in the time of Zygmunt III, the region of Mazowsze, including Warsaw, was detached from their influence. In 1525, at the dawn of the Reformation, Janusz, the Mazovian prince, issued a special decree which prohibited the profession of the Lutheran faith, the founding of communities, the building of churches, and the conducting of services.[1] Due to this the Protestants living in the capital were put under the care of a brotherhood of foreigners dedicated to St. Benon which allocated part of their lands, mainly destined for a cemetery, to the Protestants. Lutheran services on the other hand, were held in Węgrów Podlaski, the nearest town outside Mazowsze and the area of prohibition. The Warsaw community was also aided by foreign representatives from Prussia and Denmark, who offered their facilities for religious practice. The breakthrough came in 1786 with the Warsaw Treaty which changed the status of Protestants and forced them to codify the principles of their church. The community was at that time administered by a council of elders. After 1776 this body was known as the College of the Church. At that time many wide-ranging problems were taken up including charitable work. In 1778 the Charitable Section, which a hundred years later was renamed the Care Section, was founded. The section was occupied with attending to the poor and supervising charity institutions. The hospital was the oldest of these and was, for a long time, the most prominent.

The budget of the Care Section consisted of endowments, donations, single contributions, collections, etc. In order to administer the growing hospital a separate Hospital Section was established in 1872. The beginnings of this institution, however, go back to 1736 when a wooden house was built on the premises of the cemetery (at the intersection of Karmelicka Street and Mylna Street) meant as a flat for the overseer and simultaneously as a kind of hostel for travelling Protestants passing through Warsaw. Some poor or sick members of the community found shelter there for a considerable time. In 1741, a second house was built containing eight rooms.[2] The caretaker was the head of the hospital, but it was also under the authority of the Warsaw central hospital administration.[3]

In 1777 an internal statute of the hospital was formulated defining the duties of the staff and hinting at methods of curing, hygiene, and the nourishment of patients. Among the most common cures was letting of blood (in 1778 100 cases were registered) which cost 1 zloty (zł) a time. Herbal compresses and salves were also used frequently. It was recommended to burn incense and air the wards carefully, even twice a day when neccessary.

Although the hospital from its earliest days had the character of a charitable institution, the staff were paid for their efforts. The payroll was headed by the surgeon and his assistant, who in 1784 earned 540zł per year, while the nurses got 120zł per year. In 1788, the total expenditure of the hospital reached 9498zł. This sum included the purchase of meat – 558zł; bread – 520zł; and beer – 412zł.[4] The staff and the patients were daily provided with 20kg beef (for 5 zł); beer (8 to 10 casks a month) was bought for 0.29zł a cask. The number of patients amounted at that time to about 300.[5]

In 1792 a new cemetery was founded in the Wola district and after that the premises belonged solely to the hospital.

At the beginning of the nineteenth century the hospital found itself in a financial crisis which was solved only partially through donations, collections, and a special tax on theatre tickets introduced in 1814. In 1821 the enlargement of the hospital was initiated. Household appliances, sheets for the patients, and medical devices were presented by the parishioners. In 1838 the patients had to pay a daily fee of 0.38zł,[6] whereas the treatment was free for travellers. The hospital was open for patients of all faiths, a fact which often led to various complications.[7] From 1832 the hospital was under the authority of the Chief Tutelary Council.[8] Soon, rebuilding, which lasted until 1837, was started. Although the new building was furnished with 100 beds, it was regarded as one of the poorest charitable institutions in Warsaw because its income of 3,788 rubles consisted of interest on the capital and the remaining takings were unstable and dependent on voluntary payments.[9] Thus the financial base comprised fixed sums (endowed capital invested in property or located in the bank) and fluctuating ones (collections, payments by patients, etc.).

Books kept by accountants in 1829 provide information about the expenditure on food. We can conclude therefore that the diet was based on grain products – mainly bread, rice, cereals and meat, sometimes fish, vegetables or beer.[10]

The total population of Warsaw in 1826 is estimated at 131,000 and the Protestant hospital cured on average 644 people a year.[11] In 1834 the cost of maintaining one patient amounted to 1zł daily. New items were included on the food list such as pork, veal, bacon, butter, bread rolls, potatoes, cabbage, carrots, peas, turnips. It was confidently asserted that 'food given to the patients is fresh and healthy'. Every patient was served breakfast, dinner, and supper.[12] Half a portion consisted of 0.5 lbs meat, a quart of vegetables and 1 lb of bread. The full portion was considerably larger. A quarter of a portion was soup, either clear or with tiny Cracovian cereal. Apart from this the patients were served rolls of bread, plums, wine, consommé with eggs or beer caudle according to the directions of the head doctor resulting from the morning inspection.

The dinner of the hospital staff consisted in 1835 of 1lb of meat, 1.5lbs of bread, barley soup and vegetables. Every Sunday 1lb of pork was served and at the end of the month roast meat. Convalescents were allowed to have a double portion of consommé or barley soup and dishes described as 'harmless'.[13]

After 1837 the patients were charged 1zł a day; later there was an attempt to introduce subscriptions of 3 rubles a year. Patients from the countryside were enrolled after paying an overall sum or producing a guarantee issued by the owner of the property or the chief of the parish. Servants had to be guaranteed by their masters. Beggars, tramps and poor people were, however, admitted free if they could produce a document certifying their condition. The community spent considerable sums on this purpose, amounting to 30 per cent of total expenditure.[14] The chief doctor earned at that time 150zł a month.

After the mid-nineteenth century the food, previously purchased by one of the members of the Council for Particulars, was bought by auction. Milk appeared as a new item on the food list (1,680 jugs for 1,313 patients per year), but beer, amounting to 4 casks monthly, remained a prominent item in the diet. It was used as a drink (0.5 quart a day), but also for preparing the beer caudle which was served twice a week. The staff, i.e. the steward and the surgeons, received two bottles a day.[15] Throughout the nineteenth century beer is mentioned in the documents as possessing curative qualities.

A weekly menu from 1846 has come down to us and we can conclude from it that for seven days the patients received 8 oz. wheaten bread, 7 oz. wholemeal bread, 24 oz. black bread, 0.5 oz. butter for breakfast and supper everyday; supplemented 4 times a week by 0.5 lbs of beef, porridge, semolina, pearl barley c. 1.25 quarts, potatoes, carrots and vegetables 1 quart each, 0.25 quarts of salt. The meals consisted of full portions, half portions (which included no other vegetables apart from carrots) and extra portions including wine caudle, rice with beer, fine cereal, fruit or rolls of bread.[16]

Certain restrictions for the staff were introduced in 1850 which eliminated cereals, milk and coffee from their breakfasts and beer from dinners. However, the salaries were raised instead.[17]

Pots of clay were replaced by new ones, made of sheet iron and glazed on the inner side. Copper pottery was at that time believed to be much better, but it was very expensive.

In 1875 a conflict over the matter of food arose in the Protestant hospital. Patients of Jewish faith refused to accept the meals provided and had kosher food delivered from outside. This procedure violated a rule created on 18 February 1842 which stated that patients were only allowed to have food delivered by the hospital kitchen and doctors. This was the reason for the proposal that Christian hospitals should only admit Jews who accepted hospital food, especially as there existed a Jewish hospital in Warsaw.

The maintenance cost of one patient in 1876 was about 54 kopecks, but he paid only 22.5 kop., when occupying a common ward or 27.5 kop. when residing in the so-called 'excellent' one. Great importance was attached to hygiene and disinfecting rooms, and clothing, sheets and other things were treated with hot air.

In 1847 the post of head doctor was taken over by Dr Tytus Chałubiński, who remained in this position for ten years. There was a requirement for daily reports on people admitted and discharged. In 1867 gas light was installed, and a water supply followed two years later.[18] From this point onwards the hospital was progressively modernized. In 1893 a new brick building, facing Karmelicka Street, was erected. The out-patients' department was situated on the ground floor while the gynaecological ward and nurses' rooms occupied the first and second floors respectively. Apart from sick people, the hospital also admitted the aged, who could stay after paying a certain fee and in some cases after transferring the ownership of a property to the institution on death.

This procedure urged the authorities of the community to found a separate institution providing lifelong shelter for elders of both sexes. It was founded symbolically on 3 May 1841, when the new regulations came into power.[19] The Home for the Aged was established on 25 August 1842, in the buildings of the 'Red Palace',[20] purchased by the community from Count Józef Krasiński. After this estate was sold in 1852, the home was transferred to the newly bought building in

Erywańska Street, formerly owned by the Polish Bank, next to the church. The Home for the Aged was placed here together with the school. It was looked after by the Charitable Section and the members performed monthly duties – buying clothing and food.

Soon, the post of supervisor of the Home for the Aged (from 1855 named the Inspector) was established. His duties included looking after the larder and the cellars, keeping books and dealing out food to the kitchen. His wife acted both as the housekeeper and the cook. In the 1870s the posts were occupied by the Billis, parents of six children. Their combined salary amounted to 374 rubles. This was a considerable sum, especially as they were allowed to take food for the children from the larder (worth 165 rubles). At that time the maintenance of one elder cost 15.5 kop. a day. In 1850 23 loaves of bread daily, 6 casks of beer and 4 gallons of vodka were used monthly for 87 people. Dinner consisted of cereals, potatoes, vegetables, and meat. Alcohol appeared only among the expenditure for old people.[21]

In 1853 the Ladies Society, inspired by Dr V. Oettingen, was founded in order to provide care for orphans and the children of poor Protestants. The budget consisted of collections, endowments, and donations.[22] Originally it was proposed that orphans should be placed privately with families well-regarded by the community. However, in 1857 it was decided that a Home for Orphans would be organized in two spacious rooms of the Home for the Aged, which were to be refurnished so as to meet the new demands.[23] Twenty boys and ten girls found shelter there in 1866. Apart from this 50 children stayed with foster families.[24] This state of affairs remained unchanged for 50 years due to the lack of appropriate premises.

The above-mentioned Ladies Society, however, expanded its activities. The efforts resulted in 1869 in the foundation of the Nursery no. 1 for the children of poor Protestant families.[25] In the 1880s a two-storey building was erected in Erywanska street and the nursery moved there for a time. The legacy of August Schoenfelder (10,000 rubles) made it possible for the nursery to be moved to its own building, which was erected in 1898 on the premises of the community.[26] The Nursery lacked its own code of principles and functioned according to the rules of the Warsaw Society for Charity, codified in 1892. It was open for eight to ten hours a day and admitted children aged three to seven years. To feed one child in the Nursery cost 1.75 kop., while the Home for Orphans spent 11.5 kop. daily on this purpose. No documents carrying detailed information about the composition of the diets have been preserved.

Poor girls aged 10 to 18 gained the opportunity of learning a trade when the tailoring school was set up. The girls, being charged a modest fee (5–20 kop. per week, were taught sewing, mending garments and embroidering, together with religion and singing. A hot meal consisting of soup with bread was served daily.

Adult women could find protection in the Shelter for Solitary Women, which was established in 1903 and occupied three rooms and a kitchen. Persons aged 16 to 36 stayed there, including those who came to Warsaw in search of a job. The inmates paid small fees and were provided with food and accommodation.[27]

For infants aged one to four another nursery was established in 1905. The diet consisted in 1916 of a jug of gruel for breakfast and supper respectively, and 2 pints of thick soup for dinner.[28] In the 1930s the number of children cared for amounted to 120. Their parents were charged 6zł per month.[29] A document specifying the orders for food for three months in 1932 reveals detailed information about the diet – 60 kgs of bread, 80 kgs of pearl barley, 1200 kgs of potatoes, various vegetables, meat and a number of products entirely new on the food lists of the kitchens of charity institutions, for example soya oil (15 litres).

Older children in the Home for Orphans were fed in 1917 in the following way: breakfast at 7 – soup (barley, potato or borsch); lunch at 12 – soup and vegetables (carrots, turnip-rooted cabbage, cabbage, potatoes, rarely cereals), meat on Sundays; afternoon snack at 3.30 – bread without butter or rye groats; supper at 6 – soup (the same as for breakfast) and bread. This menu entirely lacked dairy products, fat and dishes based on flour. These shortcomings were known to the staff but the difficult conditions of life during wartime made them extremely hard to improve on.[30]

A few years later, in 1922, 50 kgs of rice, 100 kgs of groats, 80 kgs of beans and 80 kgs of sugar were used monthly for 75 children; 24 kgs of flour were used daily for baking bread. As far as drinks are concerned, the children got chicory groats, tea, cocoa, milk.[31] One kilogram of fat was spread daily on bread. In 1932 the list was extended to include peas. Much meat and cabbage was also being bought at that time.[32] The children were also given doses of cod-liver oil.

The Shelter for Solitary Women served three meals daily. In 1920 breakfast included bread and coffee (butter required a small extra fee); dinner consisted of soup and vegetables, with meat available once a week; and supper included soup and bread. Inmates, who paid an extra fee, could get meat three times a week.

The above-mentioned Protestant hospital gradually raised the fees, varying them simultaneously. In 1906 the food cost 23 kop., but in 1907 the price was already 1 ruble and, in 1912, 2 to 3.50 rubles. These differences can be accounted for not only by the differentiation of standards but also by the various kinds of food served. The documents reveal that patients paying more could get rolls of bread instead of bread (butter was also free for them), ate meat more frequently and were served full portions. In the early 1920s the amount of vegetables (potatoes, beetroot, carrots, cabbage, parsley, onions) and dairy products purchased rose steadily. By the end of the 1930s the menu must have been quite diversified for the food lists display also fruit (plums, apples, lemons, oranges), marmalade, honey, herrings, and plenty of spices (cinnamon, citric acid, pepper, cloves, pimento, muscat). Additionally, a lot of salt was always used. In 1922 90 kgs, and in 1933 70 kgs of salt were bought monthly for 180 and 200 people respectively. Unfortunately, however, no food quotas and sample menus have been preserved from that time.

In the 1920s the menu in the Home for the Aged consisted of chicory groats, tea, rice, a lot of potatoes, plenty of vegetables, sauerkraut, meat and bread.[33] In 1933 the list was enriched with meat products.[34]

By comparison with the nineteenth century, beer disappeared completely and coffee (either chicory or ersatz), milk, and, rarely, tea were introduced for adults. There was still plenty of bread consumed, at first dry, later with butter and finally with marmalade, honey and meat products. Groats were gradually given up for potatoes and rice was eaten more frequently. The amount of vegetables used grew steadily and though they were still only served with dinner the choice was now much richer. Finally, by the end of the period surveyed, fruits appeared in the kitchen.

For a final evaluation of the diets maintained in the charity institutions of the Protestant community it is necessary to compare them with modern standards. Such a comparison suggests that – especially in the eighteenth and nineteenth centuries – the nourishment was insufficient. It lacked the right amount of animal protein and fat necessary for correct functioning of the human organism. The overall amount of protein was much more satisfactory as a result of the high level of the consumption of vegetable products. The consumption of carbohydrates was closest to the required amounts. These proportions changed in time as the amounts of food consumed increased.[35] In this connection four sub-periods can be distinguished. The first, up to the 1850s, displays extremely poor nourishment; the second, transitional, slightly richer but still insufficient; the third, including the final decades of the nineteenth and the initial years of the twentieth century, shows very desirable changes in the menu; and the fourth, ranges from 1930 to 1939. This last sub-period is characterized by the diversification of food, with the introduction of fruits and spices.

The lack of complete documentation makes a detailed analysis impossible, especially where food quotas are concerned, though we are able to get an insight into the shape of the menus, the importance attached to meals, their daily schedule and what was considered to be the necessary minimum for existence according to the beliefs at that time. In conclusion, it ought to be stressed that the above-mentioned menus tended towards the minimal quotas of food needed for survival because of the charitable character of the institutions discussed.

Notes

1. *Zwiastun Ewangeliczny* [Evangelic Herald], 1864, p. 311, on the History of the Protestant Augsburgian Community in Warsaw.
2. E. Kneifel, *Die Pastoren der Evangelisch–Augsburgischen Kirche in Polen* [Pastors of the Protestant Augsburgian Church in Poland], Eging, 1967.
3. Main Archive of Old Documents (AGAD), Protestant Augsburgian Community, sign. 7, p. 28.
4. Ibid., sign. 2174, pp. 24–8.
5. Ibid., p. 55.
6. The calculations are based on payments for drugs and medical assistance which in 1799 amounted to 367 zł.
7. AGAD, Protestant Augsburgian Community, sign. 262, p. 111.
8. Ibid., sign. 2174, p. 169.
9. Ibid., sign. 2174, p. 200.
10. Ibid., sign. 108.
11. Irena Pietrzak (ed.), *Wielkomiejski rozwój Warszawy do 1918r* [The evolution of Warsaw into a large city before 1918], Pawłowska, 1973, p. 13.
12. AGAD, Protestant Augsburgian Community, sign. 2174, p. 187.
13. Ibid., p. 202.
14. Ibid., pp. 306–14.
15. Ibid., p. 268.
16. Ibid., sign. 260, the 1846 kitchen menu.
17. Ibid., sign. 261, p. 202.
18. Ibid., sign. 2174, p. 489.
19. Ibid., sign. 261, p. 87.
20. Ibid., sign. 378, p. 39–42.
21. Ibid., sign. 764, p. 29.
22. Ibid., sign. 461, Part II, p. 1.
23. Ibid., p. 14.
24. L. Heintze, 'Parafialne zakłady opiekuńczo–charytatywne i wychowawcze' [Charity and Care Institutions in the Community], in *Jubileusz parafii ewangelicko – augsburskiej Św. Trójcy w Warszawie 1581 – 1781 – 1981* [Jubilee of the Holy Trinity Protestant Augsburgian Community in Warsaw 1581 – 1781 – 1981], Warsaw, 1981, p. 67.
25. AGAD, Protestant Augsburgian Community, sign. 2093, p. 92.
26. At the crossing of Żytnia Street and Karolkowa Street.
27. AGAD, Protestant Augsburgian Community, sign. 2139, a 1920 report.
28. Ibid., sign. 2093, p. 30.
29. Ibid., p. 71.
30. Ibid., sign. 2054, a report of the management of the Home for Orphans 1916–1917.
31. Ibid., sign. 2143, p. 67.

32. Ibid., sign. 2095, p. 34.
33. Ibid., sign. 2143, 1922 registry of food products.
34. Ibid., sign. 9095, 1933 registry of food products.
35. Similar conclusions were drawn by Tadeusz Sobczak in his book *Turning point in the consumption of food products in the Polish Kingdom during the nineteenth century*, Wrocław, 1968.

16 Diet in Sweden during industrialization, 1870–1939: changing trends and the emergence of food policy

Mats L. W. Morell

Basic characteristics of pre-industrial Swedish diets

Pre-industrial diets in Sweden were strongly regionally varied, due to ecological and cultural differences. Whether food items were bought, received as remuneration or produced at home, food preparation was carried out mainly within the households. Diets were based upon preserved and stored items. The storing of food provided security and expressed social differentiation.[1]

In the mid-Swedish plain lands and towns hard rye-bread, porridges and gruels together with small beer constituted the basis of the diet. Dried or salted beef – less pork – and fish were added. Dairy products were sparingly eaten; more was consumed in forestry areas and further north, where yoghurt-type products and sour-milk cheeses were important. Among vegetables, peas, cabbages, carrots and turnips were much consumed.[2]

The dominance of grain in diets increased in the run up to the early nineteenth century. By then the potato gained importance and this strengthened the tendency of 'vegetabilization' of diets. Diets became more one-sided. Among farm-hands on large estates, the share of consumed energy derived from vegetable sources rose from 70 per cent in the sixteenth to almost 90 per cent in the seventeenth and eighteenth centuries. Developments were similar in institutional households.[3] The background to these changes was the expansion of grain cultivation. As the population grew, pastures and meadows were transformed into rye fields. Livestock rearing declined.[4]

Peasants and workers suffered badly from recurrent crop failures; institutionally provided people were more protected. Among studied groups intakes of energy and protein seem to have been largely sufficient in normal years, at least after the 1730s. Diets were low in fat and the composition of fat was favourable as large shares of it came from fish and very little from milk. In the studied institutions 15 per cent of energy was derived from fat, 10–15 per cent from protein and 70–75 per cent from carbohydrates. The intake of fibre was definitely satisfactory as whole grain flour was used. However, the lack of milk products possibly resulted in under-consumption of calcium and vitamin A. The intake of vitamin C was certainly unsatisfactory during winter and spring before the emergence of the potato.[5]

Industrialization and urbanization – dietary change . . .

It is commonplace to date Swedish industrial take-off to the 1870s, when exports of sawn wood and pulp grew considerably together with the engineering industry, while urbanization gained pace. At the turn of the century the value of industrial production surpassed the value of agricultural production. The proportion of the population living in towns was 10 per cent in 1800, 13 per cent in 1870, 21 per cent in 1900 and 30 per cent in 1920. Stockholm housed merely 75,000 inhabitants in 1800 and 136,000 in 1870 but 301,000 in 1900 and 419,000 in 1920. By the mid-1930s more people were employed in industry than in agriculture.[6]

Figures 16.1 to 16.3 show what happened with per capita consumption of food from 1870 to the outbreak of World War II, when Sweden clearly could be reckoned among industrial countries.

Per capita consumption of potatoes grew up to the 1870s, to stabilize at a level of 150–160 kg per person a year. Consumption per head of bread grain also increased until it stabilized at a similar level around the turn of the century. Wheat tended to replace rye. Consumption of green vegetables grew at least after 1920, but the only important food item of vegetable origin of which per capita consumption increased substantially during the industrialization era was refined sugar. From 9.2 kg in 1876/85, annual per capita consumption of sugar approached 50 kg by the 1930s.[7]

Per capita consumption of beef increased up to the 1890s, but stagnated from then on. Instead, consumption of pork grew strongly, from around 10 kg per head a year in 1876/85, to roughly 20 kg – i.e. on a par with beef consumption – in the 1920s and 1930s. The most spectacular increase, however, concerned dairy products and fats. Consumption of fresh milk rose from 150 kg per person a year in the 1870s, 1880s and 1890s to 250 kg in the 1910s. Consumption of butter increased from about 4 kg per head a year around 1880 and 1890 to

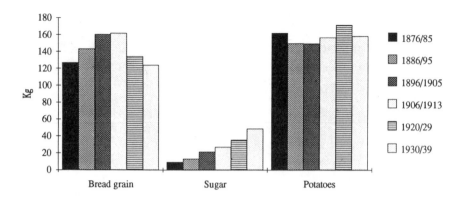

Source: Juréen, L., Sveriges jordbruksproduktion och försörjning med livsmedel. Statens Jordbruksnämnd.

Figure 16.1 Annual per capita consumption of bread grain, sugar and potatoes in Sweden, 1876/85–1930/39. Ten-year averages, in kg.

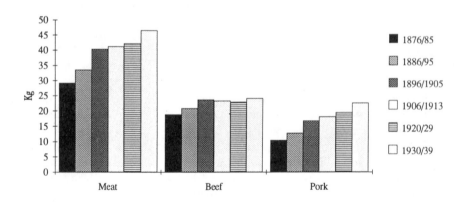

Source: Juréen, L., Sveriges jordbruksproduktion och försörjning med livsmedel. Statens Jordbruksnämnd. (Meat = beef + pork)

Figure 16.2 Annual per capita consumption of meat, beef and pork in Sweden, 1876/85–1930/39. Ten-year averages, in kg.

roughly 10 kg in the 1920s and 1930s. To this margarine should be added. At the turn of the century 2 kg per capita a year was consumed. In the 1930s the corresponding figure was 8.8 kg. Thus per capita consumption of fats increased almost fivefold from around 1880 to the 1930s. Consumption of cheese also grew substantially.[8]

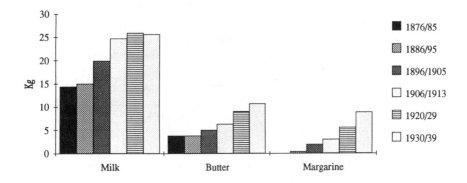

Source: Juréen, L., Sveriges jordbruksproduktion och försörjning med livsmedel. Statens Jordbruksnämnd.

Figure 16.3 Annual per capita consumption of milk, butter and margarine in Sweden, 1876/85–1930/39. Ten-year averages, in kg (milk in kg/10).

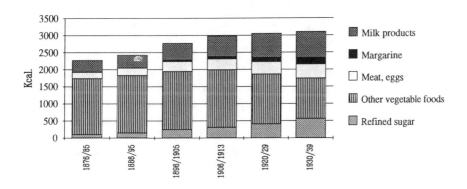

Source: Juréen, L., Sveriges jordbruksproduktion och försörjning med livsmedel. Statens Jordbruksnämnd.

Figure 16.4 Energy consumption per capita and its distribution between different foodstuffs in Sweden, 1876/85–1930/39. Ten-year averages, in Kcal.

Sugar, fats and pork thus replaced traditional energy suppliers, notably grain and potatoes. Figure 16.4 shows daily per capita intake of energy from different groups of foods. Total per capita intake of energy increased until around 1910 but ceased to grow from then onwards. The share of consumed energy derived from sugar increased from 5 per cent around 1880 to almost 20 per cent in the 1930s, whereas the share from vegetable sources other than sugar decreased from around 70 per cent to less than 40 per cent and the share from meat and eggs increased from 8 to 13 per cent. The share of milk products and margarine rose from 15 per cent around 1880 to 29 per cent in the 1930s.

It may be added that coffee-drinking grew quickly, particularly from the 1880s onwards. In the 1870s 2–2.5 kg unroasted coffee per person was imported annually. Just before the outbreak of World War I, the corresponding figure was 8–9 kg. Only in the 1960s was this figure more than temporarily surpassed. Likewise, imports of tropical and subtropical fruits – particularly oranges – grew, but almonds, nuts, raisins and other dried fruits remained more important.[9]

. . . for better or for worse?

It is certain that provisioning became more stable. More milk products meant more vitamin A and calcium. The diet became more varied and more valuable proteins were consumed. Increased consumption of vegetables and fruits contributed more vitamins and minerals. The per capita intake of energy seems to have been so low during the first decades of the industrialization period that severe malnutrition most probably occurred among certain groups. It was thus advantageous that the levels of energy intake rose. However, the figures shown represent crude averages and the variation around them may have been considerable. Therefore in certain social groups and in certain regions under-consumption of energy as well as serious risks of vitamin deficiencies may well have persisted at the end of the period. A less favourable side of the changes was that consumption of fat increased and by the end of the period approached the worrying levels of recent years (see Figure 16.5).[10] Neither was it favourable that more and more of the energy needs were fulfilled by 'empty' sugar calories. Finally the dietary changes reduced the intake of fibre.

In some respects then, the new urban diet was inferior to the traditional peasant diet. According to the household budget survey of 1907/08 the Stockholm diet was too fat, too sweet and unnecessarily extravagant as far as meat was concerned. Too much coffee and alcohol was drunk. Above all, the diet gave too little energy; only 2,500 kcal. per consumption unit on average and less than 2,200 kcal. in the lowest studied income-group (1,200–1,500 crowns per year per household). In many individual households less than 2,000 kcal. per consumption unit were consumed.[11] Workers' households dominated this survey, but the poorest were hardly represented. Thus, it is likely that dietary situations in several cases were systematically worse than depicted.[12]

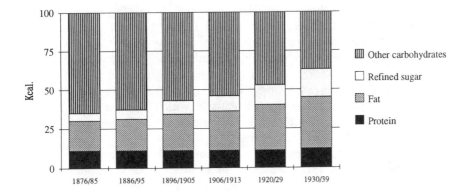

Source: Juréen, L., Sveriges jordbruksproduktion och försörjning med livsmedel. Statens Jordbruksnämnd.

Figure 16.5 Percentage distribution of consumed energy in Sweden, 1876/85–1930/39. Ten-year averages, in per cent.

Judging from what little there is of household budgets and similar specific data from the decades before 1907/08, and from the movement of wages, prices and employment, workers' families' dietary standards deteriorated during the latter half of the 1870s and in the 1880s. From then on the situation seems to have improved more or less continuously up to the outbreak of World War I, and again from the end of that war up to the eve of the next – at least as far as urban populations are concerned.[13]

General explanations

It is easily demonstrated that the dietary changes described above were related to urbanization and industrialization. In the 1890s the diets of rural workers approximately resembled the traditional peasant diet. Farmhands ate more bread, porridge and potatoes than town-dwellers did, but less meat, fats, dairy products and sugar. Still, according to the national household budget survey of 1913/14, the industrial town-dweller ate fatter food than the average rural person. Whereas the average household in Stockholm derived 13 per cent of its consumed energy from protein, 42 per cent from fats and 45 per cent from carbohydrates, the corresponding figures for Sweden as a whole were 12 per cent, 31 per cent, 57 per cent. The total intake of energy per consumption unit was considerably lower in the average Stockholm household compared to the national average. Differences tended to diminish according to a new survey in 1922, but they nevertheless persisted. According to household surveys and medical reports from the early 1930s, the rural population in general ate more potatoes and drank more milk than town-dwellers, whereas the latter ate more meat, butter, margarine, fruit and vegetables. By then urban diets had become superior at least to low-income diets in the countryside. Above all, the reports from the 1930s indicated a precarious situation for poor (particularly rural) families with many children. Vitamin, iron and energy deficiencies among members of such families seem to have been common.[14]

The general dietary changes in connection with industrialization and urbanization can be explained from four interrelated viewpoints. First they reflect changes in the volume and emphasis of agricultural production. During the nineteenth century land was enclosed, land ownership and land use was made more exclusively private, and according to one interpretation this laid the foundation for rationalized farming. Reclamation continued and grain production increased, but this mainly concerned oats, used for animal fodder. Crop rotations with clover, timothy and fodder roots spread. The horse replaced the ox for draught power and thereby one motive for keeping oxen disappeared. The supply of feeding stuff for dairy cows and pigs increased and breeding associations helped farmers to acquire high-yielding stocks.[15]

Price signals strengthened the tendencies of increased emphasis on animal production. The transport revolution – railroads and steamships – made cheap transatlantic and East European wheat available in Western Europe. Rising per capita incomes in industrialized countries turned food demand from cheap basic items towards dearer products such as bacon, cheese and butter. Grain prices fell in the 1870s and 1880s, while prices of animal products stayed up. From then on the movement of prices favoured animal husbandry right up to the 1930s when price regulations and import restrictions shielded Swedish agriculture from direct effects of the world market as well as from domestic consumers.[16]

Thereby we have arrived at the second point, and that is income change. In all countries having gone through industrialization and where per capita incomes thereby increased, the following pattern can be observed: at first per capita consumption of energy from both animal and vegetable origin increases; later the intake of energy from vegetable sources becomes stable or even falls, while total intake of energy and above all, intake of animal energy continues to increase. In the next phase total consumption of energy ceases to grow or even diminishes.[17]

This is an expression of Engels' law, according to which households with rising incomes spend smaller and smaller proportions of their earnings on basic goods, e.g. food. However, they normally do spend absolutely more even on food, when incomes grow. As far as food spending in particular is concerned, the shares used for procuring potatoes and flour – cheap, filling foodstuffs, rich in energy for the money spent – will diminish, while shares used for procuring meat, cheese, semi-finished foods and restaurant visits will increase.

These regularities are reflected in a cross-section analysis of the Stockholm survey of 1907/08. According to this, food expenditure amounted to 50 per cent of the total incomes in the lowest earning income group (with 1,200–1,500 crowns per year per household) and only 35 per cent in the richest category investigated (4,000–4,500 crowns per household per year). The intake of energy per consumption unit (c.u.) grew with household income, up to the third income group (1.700–2,000 crowns per household). Richer households received far less calories per crown spent. All three social groups into which the sample was divided – workers, civil servants and 'middle class' households – used, between them, similar shares of total food spending on meat, dairy products and fats, cereals and bread and on sugar and spices, but the richer groups bought more fruits and green vegetables. The richer households consumed less preserved or canned meat and sausages than the workers, but more veal, lamb, game and poultry, more fresh meat and more cheese, cream and butter. Workers ate more potatoes, more pure sugar but less spices and confectionery than the rich did. Workers drank more coffee, much more small beer, but less lemonade and wine. All average households indulged in alcohol, but whereas the rich drank brandy and sweet punch, workers had to make do with ordinary vodka.[18]

According to the household budget survey in 1922, these differences in food consumption and food spending had evened out to some extent.[19] Differences of class and income began to be expressed in other ways. This is a sign of generally rising incomes. Some differences persisted however, as was shown by similar national surveys 1932–34, although these reports rather stress that households with many children tended to spend less money per c.u. on food but still larger shares of their income on food than others, indicating that nutritional standards – as well as other aspects of living standards – were unsatisfactory in such families.[20]

We move on to the third point: changes in popular diets were connected to the industrialization of production, preparation and handling of food. Beet-sugar refineries trace their origins to the 1830s but their massive breakthrough came in the 1880s. National self-sufficiency in sugar was soon achieved. The dairy industry expanded simultaneously. By 1915 the amount of milk delivered to dairies was twice as large as in 1890. By the end of the 1890s seven margarine factories existed and this number remained stable, but annual production grew from 400 metric tonnes annually in 1886/90 to around 18,000 tonnes in 1920 and 60,000 tonnes in 1939. Production of canned fish doubled between 1920 and 1939, while production of other canned food increased fivefold. Industrial production of chocolate, cocoa, confectioneries, jam and lemonade increased substantially from the 1910s onwards. The size of milling and slaughtering units grew and the number of workers employed in the food industry rose from approx. 7,000 in the 1870s to 34,000 in 1906. In the 1930s co-operative dairies and slaughterhouses controlled by the farmers increased their share of production profoundly and processing was centralized; the small dairy disappeared, as did the home-making of butter.[21]

The industrialization of food processing and food distribution made much more food and a few new items (margarine) available on the market. It also changed the price ratios between certain foodstuffs dramatically (e.g. imported fruits and sugar became much less expensive) and this directly affected dietary choices. The essence of the industrialization of food production and food trade was, however, that productive activity was being transferred from households and the agricultural sector to factories and the industrial sector.

This leads to the fourth and final point: one implication of urbanization and industrialization was that the family or the household lost its role as productive unit. Work was removed from the home and drawn into the factory. Waged work spread and foodstuffs were trans-formed on a massive scale to commodities being produced primarily in order to create profit, not to fulfil needs. (At a somewhat later stage this meant that food habits could be strongly exploited by, and even altered by producers through marketing, competition by brand names, creation of very superficially different items etc.) A growing share of the remuneration for work-effort took the form of a money wage. The worker's family was to cover the main part of its food needs by buying more or less prepared foods in the market. Less than before the worker's family disposed of its time at will. This, in combination with changed working conditions, housing conditions and storage conditions, reduced the workers' families' real possibilities to prepare or store food or to produce food on garden plots or by keeping animals.[22] Meal habits and dietary choices were determined by factory work rhythms and workplace conditions. The number of one-person-households increased, as did the number of households where all adults worked outside the home. Eating out in one way or another became more common, ready-made canned foods became popular, stimulants like coffee and alcohol as well as quick and concentrated energy suppliers like sugar, fats and fat pork came into the foreground.

Complementary explanations

Basically, impersonal social processes determined the major trends in dietary change during industrialization, but the impact of legislation, ideological factors, media and the influence of an aspiring body of nutrition scientists should not be totally disregarded. As more and more consumables passed through the market, people faced – within budget constraints – an increasingly 'free' choice of food. The widespread view that people in general lacked knowledge about the market alternatives to choose from – at least knowledge of how to make optimal choices from nutritional or economic points of view – created opportunities (or pretexts) for 'experts', national or local government, food producers and food distributors to try to influence dietary habits. The social processes also resulted in the formation of new classes and political parties willing to interfere in the play of market forces and more generally a rising interest in the conditions of the working masses. Simultaneously, advances in chemistry and medicine made possible a more successful assessment of the nutritional needs of humans in varying circumstances.[23] Did this conjuncture of social, political and scientific developments determine to any perceivable extent the dietary changes related above?

Certainly many books and pamphlets with household advice, lists ordering food items according to their nutritional value in relation to price, cookbooks and so on, were widely read. The flourishing weekly press contained much similar stuff. Clearly this literature and the emerging household schools – signs and means of the shaping of new images of the ideal woman as the good housewife, more firmly than ever placed at the stove – had an impact upon household behaviour and eating habits and contributed to the rise of the *husmanskost* – today's 'traditional' Swedish diet made up from past time everyday dishes of upper classes.[24] Public interventions in distribution of milk and meat in particular were important from a sanitary point of view.[25] It is hard, however, to trace any influence of this on the broad changes in dietary composition. Rather, increased demand, distribution and consumption of milk and meat, necessitated sanitary arrangements.

In one field the emerging nutritional experts were given a free hand to formulate diets 'on rational grounds'. This concerned inmates, patients and staff in public institutions such as hospitals and orphanages.[26] If general dietary changes in the industrialization period were to some extent the outcome of actions ultimately motivated by the experts, then institutional diets ought earlier to have taken the shape general diets later were to take. From Abukhanfusa's work on institutional menus 1800–1930 it seems clear that institutional diets developed similarly to general diets and nothing indicates that these changes of the institutional diets predated general dietary changes. A comparison rather confirms that changes in institutional diets fairly well reflected general dietary changes and that there were some peculiarities with institutional diets.[27]

'Social engineering', agricultural regulations and the birth of a positive food policy

The new social democratic government formed in 1932 presented a series of proposals for social reforms generally based upon penetrating parliamentary investigations. Fears of the consequences of the fall in birth rates secured conservative support for such investigations; in fact the great Commission on Population was launched in 1935 on a conservative proposal. In three years it produced a massive series of reports with proposals concerning various social and moral issues, most of which were accepted by the parliament. A circle of young academics dominated the discussions, but none were as influential as Alva and Gunnar Myrdal.[28]

In essence the Myrdals and their fellow 'social engineers' argued that the low birth rate was explained by the fact that the rearing of children strained the resources of the families and pressed down their living standards. Not only was it irrational to have more children than one could afford to raise properly, but infant mortality took a large toll and many children suffered long-term defects from sub-optimal diets during school years. Two strategies were envisaged to solve these problems. Firstly, the social engineers were optimistic about the possibilities of reshaping people through education. The building up of networks of mother and child care centres, the appointing of school doctors, household education in schools and the foundation of institutions responsible for information, research, testing and controlling food, making nutrition surveys etc., were aspects of this enlightenment strategy.[29]

The second strategy involved redistribution of resources. 'Socialization of the costs of children' – implying that people without children should help finance child rearing – was envisaged. Day-care centres, functional housing and rationalized household work should make it possible for mothers to enter the labour market. It was argued that a 'consumption reserve' prevailed when consumption levels (concerning housing and nutrition) were sub-optimal in certain families because of the lack of finance. According to the idea of 'socialism from the consumption side', effective demand should be created socially. As far as nutrition was concerned the Commission on Population suggested that this should be achieved by the free provisioning of 'protective foods' (i.e. food items rich in specific essential nutrients such as protein, minerals and vitamins) on prescription to pregnant and breast-feeding women and pre-school children, by way of free school meals and through discounted food prices for certain population groups – particularly families with many children.

School meals were of particular relevance in rural Sweden since hundreds of thousands of children had to walk long distances to and from school daily. Many had to start too early in the morning to have time for a full meal before leaving home. In school they had access only to the cold sandwiches and milk they had brought with them and commonly they arrived home late, being too tired to make full use of a proper meal, if such was offered.[30]

By the mid-1930s some districts already provided free school lunches, but only 6 per cent of all schoolchildren, most of them in towns, benefited from this. From 1946 onwards local authorities unconditionally received central government support to finance school meals, and they invariably used this opportunity. The school-meal system, therefore, became universal much quicker than the Commission on Population – which for financial reasons proposed a gradual development – had anticipated.

As a part of the programmatic construction of the welfare state and in the context of various other reforms motivated by a specific ideology of societal change, a positive food policy was thus born – but too late to influence the general changes in diet up to World War II.

These reforms had implications for agriculture as well. Up to the 1930s agricultural policy was directed towards increased national sufficiency in food. To meet this end – as well as a few others – governments from the end of the nineteenth century supported reclamation and the formation of smallholdings, particularly in the north.

The regulations of the domestic agricultural market, the import restrictions and the export subsidies introduced in the early 1930s in order to help farming incomes during the world crisis stimulated a substantial increase in agricultural output. The threat of general overproduction in all major branches of agriculture became a reality. By keeping prices up, the regulations pressed down domestic consumption and so did export subsidies as they were financed by fees on domestic sales. Thus the support for farmers' incomes was regressively financed; it hit poor, large families – spending larger shares of their incomes on food – disproportionately hard.

Most policy-makers of the 1930s thought it unrealistic to force Swedish farmers to compete with farmers from abroad without any state support. This would have led to a sharp contraction of the farming sector. Gunnar Myrdal in particular saw nothing holy in free world market prices especially as they remained a fiction as long as most countries stuck to dumping or import restrictions or both. The farming sector should shrink, but it had to do so at a tempo determined by the expansion of industry which was to take over its surplus labour force. During this process – which he thought would slow down temporarily for demographic-structural reasons – the huge agricultural population (approximately 2 million people or well over a quarter of the entire population) needed income support, especially as living standards generally were lower in rural areas than in towns.[31]

To carry on export dumping was risky as the unit cost of dumping would rise if the quantity dumped had to be increased and/or if foreign prices fell. The remaining option was to increase domestic consumption. Myrdal returned to the earlier mentioned 'consumption reserve'. Operationally it was measured as the difference in consumption levels between low-consuming families with many children and families in corresponding income groups without children. Such under-consuming families were more sensitive than others to price changes. In order to increase domestic sales, this 'consumption reserve' should be exploited.

An unconditional giving up of the price regulations would do the trick, but a fall in the living standards of poor farmers and agricultural workers would follow as well. Rationalization of production could press down prices, but if agricultural wages should be allowed to increase and profitability levels to remain unchanged, prices would hardly fall enough to stimulate a sales increase which would match the growth of output implied by rationalization. Thus the gap between production and sales would widen.

Instead Myrdal pleaded for a low-price policy. Price support should be withdrawn, prices should fall and consumption increase. Farmers' income should be kept up by government subsidies either designed to lower production costs or functioning as pure sales premiums. As sales would increase, unit production costs would fall somewhat, and thus – apart from not producing socially distorted results – this way of supporting agriculture would be cheaper than the previous method. A political obstacle remained, however. Farmers did not take it as an advantage that the cost of support would be clearly measurable in the state budget, rather than hidden in consumer prices. As the second best alternative, the above-mentioned system of discounted food prices for certain groups in need, free school lunches and provisioning of specific food items on medical prescription, was proposed by Myrdal and the Commission on Population. The system of discounted prices was presented as one of internal, instead of external dumping.

This was quite a grand design: one set of reforms was to solve intricate and pressing problems at both ends. What then came out of it? Since the late 1940s school lunches and provisioning of certain vitamins to small children has remained general. Despite lip service paid to the dangers and great social costs of external dumping, however, export subsidies have been used recurrently. Elements of a low price line have occurred now and then, for example, concerning milk products in the 1970s, but it never became the general rule. A complete gradual abolition of domestic market regulations concerning agriculture, with only temporary income support to farmers was decided in 1990, but the full implication of this decision has been argued about as Sweden later applied for membership of the European Community, which would necessitate an adaptation to its Common Agricultural Policy.

Notes

1. E.F. Heckscher, 1935, I:1, pp. 84 ff.; Heckscher, 1963; Morell, 1987. Cf. Olsson, 1958.
2. Morell, 1989. Cf. Fjellström, 1970. Concerning milk products, cf. Olsson, 1958 and Ränk, 1966.
3. Morell, 1989, pp. 288 ff.; Morell, 1987; Essemyr, 1989. Morell (1989) is summarized in English in Morell, 1990.
4. Morell, 1989, pp. 47–50, 303–4; Heckscher, 1935 I:1, pp. 120–21 and 1949 II:1, pp. 209–11; Utterström, 1957, I, pp. 444 ff.
5. Jansson and Söderberg, 1991; Morell, 1989, chapters 2 and 9. Cf. Essemyr, 1989.
6. Jörberg, 1984, *Historical Statistics of Sweden I.*
7. Juréen, unpublished, pp. 55, 57; Becker, 1984. Juréen did not incorporate vegetables, fruit and fish in his calculations. In Juréen, 1956, p. 5 it is estimated that fish and vegetables contributed 5 per cent of total energy consumption.

   Figures of grain consumption in Juréen are based upon agricultural statistics which are of low credibility up to around 1910. Production in the earlier decades was underestimated, so that a fictitious increase in production occurred. Grain consumption was probably higher in the 1870s, 1880s and possibly 1890s than Figure 16.1 suggests. The stagnation of grain consumption possibly occurred already around 1880. Thus the very low per capita intake of energy reflected in the first two columns of graph 4 should probably have been closer to the level of the early twentieth century. Another effect is an under-estimation of the changes of dietary composition made evident in Figures 16.4 to 16.5. Most likely the percentage of calorie intake from 'other vegetable sources' and 'other carbohydrates' should have been higher in the early decades than according to the figures. Possibly, finally, the period of growing intake of calories of vegetable origin ended earlier than around 1910 as Figure 16.4 suggests.
8. Juréen, unpublished, p. 73; Becker, 1984, p. 245 (concerning fish).
9. Essemyr, 1991, p. 88 (coffee). *Statistisk översikt av det svenska näringslivets utveckling 1870–1915.*
10. Cf. Blix *et al.* 1965. A growing proportion of the fat originated from milk products, animal margarine and fatty bacon.
11. Hirdman, 1983, pp. 54–7, 66, 286, 289. Regarding the 1907/1908 household budget survey for Stockholm, cf. ibid., pp. 31 ff. and Neij, 1985.
12. Hirdman, 1983, pp. 27, 29, 31, 33, 51. Cf. Neij, 1985.
13. Hirdman, 1983, chapters 1–2, pp. 38–9 in particular; Gustafsson, 1965; Cornell, 1983. Fjellström, 1990, suggests that dietary standards among rural sawmill workers were far better than those experienced in Stockholm. This was because the former benefited from some domestic production and direct

trade with the surrounding peasant society. Gustafsson's and Cornell's pictures of the sawmill workers' conditions are gloomier, however.

14. Hirdman, 1983, pp. 58, 63–7; Neij, 1985; SOU 1938:6, bilaga 1, pp. 57–74.
15. Utterström, 1957, 1; Gadd, 1983; Morell, 1991.
16. Morell and Whittaker, forthcoming. Prices of animal products fell in relation to prices of vegetable products in the 1920s. However, that was largely a normalization following the disturbance of World War I when prices of animal products had sky-rocketed while grain prices had been kept down through government action. Cf. Ljungberg, 1990.
17. Juréen, 1956.
18. Hirdman, 1983, p. 32. Neij, 1985.
19. Hirdman, 1983, p. 35.
20. SOU 1938:6, bilaga 1, pp. 50–51.
21. *Statistik översikt av det svenska näringslivets utveckling 1870–1915*; Kurtman and Kristersson 1962; Dahmén, 1950.
22. According to the 1907/08 survey it was mainly civil servant households that bought flour and baked bread. Workers bought ready-made bread. Workers living in rural conditions kept up some domestic production of food for a few more decades. This is evident in probate inventories from small industrial towns and villages. Over time, however, (1920–1930–1940) the frequency of household cows or pigs among rural industry workers fell. Cf. note 13.
23. Cf. Hirdman, 1983, pp. 13, 19, 22 ff., 86 ff. and Morell, 1989, pp. 60, 364–5.
24. Hirdman, 1983, pp. 53, 61, 70 ff., 120 ff. The 'housewife ideal' was at its peak in the 1940s and 1950s. Cf. Hirdman, 1989. By way of its rather elaborate recipes, contents and variety, the 'husmanskost' style of eating was in marked contrast to the pre-industrial diet of the lower classes.
25. Hirdman, 1983, p. 168 has shown that the 'meat pathos' of one of the turn-of-the-century nutritionists (August Almén), turned him against sanitary regulations concerning meat-handling since such regulations would make meat more expensive to the labouring poor.
26. August Almén quoted by Abukhanfusa, 1977, p. 21.
27. Abukhanfusa, 1977. Cf., concerning pre-industrial institutions, Morell, 1989, pp. 289–94.
28. Hirdman, 1989, pp. 92 ff.
29. For this and the following paragraph, see Hirdman, 1989, pp. 185–6; and SOU 1938:6 passim.
30. SOU 1938:6, bilaga 4.
31. For this paragraph and what follows, see SOU 1938:6 passim and Myrdal, 1938.

Bibliography

Abukhanfusa, K. *Från ölsupa till blancmange. Institutionskostens utveckling 1800–1930*, duplicated, Historiska Institutionen, Stockholms universitet, 1977.
Becker, W. Livsmedelskonsumtionen i Sverige. In L. Abrahamsson *et al.*, *Näringslära för högskolan*, Uppsala, 1984.

Blix, G., A. Wretlind, S. Bergström, S.I. Westin, Den svenska folkkosten, *Vår Föda* 1965:17.

Cornell, L. *Sundsvallsdistriktets sågverksarbetare 1860–1890. Arbete levnadsförhållanden rekrytering.* Göteborg, 1983.

Dahmén, E. *Svensk industriell företagarverksamhet.* I. Stockholm., 1950.

Essemyr, M. *Bruksarbetarnas livsmedelskonsumtion.* Forsmarks bruk 1730–1800. Uppsala, 1989.

Essemyr, B. Prohibition and diffusion – Coffee and coffee-drinking in Sweden 1750–1970. In D. Ball (ed.), *Coffee in the Context of European Drinking Habits.* Zurich, 1991.

Fjellström, C. *Drömmen om det goda livet.* Umeå, 1990.

Fjellström, P. Nord- och Mellansvenskt kosthåll i kulturekologisk belysning. In N-A. Bringeus, (ed.), *Mat och Miljö. En bok om svenska kostvanor.* Lund, 1970.

Gadd, C-J. *Järn och potatis. Jordburk, teknik och social omvandling i Skaraborgs län 1750–1860.* Göteborg, 1983.

Gustafsson, B. *Den norrländska sågverksindustrins arbetare 1890–1913. Arbets- och levnadsförhållanden.* Uppsala, 1965.

Heckscher, E.F. *Sveriges ekonomiska historia från Gustav Vasa.*I:1–II.2. Stockholm, 1935–1949.

Heckscher, E.F. *An Economic History of Sweden.* Cambridge, Mass. 1954.

Hirdman, Y. *Magfrågan. Mat som mål och medel. Stockholm 1870–1920.* Stockholm, 1983.

Hirdman, Y. *Att lägga livet till rätta – studier i svensk folkhemspolitik.* Stockholm, 1989.

Historical Statistics of Sweden. I. Population. SCB, Stockholm, 1969.

Jansson, A. and Söderberg, J. Priser och löner i Stockholm 1600–1719. In A. Jansson, L.A. Palm and J. Söderberg, *Dagligt bröd i onda tider. Priser och löner i Stockholm och Västsverige 1500–1770.* Institutet för lokalhistorisk forskning, Göteborg, 1991.

Juréen, L. *Sveriges jordbruksproduktion och försörjning med livsmedel.* Unpublished manuscript. Statens Jordbruksnämnd, Jönköping.

Juréen, L. Long-Term Trends in Food Consumption: A Multi-Country Study. *Econometrica*, 1956, vol. 24:1.

Jörberg, L. *Den svenska ekonomiska utvecklingen 1861–1983.* Meddelanden från Ekonomiskhistoriska institutionen Lunds universitet, 1984.

Kurtman, C.W. and Kristersson, H. Förädlingsindustrier. In *Svenskt jordbruk och skogsbruk 1913–1962.* Uppsala, 1962.

Ljungberg, J. *Priser och Marknadskrafter i Sverige.* Lund, 1990.

Morell, M. and Heckscher, Eli F. The 'Food Budgets' and Swedish Food Consumption from the 16th to the 19th Century. The Summing up and Conclusions of a Long Debate, *Scandinavian Economic History Review, XXXV:1*, 1987.

Morell, M. *Studier i den svenska livsmedelskonsumtionens historia. Hospitalshjonens livsmedelskonsumtion 1621–1872.* Uppsala, Almqvist & Wiksell, 1989.

Morell, M. Studies in the History of Swedish Food Consumption: Food Consumption Among Institutionally Supported Paupers, 1621–1872. In E. Aerts and H. Van der Vee, (eds), *Proceedings of the Xth International Economic History Congress, Leuven, 1990. Recent Doctoral Dissertations.* Leuven, 1990.

Morell, M. Family Farms and Agricultural Mechanization in Sweden Before World War II. In K. Ullenhag, (ed.), *A Hundred Flowers Bloom. Essays in Honour of Bo Gustafsson.* Uppsala, 1991.

Morell, M. and Whittaker, J. The Productivity and Performance of the Agricultural Sectors in Sweden and the UK in the Interwar Years. In R. Lewis and L. Magnusson, (eds), *Productivity and Performance of the British and Swedish Economies in the Interwar Years.* Exeter University Press (forthcoming).

Myrdal, G. *Jordbrukspolitiken under omläggning.* Stockholm, 1938.

Neij, B. *Stockholmshushållens livsmedelskonsumtion 1907–1908.* Duplicated. Ekonomiskhistoriska institutionen, Uppsala Universitet, 1985.

Olsson, A. *Allmogens kosthåll. Studier med utgångspunkt från Västnordiska kostvanor.*, Göteborg, 1958.

Ränk, G. *Från mjölk till ost. Drag ur den äldre mjölkhushållningen i Sverige.* Lund, 1966.

SOU 1938:6. *Betänkande i näringsfrågan avgivet av befolkningskommissionen.* Stockholm 1938.

Statistisk översikt av det svenska näringslivets utveckling 1870–1915. Kommerskollegium, Stockholm, 1919.

Utterström, G. *Jordbrukets arbetare. Levnadsvillkor och arbetsvillkor på landsbygden från frihetstiden till mitten av 1800-talet.* Vol 1–2, Stockholm, 1957.

PART 6: THE EFFECT OF THE EC ON EUROPEAN FOOD

17 The EC's policies and its food

Alan Swinbank[1]

Introduction

In the early 1990s, most citizens of the European Community (EC) undoubtedly enjoy a wider range of quality, safe foods, at lower real prices, than at any time in history. This is not to say that perfection prevails. In particular:

- the common agricultural policy (CAP) may push food prices to too high a level;
- insufficient resources may be devoted to the safety of the food supply (but 100 per cent safety is an unattainable objective);
- some individuals may ingest an inappropriate diet;
- some households may be unable to afford an appropriate diet; and
- some car-less, and immobile citizens, may not have access to the cornucopia of products on sale in the modern out-of-town store.

There are two factors which in the main explain this success. First, the unprecedented level of economic growth enjoyed by these economies in the post-war world, coupled with their relatively low rates of population growth, has allowed the EC's citizens a level of material prosperity undreamt of in earlier years.[2] Secondly, new technologies affecting agricultural production, and food processing, storage and distribution, have vastly increased the world's food supply, so for the moment keeping at bay the Malthusian prospect of dwindling per capita food supplies. Of course, there are millions of malnourished and underfed people in the world, for whom the Malthusian nightmare is all too real; but for the

EC's citizens, with their international spending power, the prospect of food shortages is not a cogent threat.

There are also subsidiary factors which are of importance: particularly the fact that the EC participates in a relatively liberal world-trading system, with convertible currencies, and has physically secure trading links with its main trading partners. These subsidiary factors are not, of course, unconnected with the high levels of economic prosperity enjoyed by the EC; but they are none the less necessary. Food security, sometimes crudely equated with self-sufficiency, will be of concern to any economy which faces a military or economic blockade; and an economic system that is capable of putting goods into the shops, combined with convertible currencies that permit consumers to exercise their spending power on world markets, is also an important requirement, as the recent experiences of a number of former communist countries testify.

A particular feature shaping the food supply in the UK today is the role of the supermarkets, and their market power.[3] The growth of the supermarkets, though probably unstoppable once they had access to modern distribution technologies, was influenced by (and in turn influenced) the competitive environment in which they operated. Planning controls could have inhibited the growth of large business units, and determined their location; and a different approach to competition policy might have produced other outcomes. For example, although Maunder claims that the 'bargaining power' of the retail chain stores 'was important in the demise of resale price maintenance' (RPM), in that 'RPM was of diminishing importance in the case of many food grocery products by the time that the then Secretary of State for Industry and Trade . . . vigorously sponsored the 1964 Resale Prices Act', he also points out that the failure of five major suppliers of chocolate and sugar confectionery, in the Restrictive Practices Court in 1967, to sustain the practice of RPM for their products, was 'a significant part of of the post-war quest for freer competition'.[4]

EC policies and the food supply

Where then, after this lengthy introduction, does this leave the European Community? First, we can acknowledge that the existence and membership of the EC has had a positive impact on the levels of material prosperity and political stability enjoyed by its citizens today; but an exploration of that theme is not the intent of this chapter. Second, we can note that EC agriculture has contributed to the growth in world food production throughout the post-war period, and that some of this growth in the EC can be ascribed to the agricultural policies pursued, notably the CAP. The CAP affects the volume of raw material supplies from our farms. However, it is important to note that it is the European Community's international spending power, and the world-wide growth in farm production, which predominantly determines the range and quality of foods available in our stores. Thirdly, it can be noted that some of the subsidiary factors identified in my introduction to this chapter remain the prerogative of the Member States, and not the EC. Planning controls, for example, are still determined at national level; and EC competition policy has as yet had only a marginal impact on food industries.[5]

This chapter, then, is not concerned with the big question: 'What impact has the EC had on the spending power of its citizens, and hence on their food supply?' Rather, it is concerned with questions of detail. In particular, three interrelated aspects of EC policy will be examined:

- the customs union, and the determination of a common external tariff;
- the adoption of a common agricultural policy; and
- the move towards a single market: an objective now known as the '1992' programme.

The customs union

The basic framework of the EC is that of a customs union. Thus, Article 3 of the Treaty Establishing the European Economic Community[6] specifies that, *inter alia*,

the activities of the Community shall include, . . .

(a) the elimination, as between Member States, of customs duties and of quantitative restrictions on the import and export of goods, and of all other measures having equivalent effect;

(b) the establishment of a common customs tariff and of a common commercial policy towards third countries;

. . .

And Article 38 goes on to confirm that 'The common market shall extend to agriculture and trade in agricultural products'.

By contrast, the 'rival' European grouping, EFTA (The European Free Trade Association), was a free-trade area, not a customs union; and it specifically excluded trade in agricultural products. In a free-trade area it is only products which originate within the member states which can be freely shipped from one member state to another. With respect to trade with third countries, national trade restrictions remain in force. An unsophisticated rule was devised for the EC's common customs tariff: it was to be the simple 'arithmetical average of the duties applied in the four customs territories comprised in the Community', as applied on 1 January 1957.[7]

The implications of these measures for a nation's food supply, if fully implemented, were significant. With recent experience of post-war food and foreign exchange shortages, the adherence to a rule of no quantitative restrictions on the export of food products to partner states was an important step. But of equal importance in the longer run was the opening up of national markets to the products of one's partner,[8] and in a number of instances adopting less restrictive trade barriers against third country produce. These measures are particularly important for seasonal, perishable, products like fruit and vegetables where a government, in an attempt to protect its own growers, might seek to restrict imports of out-of-season produce. Thus, for example, in a small country with little climatic or geographic diversity, strawberries might be available for only two or three weeks a year from the local crop; whereas in a customs union covering many different climatic regions, strawberries could be available throughout the year.[9]

Subsequent enlargements of the Community have reinforced this tendency; though in the case of the Iberian Enlargement of 1986 the full consumer benefits of freer access to Spanish produce will not all be gained until the end of the transition period in December 1995. Although it is hard to build a cast-iron case, for the counter-factual position is impossible to establish, it could be claimed that EC membership has had a beneficial impact on the availability of fruits and vegetables in British supermarkets. Similarly, Greece was surprised to find that it became an importer of fruits and vegetables, including citrus, following its accession to the EC.

The Common Agricultural Policy

Ever since its formulation in the 1960s, the CAP has tended to dominate the EC's internal deliberations and its external relations.[10] As well as specifying that the common market should extend to agriculture, the EEC Treaty also explicitly provided for 'a common policy in the sphere of agriculture'.[11] Article 39 set out the objectives of the CAP as follows:

   (a) to increase agricultural productivity by promoting technical progress and by ensuring the rational development of agricultural production and the optimum utilisation of the factors of production, in particular labour;
   (b) thus to ensure a fair standard of living for the agricultural community, in particular by increasing the individual earnings of persons engaged in agriculture;
   (c) to stabilise markets;

(d) to assure the availability of supplies;

(e) to ensure that supplies reach consumers at reasonable prices.

Most commentators would agree that policy-makers have focused their attention upon policy objective (b), though many would add the rider that the objective has not been met. It is difficult to believe that, in the absence of the CAP, member states would not have pursued their own national farm policies; but, viewing the CAP in isolation, it can be said to have:

- raised the price of farmland;
- sustained a larger number of people on the land than could otherwise have earned a living in farming;
- increased the volume of EC production, which might superficially be thought to be in line with objective (d);
- Maintained farm-gate (and hence food) prices at higher levels than would otherwise have been achieved, in apparent contradiction of objective (e);
- stabilized farm-gate (and hence) food prices, in line with objective (c); whilst
- de-stabilizing, and reducing, world market prices.

In addition, the CAP has probably altered the product mix coming off EC farms, and the relative levels of some food prices.

The prime, if unattained, aim of the CAP is to increase farm incomes. In the main, until the 1990s, it attempted to do so by maintaining farm-gate prices well above those prevailing on world markets. Although there are a number of variations on the theme, and some significant exceptions to the general rule, CAP price support has three basic mechanisms, as illustrated in Figure 17.1.

First, imports are subject to an import tax, usually in the form of a variable import levy, designed to bridge the gap between the prevailing world market price and an EC determined minimum import price (known as a threshold price in most commodity regimes). Second, exports are subsidized. And third, various intervention mechanisms, such as intervention buying, usually apply to sustain domestic market prices.[12]

Because these policy mechanisms encourage an enhanced level of EC production, their impact, as mentioned earlier, is to depress world market prices. But this effect will vary from product to product, so neither the hierarchy of present world market prices, nor that of farm-gate prices observed within the EC, gives a good indication of the price hierarchy that would prevail in the absence of the CAP.[13]

Four price-related effects can be identified. First, the overall cost of food is increased by the CAP; though it should be remembered that

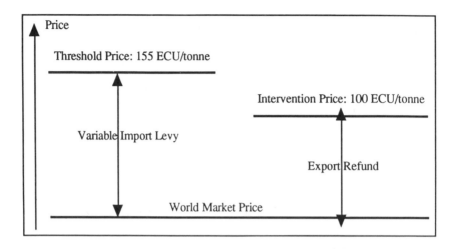

Figure 17.1 CAP price support for cereals (prices to apply in July 1995).

processing and distribution costs together account for the larger share of the retail price. For some low-income families, this increase in food prices is a serious matter; but for the majority of the EC's citizens it probably has only a marginal impact on the range and quality of food they eat.[14]

Second, it alters the price relationships between foods – though in a manner difficult to disentangle. Thus, it is probable that sugar and butter fats are more heavily taxed than are most other food products. Consequently, as a result of these price effects, the CAP has probably had some impact on diet, possibly for the better.

Third, by ensuring that the minimum price at which imports can be obtained is well in excess of intervention prices (see Figure 17.1), the quality characteristics of certain foods can be affected. Two products are commonly cited: long-grained rice, and hard wheat. Although the UK is now more than self-sufficient in wheat, millers still import some bread-making wheats from Canada, despite a considerable price penalty, because of certain baking characteristics that cannot be found in EC-grown wheats; and this has induced the baking industry to search for new bread-making techniques which minimise the use of the (artificially) more expensive imported product.

Fourthly, by using a *variable* import levy (and export refund) which bridged the gap between a fluctuating world market price and a fixed minimum import price, prior to the May 1992 reforms the domestic market had been largely insulated from world market price fluctuations.

The resulting domestic price stability was – it was said – highly prized by the EC's citizens. The 'downside' of the policy was that world market price fluctuations were likely to be accentuated as a result of the EC's policy mechanisms, to the acute annoyance of its trading partners; and – for EC citizens – prices tended to be 'stabilized' at an excessively high level.

The CAP's high prices have encouraged the EC's farmers to produce a greater volume than would otherwise have been the case. However, whilst it is clear that certain industrial interests, notably milk processors and sugar-beet refiners, have benefited from this, the overall impact on food supplies in the shops has been slight. In the EC's free market economy, despite the *dirigiste* mechanisms of the CAP, the primary factor determining the volume and variety of foods in the shops is the country's ability to pay for those goods on world markets, not the local agriculture's productive capacity. Imported products have been crowded or priced out of the market, as with Australian dairy products and canned fruits in the UK, and thus it might be claimed that the range of origins and qualities is diminished; but the consumer is neither forced to buy all of the produce of EC farms (witness the intervention stocks, and export sales), nor forbidden to buy imported goods.

Similarly, it cannot really be claimed that the high levels of self-sufficiency experienced in most branches of EC agriculture make a positive contribution to the level of food security enjoyed by the EC's citizens. It is helpful to draw a distinction between self-sufficiency in production, and a self-sufficient farming system. The EC's high levels of self-sufficiency in production are often dependent upon heavy use of imported (or exportable) animal feeds and fuels which are just as susceptible to economic or military blockade as are the foods they produce; and provide no relief for local harvest failure. The pursuit of food security would involve first an integrated policy combining some minimum capacity to produce food domestically under a worst-case scenario; strategic stocks of food, possibly co-ordinated on an international basis; third, the physical infrastructure to facilitate trade; and fourthly, selfishly, foreign currency reserves to enable the country to purchase its requirements on international markets.[15]

In summary:

- the CAP is a farm policy, not a food policy;
- which affects the volume and composition of raw materials produced by farmers, but has little effect on the range or quality of foods on sale in the shops; though
- it does increase the overall price of food and influence the price of one foodstuff in relation to another.

The single market

The EC's vocation has always transgressed the confines of a customs union with certain common policies, such as the CAP. Thus Article 2 of the EEC Treaty declares:

The Community shall have as its task, by establishing a common market and progressively approximating the economic policies of Member States, to promote throughout the Community a harmonious development of economic activities, a continuous and balanced expansion, an increase in stability, an accelerated raising of the standard of living and closer relations between the States belonging to it.

Article 3, heading (a), cited above, referred not just to the elimination of customs duties and quantitative restrictions on trade between the member states, but also to 'all other measures having equivalent effect'. Article 3 also referred, *inter alia*, to:

(c) the abolition, as between Member States, of obstacles to freedom of movement for persons, services and capital;
. . .
(h) the approximation of the laws of Member States to the extent required for the proper functioning of the common market;
. . .

and Article 8(1) went on to declare that

The common market shall be progressively established during a transitional period of twelve years.

Subsequent paragraphs of Article 8 allow for an extension of the transitional period to a maximum of 15 years (that is until 31 December 1972), and paragraph 7 declares:

Save for the exceptions or derogations provided for in this Treaty, the expiry of the transitional period shall constitute the latest date by which all the rules laid down must enter into force and all the measures required for establishing the common market must be implemented.

Elimination of quantitative restrictions and tariff barriers, on trade between member states was relatively easily achieved compared to the elimination of non-tariff barriers. In the food sector it was quite understandable that non-tariff barriers should have arisen. In order to protect consumers from fraud or deception, or to safeguard their health, countries had adopted a range of food laws which, though having common objectives, often contained incompatible measures such that a product manufactured to the standards laid down in one country did not meet the legislative provisions of a second. Similarly, legislation concerning plant and animal diseases, animal welfare, and the environmental aspects of food and drink packaging, can easily result in trade barriers between countries.

In the early days of the Community, 'the approximation of the laws of the member states to the extent required for the proper functioning of the common market', under Article 100 of the EEC Treaty, seemed to be the appropriate way forward. Indeed, the food sector led the way, with in 1962 a directive on food colours.[16] However, Article 100 required the unanimous consent of all member states, which was not easily mustered; and the prospect of Euro-beer and Euro-bread, made to harmonized EEC standards, rather than a diverse range of national products made to meet local standards, was not politically attractive. Together with the adjustment problems of the first Enlargement, and the OPEC oil shock of the early 1970s, these factors combined to render the original timetable for completion of the common market, across all sectors including food, hopelessly optimistic. Although some slow progress was made, by the mid-1970s it was generally acknowledged that the harmonization programme had run into the sand.

However, the EEC Treaty did make other arrangements for completion of the common market. In particular, though tempered by the provisions of Article 36, Article 30 of the EEC Treaty said:

Quantitative restrictions on imports and all measures having equivalent effect shall, without prejudice to the following provisions, be prohibited between Member States.

As the 1970s progressed it became evident that the European Court was willing to interpret this Article in a liberal fashion. Again the food sector was to the fore, and one of the most quoted cases concerned the blackcurrant liqueur *Cassis de Dijon*.[17] The case stemmed from the fact that sales of this French-made product had been forbidden in West Germany because it contravened German legislation designed to protect the consumer from deception. Its alcoholic content was too low for it to be sold in Germany as an alcoholic beverage. However, the European Court decided that although the German authorities were entitled to adopt reasonable measures to protect the consumer, this outright ban was unreasonable. Adequate labelling would serve to protect the consumer interest, and the free-trading principles of Article 30 should prevail. This, and a string of similar rulings, led the Commission of the European Communities to enunciate the principle of 'mutual recognition':

The Court of Justice has developed this principle in its case law, notably in the *Cassis de Dijon* judgment. It signifies acceptance by all Member States of products lawfully manufactured and sold in any other Member State, even if such products are manufactured on the basis of technical specifications different from those laid down by national laws in force in so far as the products in question protect in an equivalent fashion the legitimate interests involved.[18]

It should be emphasized that 'mutual recognition' does not imply a free-for-all with unsafe, inferior products dominating all EC markets – though consumer groups have expressed some concern. It is not a new piece of legislation binding the member states: it is simply the Commission's articulation of how, in its view, the European Court is likely to interpret existing EC Treaty provisions, in particular Articles 30 and 36 of the EEC Treaty. Member states are still entitled to defend their own actions before the European Court on the grounds that such:

prohibitions or restrictions on imports, exports of goods in transit [are] justified on grounds of public morality, public policy or public security; *the protection of health and life of humans, animals or plants*; the protection of national treasures possessing artistic, historic or archaeological value; or the protection of industrial or commercial policy. *Such prohibitions or restrictions shall not, however, constitute a means of arbitrary discrimination or a disguised restriction on trade between Member States.*[19]

Thus the Commission's strategy has become that of establishing a framework of legislation at EC level, dealing with public health, consumer protection, and enforcement procedures, while leaving national authorities free to determine detailed provisions, and trusting to the principle of 'mutual recognition' to ensure that products lawfully manufactured and sold in one member state can be sold in all others.[20] This procedure was much facilitated by the adoption of the Single European Act, which inserted Article 100A into the EEC Treaty allowing the Council of Ministers to adopt harmonization measures by qualified majority vote.[21]

'Mutual recognition' has been discussed elsewhere.[22] As far as the EC's food supply is concerned it implies a wider range of types and qualities of food products on sale in our stores. Member states will still be able to defend legitimate consumer interests, but in a manner proportional to the desired end. Thus, it is difficult to see what role nationally determined compositional standards (sometimes referred to as 'recipe law') will play in the future. If products lawfully manufactured to the standards laid down in another member state are on sale alongside products from the 'home' country, then the purchaser has to have recourse to the label to determine the competing products' composition.

Nationally determined compositional standards would inhibit industry's capacity to compete, for 'mutual recognition' while breaking down trade barriers does not result in a single market. Rulings of the European Court have not overturned national legislation as such, but rather they have forced the 'home' country to accept products manufactured in other member states. Products manufactured, and sold, in the 'home' country, or products imported from third countries, are still subject to the 'home' legislation. Thus, potentially if unlikely, products manufactured to 12 different national standards could be legally on sale at any one time – itself a major problem for the national Courts and enforcement agencies, for it is far from clear how infringement of legislation could either be monitored or prosecuted.

The potential response of manufacturers, who face stringent regulations on the 'home' market, is threefold. First, they might seek to relocate their manufacturing activity in a member state with less stringent rules. Second, they might lobby their 'home' government for repeal of the national legislation which impedes their competitive position, and such a 'competitive' scramble for de-regulation is, in my view, likely to lead sooner or later to pressure to introduce harmonized EC standards. Third, the 'home' manufacturer may lobby the 'home' country to press the EC to adopt at the outset harmonized EC standards which protect the 'home' country's products. Reflecting the UK's rather more liberal legislation, for example with respect to 'imitation' dairy products, the UK's Food and Drink Federation has expressed its concern that:

. . . there are still those in the Community who consider that mutual recognition will threaten their economic or political interests and who therefore attempt to undermine it principally through demands for a return to compositional or 'recipe' legislation. FDF has taken every opportunity to resist this approach which would segment markets, restrict new product developments and reduce consumer choice.[23]

Certainly, over the years, the French Government has voiced its concerns about the Commission's new approach. Thus, in a memorandum to the Council in 1988 it declared:

The French authorities recognise that it is neither possible nor realistic to carry out sectorial harmonization for all foodstuffs. The time this would take would be incompatible with the objective of completing the Internal Market by 1992, particularly since this sector is becoming daily more diversified with the appearance of new manufactured products.

None the less, *exclusive recourse to mutual recognition of national standards and technical rules* (author's emphasis) involves risks for fair trading and will sooner or later lead to alignment on the least demanding quality requirements. Mutual recognition will also not prevent one and the same name, which constitutes an essential 'cultural' reference for the European consumer, being placed on products whose composition may well differ fundamentally from one State to the other.

Thus the debate is far from resolved, and the overall impact of the internal market programme on the EC's food supply has yet to be determined.

Before concluding this section it is, perhaps, of importance to comment briefly on '1992'. As noted earlier in this chapter, the original intent of the EEC Treaty was that a common market should have been fully established by the early 1970s. However, those initial aspirations, while not forgotten, were none the less unrealised. From time to time the Commission reminded the member states of their commitments under the Treaties. It was not, however, until the arrival of a new college of Commissioners in January 1985, headed by Jacques Delors and with Lord Cockfield in charge of the internal market, that the new campaign to complete the internal market fired the political imagination. It is Lord Cockfield's 1985 white paper which is now credited with launching the '1992' programme, a date that came to prominence in that in the Single European Act of 1986 the member states inserted a new Article [Article 8A] into the EEC Treaty which declared:

The Community shall adopt measures with the aim of progressively establishing the internal market over a period expiring on 31 December 1992, in accordance with the provisions of this Article . . . and without prejudice to the other provisions of this Treaty.

The internal market shall comprise an area without internal frontiers in which the free movement of goods, persons, services and capital is ensured in accordance with the provisions of this Treaty.

The '1992' programme has progressed to such an extent that various Federal governments throughout the world are examining the degree to which free movement of goods, services, persons and capital is permitted in their territories. In Australia for example, prompted by the thought that the EC market would be more unified than its own, the State Governments agreed 'to dismantle barriers which have restricted interstate movement of goods and labour for almost a century'.[24]

Conclusions

In this chapter we have argued that the EC has affected the range, quality, composition and price of food in our stores; and that involvement is likely to grow in coming years. In the limited space of a short chapter only a few of the EC's policies have been mentioned: for example, we have not discussed transport, taxation or competition policy in any depth. What is certain, however, is that the CAP, despite its massive impact on raw material supplies, does not have a dominant role in determining the food we eat: our international buying power, and the ready availability of foods on world markets, are more potent considerations.

Notes

1. An earlier version of this chapter was first published in *Food Policy*, vol 17, no. 1, February 1992, pp. 53–64, and it is reproduced here with the permission of Butterworth-Heinemann, Oxford, UK.
2. It could of course, with some justice, be claimed that economic growth has focused on goods and services exchanged in the market-place, at the expense of non-market goods and services, and the quality of life in general.
3. See, for example, Mason, 1986, for a review of one supermarket chain's role in influencing the range and characteristics of foods on sale; and Atkinson 1986, and Howe, 1988, on the buying-power of the main companies.
4. Maunder, 1983, p. 197.
5. For a discussion, see Vaughan, 1988.
6. Throughout this chapter the term 'European Community', or EC, will be used except where, as in this instance, the individual Treaties are relevant. There are in fact three European Communities, with common institutions and membership: the ECSC (The European Coal and Steel Community), the EEC, and Euratom [The European Atomic Energy Community]. The Maastricht Treaty, not ratified at the time of writing, whilst creating an overarching European Union and renaming the EEC as 'The European Community', would not directly affect the policy measures described in this chapter.
7. Article 19 of the EEC Treaty. The Benelux customs union pre-dated the Community.
8. The CAP has, none the less, often acted to counter the benefits of such trade creation.
9. Customs union theory implies that the more similar the participating states, the greater (or more likely) the economic benefits to be be reaped from the formation of a customs union. Here, we are assuming that imports of strawberries were not permitted prior to the customs union: thus trade creation, and not trade diversion, will predominate.
10. For a detailed, if dated, review of the CAP see Harris *et al.*, 1983.
11. It may seem somewhat artificial to draw a distinction between the CAP and the EC's customs union. For a discussion of the issues involved see Swinbank and Ritson, 1991.
12. In May 1992 the EC adopted quite radical changes to the pricing mechanisms for cereals. The level at which prices are to be supported was substantially reduced, and in return farmers became eligible for acreage

payments, determined on a regional basis, on most of their arable area. Larger farmers are to be obliged to 'set-aside' (not use) 15 per cent of their arable land. These changes will be fully operative from July 1995, and are reflected in Figure 17.1.

13. For a fuller discussion, see Swinbank, 1992.
14. In the UK this effect is partially offset by the fact that food is zero rated for VAT, whereas most other consumer goods attract VAT at 17.5 per cent.
15. For a detailed review of the issues involved see Ritson, 1980.
16. See Gray, p. 111.
17. Judgement of 20 February 1979 in Case 120/79, *European Court Reports*, 1979, p. 649. For a review of the European Court's evolving interpretation of Article 30 see Mortelmans, 1991.
18. Commission of the EC, 1988, p. 24.
19. Article 36 of the EEC Treaty; author's emphasis.
20. A definitive account of the Commission's strategy is to be found in Gray, 1990.
21. The Single European Act was re-printed in Supplement 2/86 to *Bulletin of the European Communities*.
22. See for example Burns and Swinbank, 1991.
23. Food and Drink Federation, 1991, p. 6.
24. *Financial Times*, 1 August 1991.

Bibliography

Atkinson, A.G. 'Competition and the Food Industries', in J.A. Burns and A. Swinbank (eds), *Food Policy Issues and the Food Industries*, Food Economics Study no 3, Department of Agricultural Economics and Management, University of Reading, 1986.

Burns, J.A. and Swinbank, A. 'An Exploration of the Economic Implications of "Mutual Recognition" in the Food Sector', in D.K. Kelch (ed.) *EC 1992: Implications for World Food and Agricultural Trade*, AGES 9133, Washington DC, US Department of Agriculture, 1991.

Commission of the European Communities, *Completing the Internal Market*, COM(85)603, Brussels, CEC, 1985.

Commission of the European Communities, *Completing the Internal Market: An Area Without Internal Frontiers. The Progress Report Required by Article 8B of the Treaty*, COM(88)650, Brussels, CEC, 1988.

Food and Drink Federation, *Annual Report 1990*, London, FDF, 1991.

French Government, *Contribution to the Completion of the Internal Market in the Field of Foodstuffs*, Memorandum from the French Government to the Council of the European Communities, January 1988.

Gray, P. 'Food Law and the Internal Market. Taking Stock', *Food Policy*, 15(2), pp. 111–21, 1990.

Harris, S.A., Swinbank, A. and Wilkinson, G.A. *The Food and Farm Policies of the European Community*, Chichester, John Wiley, 1983.

Howe, M. 'UK Competition Policy and the Food Sector', in J.A. Burns and A.

Swinbank (eds), *Competition Policy in the Food Industries*, Food Economics Study no 4, Department of Agricultural Economics and Management, University of Reading, 1988.

Mason, T.J.R. 'The Tesco Healthy Eating Programme', in J.A. Burns and A. Swinbank (eds), *Food Policy Issues and the Food Industries*, Food Economics Study no 3, Department of Agricultural Economics and Management, University of Reading, 1986.

Maunder, W.P.J. 'Competition Policy in the Food Sector', in J.A. Burns, J.P. McInerney and A. Swinbank (eds), *The Food Industry. Economics and Policies*, London, Heinemann in Association with the Commonwealth Agricultural Bureaux, 1983.

Mortelmans, K. 'Article 30 of the EEC Treaty and Legislation Relating to Market Circumstances: Time to Consider a New Definition?', *Common Market Law Review*, 28(1), pp. 115–36, 1991.

Ritson, C. *Self-sufficiency and Food Security*, Centre for Agricultural Strategy, University of Reading, 1980.

Swinbank, A. 'The CAP and Relative Food Prices', in *The CAP and Healthy Eating: Help or Hindrance*, Seminar Proceedings, Department of Agricultural Economics and Management, University of Reading, June 1992.

Swinbank, A. and Ritson, C. 'The CAP, Customs Unions and the Mediterranean Countries', in C. Ritson and D.R. Harvey (eds), *The Common Agricultural Policy and the World Economy*, Wallingford, CAB International, 1991.

Vaughan, D.A.J. 'EEC Competition Law in the Food Sector', in J.A. Burns and A. Swinbank (eds), *Competition Policy in the Food Industries*, Food Economics Study no 4, Department of Agricultural Economics and Management, University of Reading, 1988.

Index